opposing viewpoints SOURCES

foreign policy

1987 annual

David L. Bender, *Publisher*
Bruno Leone, *Executive Editor*
M. Teresa O'Neill, *Senior Editor*
Bonnie Szumski, *Senior Editor*
Janelle Rohr, *Senior Editor*
Lynn Hall, *Editor*
Susan Bursell, *Editor*
Julie S. Bach, *Editor*
Neal Bernards, *Editor*
Thomas Modl, *Editor*
Karin Swisher, *Editorial Assistant*

greenhaven press, inc.

577 Shoreview Park Road
St. Paul, MN 55126

ISBN 0-89908-528-8
ISSN 0748-2841

contents

The South African Government Is Oppressing Blacks

Gary A. Haugen

Must the complexity of South Africa's situation keep us from properly responding? Must it keep us from understanding, in a practical way, enough of what is happening so that we *can* respond? I say no.

Yet ever since I returned from my term of missionary service in South Africa, I have observed among American[s] . . . an almost omnipresent attitude of frustrated confusion toward the crisis there. I perceive that to Americans lost in a tangle of urgent headlines and violent pictures, getting a clear understanding of the South African situation seems almost impossible. Everywhere I go I hear the same questions: "What's *really* going on down there?" "Isn't communism the real threat?" "Why are blacks fighting each other if it's a struggle between whites and blacks?" Of those I've talked to, the only conclusion of which they seem confident is that more is going on in South Africa than meets the eye. Many tend to act as if they believe the only good way to end a discussion on South Africa is to assert how "complex" the situation is.

Media Coverage

This confusion is due in part to the rather predictable manner in which the media "discovers" international issues for us. It usually begins with a dramatic event overseas that suddenly focuses massive media attention on a longstanding problem. Whether it be a severe famine in Ethiopia that causes us to discover hunger in Africa, or the overthrow of Marcos that causes us to discover tyranny in the Philippines, the usual pattern is for the American public to be quickly captivated by a crisis, in a country the name of which we could not have spelled correctly a few days before. Once the basic story of the crisis pounds the headlines for a few months, the second stage of discovery begins. In

this stage all of the journalists, experts, and pundits begin to reveal for us everything that was missing in the first telling of the story.

The foreign affairs specialists all race to dig up the latest little-known fact, and all of the early "superficialities" (read "basic facts") are buried underneath piles of "illuminating" complexities and countercharges. By the end of the year the American public is wondering why anyone ever got so excited about such a confusing and equivocal issue in the first place.

This familiar pattern can be seen again in the way we discovered the South African crisis. Before 1984 very few Americans knew that South Africa was actually a country, and not simply the lower part of the African continent. But by 1985, most Americans knew the name of South Africa's State President Botha. Between 1982 and 1985, the number of articles published on South Africa increased by more than 1,000 percent. The situation seemed rather tragically clear at first. The South African black majority was struggling for basic political rights denied to them, on the basis of their race, by the white minority government.

Then stage two set in. In each month of 1986 more articles on South Africa were featured than had appeared in the entire year of 1985. As this happened, we discovered how superficial our initial understanding had been. We were provided with enough of the missing parts of the puzzle to see that those black-and-white moral issues might actually be deeper shades of gray. Now we are much more sophisticated, but unfortunately, we are also much more confused.

Moral Muddledness

Yet I have a hunch that our grandchildren will be less confused about the South African crisis of 1987 than we are. I believe the struggle in South Africa will be one of those issues of history in which

Gary A. Haugen, "South Africa Simplified," *Eternity*, April 1987. Reprinted by permission of ETERNITY magazine. Copyright 1987, Evangelical Ministries, Inc., 1716 Spruce Street, Philadelphia, PA 19103.

future generations will find it difficult to appreciate our moral muddledness.

Today it's difficult for us to understand why there was so much confusion in the 19th century about slavery. And why were the German people unsure whether Hitler was evil or not? Why did the American people of the 1960s have such mixed feelings about Martin Luther King, Jr. and the Civil Rights Movement? In regard to each of these issues there was sincere and honest moral confusion; but it's nearly impossible to find much sympathy for that confusion now.

Therefore, in order to avoid some rather embarrassing questions from my grandchildren, I would like to commit the sin of trying to simplify things. In regards to South Africa we have paid so much attention to the trees of complexities and countercharges that we have missed the forest of simple facts. What follows are . . . simple facts about South Africa that future generations will find most easy to understand, and a review of some of the "complexities" that they will probably find more difficult to appreciate.

One: Oppressed Blacks

The word "oppression" is a perfectly good and useful word, that used to mean something before it became the slogan of every petty crusade. To be oppressed is to suffer under the unjust or cruel exercise of authority or power. If anyone is entitled to use the word "oppressed" to describe their condition, it is blacks in South Africa.

For hundreds of years now the blacks of South Africa have suffered under the unjust and cruel authority of white South Africans. Over a period of several centuries, the Dutch boers (Afrikaners) and the British colonists conquered the native peoples of South Africa, and in 1910 established joint rule over the country. In 1948 the Afrikaners' Nationalist political party came to power, and established its particular brand of oppression called "apartheid." The Nationalists have been in control of the government ever since. In 1987 South African blacks suffer under the following injustices and cruelties:

• Though they were born and live in a "democracy," the blacks cannot vote for those who will lead the government.

• The blacks have no representation in the South African parliament.

• Although they make up nearly 80 percent of the population, the blacks have been allotted only 13 percent of the country in which they can own land.

• Many black families have been forceably separated from their breadwinners and made to exist on undeveloped, barely arable black reservations.

• Black breadwinners are not allowed to live within the major cities, but must live in poorly serviced black townships on the city perimeters.

• Blacks can be legally imprisoned and tortured

by security forces for an indefinite time without charge or trial.

• Blacks cannot freely assemble for political meetings or marches without special (and difficult to obtain) permission from the white government.

• Blacks cannot legally organize peaceful boycotts or strikes to protest government policies.

• For every South African dollar spent on educating white students, only 14 cents is spent on educating black students.

This list could and does go on *ad nauseam*, and still would reveal almost nothing of the daily humiliation of living in a racist society. The simple fact is that blacks in South Africa are oppressed.

But what about the complexities? Three kinds of counter-arguments—or "complexities"—are mentioned when the white government is accused of oppression:

The first kind of argument defends these injustices on the basis of false generalizations about the character of blacks. For example: "Blacks are too irresponsible and uncivilized to vote." Or, "Blacks don't need the educational opportunities of whites because their minds are too simple."

The second kind of argument defends the current situation on the basis of "history"—actually a mythical interpretation of history. For example: "There weren't many blacks in South Africa until the whites came and created all the job opportunities." Or, "Apartheid was set up with the good intention of keeping different cultures from clashing, and everything was working out fine until the communists started agitating the blacks."

"If anyone is entitled to use the word 'oppressed' to describe their condition, it is blacks in South Africa."

The third argument used to defend the status quo is based on a political double standard—one whites use to justify conditions they would never accept if blacks were in power. For example: A South African white will say, "Blacks can go exercise their political rights in the 'homelands'"; but the speaker himself would be totally unwilling to pack up and move onto these desolate and impoverished reservations.

The most basic and fundamental fact about the South African crisis is that the blacks are oppressed, and it is impossible to understand anything about South Africa so long as that fact is ignored or trivialized.

Two: Outraged Blacks

Black South Africans are angered and hurt by the oppression of the white government, and the upheaval we see in the news is a manifestation of that anger. Imagine how we would respond if we suffered the kinds of injustices outlined above. We certainly know how our American forefathers reacted to the relatively benign oppression of the British crown; they rioted in the streets of Boston and started killing British soldiers. So we should not be surprised when blacks in South Africa begin to challenge the white government that oppresses them.

There are two important antecedents to the present anger among South Africans. In March 1960, in the township of Sharpeville, the South African police opened fire on a group of protesters and killed 69 blacks, mostly women. In the post-Sharpeville "state of emergency," thousands of blacks were arrested or severely restricted in their movements ("banned"). Most significantly, the government imprisoned the leaders of the African National Congress, such as Nelson Mandela, and outlawed this organization that had been struggling for black rights—non-violently—since 1912. The ANC responded by abandoning its commitment to non-violence.

"Many [black] young people feel that violence is a reasonable response to the violence of the white government, and they would rather die than grow old under apartheid."

The second major event occurred in 1976, when black students in Soweto began to protest the imposition of the Afrikaans language into the schools. In the resulting unrest, hundreds of black people were killed by security forces.

As a result of these two and other similar events, an entire generation of black young people has skipped right past the innocence of a normal childhood, and has moved to the forefront of a brutal political struggle. Many of these young people feel that violence is a reasonable response to the violence of the white government, and they would rather die than grow old under apartheid.

This tinderbox of angry and politicized young people was truly ignited in 1984, with the ratification of a new constitution that gave parliamentary representation to mixed-race and Asian South Africans, but excluded any representation for the blacks—who form South Africa's largest population group. Since that time we have seen bitter protests by blacks, and cruel repression by the government. Hundreds of thousands of blacks have been detained without charge or trial, more than 20,000 of them under the age of 16. Thousands more have been killed, including hundreds of women and small children.

Acting under martial law in the townships, the security forces have killed and tortured with impunity. Because of the brutality of the security forces, thousands of black parents—who formerly shied away from involvement—have now thrown themselves into the struggle. If this all sounds too difficult to believe, I know hundreds of evangelical ministers and priests who would tell you the same.

Legitimate Complexities

But what about the complexities and countercharges? Indeed, there are some very legitimate complexities surrounding this issue of black anger and violence.

The first complexity is the issue of "black-on-black" violence. It's absolutely true that there have been numerous incidents of blacks killing other blacks, but in the vast majority of cases it is a matter of blacks and whites fighting *through* other blacks. In other words, most of the blacks killed were seen as "collaborators": black policemen working for the white government, or black township officials not elected by the residents but set in place by the white government, or blacks suspected of being informants to the white security forces. In African culture the goals of the community often run roughshod over individual rights—if you are not perceived as a loyal team player in the struggle against the white government, you may suffer for it. These acts of violence have often been gruesome and reprehensible; but still, they have been primarily motivated by anger toward the white oppressor.

Yet isn't there violence between the different black political groups? Yes, there are occasional incidents of turf violence between black political groups like the United Democratic Front, AZAPO, Inkatha, and others. There are no excuses for these incidents, and the majority of black leaders regret them when they occur.

Tribal Violence

What about violence between the different black tribes? As a factor in the South African tensions, tribalism is perhaps the most overblown. In the urban areas, where the political struggle takes place, tribal divisions are almost negligible. Tribal violence in the South African urban areas is no greater than the occasional fights in American cities between blacks, whites, Orientals, and Hispanics. In fact, even though Nelson Mandela is of the Xhosa tribe, the overwhelming majority of Zulus would welcome him as a leader for the envisioned new South Africa. The white government, on the other hand, is anxious to convince us that the blacks are hopelessly divided by primitively violent tribal loyalties. But for the majority of 1987's urbanized South African blacks, this simply is not true.

But what about the communists? Aren't they

stirring up all the unrest? This kind of questioning assumes that there can't be angry protests without communists. Yet neither the *contras* in modern Nicaragua, nor the revolutionaries in 1774 America, needed communists to convince them to fight against oppressive governments (Remember Fact No. 1 above?). If you lived under the oppression described above, would you need a communist shouting slogans in your ear in order for you to be dissatisfied with the political dispensation? It is true that there are communists, among the black political groups, who would like to exploit the situation; but thorough-going communists are a small minority, and within the ANC there is little or no interest in South Africa becoming a client of the Soviet Union. But if the ideologies of Western democracies continue to fail in bringing about political justice, the soil for communism will grow more and more fertile.

Again, black-on-black violence, political rivalry, tribalism, and communism are all complexities of the South African crisis; but under close examination one can see that they are either side issues or simple myths. The fundamental fact of which we must not lose sight is that the outraged upheaval in South Africa is occurring because the majority of the population is oppressed and discriminated against.

Three: Selfish Whites

This third fact helps explain why there is the oppression and anger described above. Blacks in South Africa are struggling to gain the power and privilege of exercising political authority, and whites are fighting back in a struggle to retain these things for themselves. This is why, despite loud claims to the contrary, the white government has not made any significant reforms. By significant I mean reforms that would relieve the oppression and anger of blacks. It might seem significant to some that blacks and whites can now be married, or that coloureds and Indians are now in parliament; but the blacks are completely unimpressed. What blacks want is a political system of power-sharing that has been hammered out in negotiations by the leaders of their choice. What the governing whites want is the pacifying *appearance* of power-sharing, over which they maintain safe control—an agreement that they would like to hammer out in negotiations with the black leaders of *their* choice. These would tend to be the goals of any minority government, whether black, white, or any other. Governments exist to exercise political power; and though it may seem immoral and unjust for a minority government to fight to retain that power, it would be unnatural for them to act otherwise.

But perhaps it sounds too simple to pin the white government's fight for political preeminence on man's fallen nature. What about the "complexities"? Indeed, there are three important ones.

The first is that the white population is struggling to retain not only political power, but also economic power and privilege—even if it is almost certain in the long run to be disadvantageous to the nation's survival. South Africa in 1987 is an instance of an established government resolutely pursuing the immediate interests of raw political power, even if at the expense of the long-term economic interests of its own constituency. The stubborn policies of the white government are destroying the economic climate of South Africa, and are steering the country toward a civil war that—if it should occur—will decimate the economy.

The Anti-Communist Argument

The second complexity, or countercharge, is that the white government's harsh measures are justified because they are anti-communist. First of all, however, the government is not primarily fighting communists. It is fighting the disenfranchised black majority. Secondly, so many of the things that we hate about communists—imprisonment and torture of political dissenters, censorship of publications and control of the broadcast media, persecution of Christians who preach a threatening gospel, forced removals of population groups—are practiced in some form by the white South African government.

"Despite loud claims to the contrary, the white government has not made any significant reforms."

The third "complicating" countercharge is that blacks in Africa don't "deserve" political power, because they have "always" governed themselves so poorly that they actually want whites to govern them. But the black government in Zimbabwe, as I discovered, is just one proof that this is not "always" true. Indeed, in not one of the African nations ruled by blacks have the leaders yet asked for the return of the white colonial rulers.

Again a simple fact emerges: the struggle of the South African minority government is fundamentally a selfish and unjust attempt to retain political dominance and privilege for itself and its constituents.

Four: Ignorant Whites

I make this observation more out of sympathy than out of condemnation. Nothing about the South African situation surprised me more than the realization of how little white South Africans knew of what was happening in their own country. Most of us are tempted to think that white South Africans are the moral ogres of the universe because they cause so much suffering—and don't care. However, the truth of the matter is they know very little of the suffering they cause. Ninety-five percent have never been inside a black township or witnessed an act of police brutality. The state-owned television system is aggressively controlled by the government in order to shield the white population from scenes of black suffering, and to portray the political turmoil as the result of just a few communist agitators egged on by the Soviet Union. With the latest press controls introduced by the government, it is illegal to report on any political unrest apart from the government's own reports—which means the white populace is told very little.

The only contact most whites have with the black world is through their black employees and servants. Unfortunately, the employer-employee relationship does not provide blacks with the freedom to tell their white bosses anything unpleasant. An American who has been watching television news for the past two years knows more about the anger and violence in the townships than the average white South African.

Dominant Demons

A second part of this ignorance is found in the fact that there is, deep within the heart of white South African society, a brooding sense of tremendous fear. The white population is tragically imprisoned by the nightmares its government has created to justify its authority. The two dominant demons in those nightmares are the teeming masses of the black population, and the faceless, formless communist conspiracy. Many of the white politicians frequently resurrect these terrors in order to justify their policies. For white South Africans to relinquish their sovereign grip over the nation, according to this scenario, would be to surrender their children's future into the hands of a godless, communist dictatorship run by uncivilized blacks, who would surely supervise the merciless rape and destruction of the whites' culture, economy, and "promised land."

With this kind of nightmarish possibility in mind, most South African whites are too scared to consider sharing their political power. Ironically, the longer they postpone doing so, the greater the blacks' anger grows, and the greater the anger grows, the closer the whites come to making their nightmare come true.

Gary A. Haugen was in South Africa in 1985-1986 as a missionary with African Enterprise. He is writing a book on the spiritual and political crises in South Africa.

> "Even South Africa's most severe critics will acknowledge that the country offers Blacks greater opportunities than does any other nation on the continent."

The South African Government Is Not Oppressing Blacks

Warren L. McFerran

The issue of South Africa is of concern to *everyone*, not just South Africans. Indeed, according to former British Foreign Secretary David Owen, it is over this issue "that the world faces its greatest challenge." Faced with such a challenge, it is time for all concerned Americans to penetrate the haze of myths and misconceptions that has been deliberately created.

Unless we wish to see a repetition of the recent tragedies of Iran, Nicaragua, and Rhodesia (Zimbabwe)—where U.S. foreign policy decisions resulted in the replacement of friendly governments with anti-American, pro-Soviet regimes—we must seek out the truth by raising pertinent questions and obtaining factual answers. In light of the Free World's hostility toward South Africa, a good place to begin is by raising a very fundamental and simple question.

A Dependable Ally

Is South Africa our friend? Although South Africans have reason to question if we are really their friends, there can be no doubt that they are ours. The Republic of South Africa allows the United States to maintain and operate space tracking stations on her soil, provides the U.S. with strategic military data on the operations of Soviet ships plying the Indian Ocean and South Atlantic, and was one of America's very few supporters during the Vietnam War.

South Africa is in fact one of our best friends in the world. Clear evidence of this can be found in the book, *United Nations Journal: A Delegate's Odyssey*, which was written by William F. Buckley Jr. and published in 1974. In the book's appendix, Buckley ranked the various member nations of the UN in the order in which they supported 14 key issues and

causes favored by the United States. According to him, South Africa was the *only* country in the world to have voted in support of the United States 100 percent of the time.

In the years since 1974, the South African delegation to the UN has not been allowed to participate in the General Assembly. Without its participation, the U.S. does not presently have even one friendly African voice. On June 6, 1986, the U.S. State Department rated all members of the UN General Assembly according to key votes of particular interest to the United States. Of 50 African nations, the highest rating was 27 percent (Ivory Coast) and the group average was 15 percent.

Despite the current efforts to portray White South Africans as "fascists" and "neo-Nazis," the truth is that South African forces fought alongside U.S. troops in World War II to help defeat Nazi Germany and the other Axis Powers. South Africa was also America's ally in World War I, the Korean War, and the Berlin Airlift. It is especially noteworthy that the United States does not have to purchase South Africa's friendship. That country has never asked for nor received any foreign aid from the United States of America.

A Success Story

How economically advanced and technologically sophisticated is South Africa? In stark contrast with all the other nations of the African continent, the Republic of South Africa is an economic and technological success story. According to a study made by the United Nations, South Africa is one of the few "developed" nations in the world and the only one on the continent of Africa. Occupying only about 3.5 percent of the surface of Africa, South Africa produces 66 percent of the continent's steel, 54 percent of its wool, and 36 percent of its maize. She also provides 40 percent of the continent's industrial output and 45 percent of its mining

Warren L. McFerran, "South Africa: The Questions That Need To Be Asked," *The New American*, March 2, 1987. Reprinted with permission.

output, has 29 percent of its railway lines and 46 percent of its passenger and commercial vehicles, and consumes 60 percent of its electricity.

Modern, interprovincial, four-lane superhighways stretch across the country. Cars, televisions, radios, and all the other conveniences of modern life are to be found in South Africa. Computers are made there, the world's first successful human heart transplant was performed there, and a method of enriching uranium was discovered there. That country has overcome threatened oil embargoes by developing a process of manufacturing oil from coal, and she has also successfully overcome an arms embargo by developing her own armaments industry.

"A free, friendly, pro-Western South Africa is fundamental to our own self-interest."

Many of the other countries on the continent as far north as Zaire are heavily dependent upon the South African economy. Not only do more than one million foreign Black Africans find employment in that country, but most of the Black-ruled nations in southern Africa are almost totally dependent on South Africa for such basic needs as transportation and electricity. In fact, it has been said that, with a flip of a switch, South Africa could plunge the rest of southern Africa into darkness.

Strategically Vital

How important is South Africa to the Free World? The Republic of South Africa is much more than a friendly, prosperous nation. She is also strategically vital to the United States. A free, friendly, pro-Western South Africa is fundamental to our own self-interest because of its valuable mineral resources and its strategic geographic position.

Although the average American seldom considers his country's strategic vulnerabilities, the truth is that our modern industrialized economy is linked to key raw materials that must be imported from abroad, especially from southern Africa. In 1980, the Subcommittee on Mines and Mining in the U.S. House of Representatives issued a report on this strategic vulnerability that was best known by the name of the Subcommittee's Chairman, Representative James Santini. In its Preface, the Santini Report asserted: "No issue facing America in the decade ahead poses the risks and dangers to the national economy and defense, presented by this nation's dependence on foreign sources for strategic and critical minerals."

Two years later, the U.S. Senate Committee on Foreign Relations issued a report on the U.S. mineral dependence on South Africa:

The Western industrial world depends heavily on Southern Africa for chrome, manganese, vanadium and platinum. A major disruption in the supply of these minerals would have a disastrous impact on oil refining and the production of a variety of specialty steels needed in such industries as aerospace and machine tools. . . . The U.S. is almost completely dependent on imports of chromium, manganese, and platinum. . . . It is particularly dependent on South Africa for imports of chrome and ferrochrome and platinum.

South Africa contains the world's largest known deposits of gold, platinum, chrome, manganese, vanadium, and fluorspar. It also contains substantial deposits of antimony, asbestos, coal, copper, diamonds, iron ore, lead, limestone, mica, nickel, phosphates, titanium, uranium, vermiculite, zinc, and zirconium. Nevertheless, even if we completely ignore the fact that South Africa is a mineral treasure house, that country is still strategically important to the West due to her geographic position. The Cape Colony was in fact first founded in 1652 precisely because it occupied such a strategic position along the trade route from the East Indies to Western Europe. Today, the Cape sea route is the busiest in the world, with more than 26,000 ships a year sailing around the Cape of Good Hope. More than 50 percent of Western Europe's oil and 25 percent of its food supplies are routed via the Cape sea route, while nearly 30 percent of all U.S. oil imports are routed around the Cape. Recent studies of world shipping routes determined that there are some 19 "choke points" around the globe where shipping could be conveniently interrupted or halted altogether. One of these "choke points" is Cape Town. Of equal significance, another seven of these world "choke points" are in the Indian Ocean area—an area where Soviet presence is effectively countered only by South African naval power.

The Need for Apartheid

What is apartheid and why was it adopted? South Africa is home to approximately 30 million people, including about five million Whites, at least 20 million Blacks (Bantu), and nearly 4 million Coloreds (mixed race) and Indians (Asians). That country is not really one nation, but is in fact many nations, each possessing its own language, cultural heritage, and loyalties. Even among the Whites, two languages are spoken—English and a unique language derived from Dutch known as Afrikaans. The Coloreds speak either English or Afrikaans, or both. Among the Asians, 65 percent are Hindus, 21 percent are Moslems, 7 percent are Christians and Buddhists, and 7 percent are officially classified as "other."

Yet the greatest tribal and cultural diversity is among the Bantu. Blacks are divided into ten major tribes, each loyal to itself and jealous of the others. Within the major tribes are sub-tribal groupings and clan divisions. The Venda, for instance, are South

Africa's most homogenous Bantu tribal group; yet they are really an amalgamation of 27 different tribes. Among the Zulu, on the other hand, there are 200 distinct tribes. The Bantu languages can be divided into four main groups, 23 sub-groups, and numerous local dialects.

The philosopher John Stuart Mill observed early in the 19th Century: "Free institutions are next to impossible in a country made of different nationalities. Among a people without fellow feelings, especially if they read and write different languages, the united public opinion, necessary to the working of representative government, cannot exist."

Instead of trying to create a great unitary state from the diverse elements within its borders, South Africa adopted in 1948 the policy of apartheid—or more properly, Separate Development—whereby each major population group was recognized as a nation entitled to develop its own political and social institutions separate from the others. According to this policy, each of South Africa's ten major Bantu homelands would evolve into a self-governing independent, democratic sovereign state.

"Instead of trying to create a great unitary state from the diverse elements within its borders, South Africa adopted . . . the policy of apartheid—or more properly, Separate Development."

In October 1976, the Republic of Transkei received its independence from South Africa, thereby becoming the first Bantu homeland to achieve sovereign status. The second Bantu homeland to receive its independence was the Republic of Bophuthatswana, which became autonomous in December 1977. The Republic of Venda became sovereign in September 1979; and, in December 1981, the Republic of Ciskei was born.

Although the rest of the world refuses to recognize these sovereign Bantu states, as of January 1987 there were six other Bantu homelands awaiting their turn for complete self-government: the National State of Gazankulu, the National State of Kangwane, the National State of Kwandebele, the National State of Kwazulu, the National State of Lebowa, and the National State of Qwaqwa.

Opportunities for Blacks

Have Blacks enjoyed the fruits of South Africa's prosperity? Because South Africa is a "meeting place" between the First World and the Third World economies, it is not surprising that a gap exists between Black and White standards of living. What is surprising to many, however, is that the gap has narrowed substantially: From 1971-1980, the real income of Blacks increased by 40 percent while that of Whites actually decreased by three percent.

Even South Africa's most severe critics will acknowledge that the country offers Blacks greater opportunities than does any other nation on the continent. As a consequence, millions of alien Blacks seek to enter South Africa every year, legally or illegally—in sharp contrast with conditions in Communist-held lands such as East Berlin, where a wall has been erected to prevent people from escaping.

Statistics released on March 28, 1980 gave a good indication of the Bantu lifestyle in the South Western Township (Soweto) near Johannesburg, where more than one million Blacks reside. The report revealed that Soweto had more than 1,600 Black-owned businesses, 300 churches, 314 schools, 115 soccer fields, 81 basketball courts, 39 children's playgrounds, 4 soccer stadiums, 6 public swimming pools, 5 bowling alleys, 11 post offices, 6 libraries, 63 day-care centers, and 2 golf courses.

According to statistics released in February 1984, one out of every three South African Blacks owns a refrigerator; 20.2 percent of the Bantu own automobiles; 11.8 percent own color televisions; 5.4 percent own washing machines; and 2.7 percent own freezers. These percentages are not high compared to the standard of living that we enjoy in the U.S., but they are high compared to the primitive conditions that exist elsewhere on the African continent.

One of the best yardsticks for measuring the standard of living is the percentage of income that has to be devoted to the most essential item of all, food. Generally, the higher this percentage, the lower the standard of living. According to the 1984 report, South African Blacks spend an average of 45.1 percent of their household budget on food, which is virtually the same percentage that goes to food among the wage earners of Italy. In fact, South African Blacks spend a smaller percentage of their household income on food than do the populations of any other African country where comparisons were possible. (In many African countries comparisons were not possible because as little as six percent of the populations were employed in wage-earning jobs.)

Respecting Human Rights

How does South Africa's human rights record compare with the record for the rest of Africa? South Africa's State President Pieter W. Botha recently issued this challenge to the world: "It is the big lie that a Black government in Africa is, of necessity, a majority government. I challenge the world to contradict me. It is a sad fact that only a minute percentage of Blacks in Africa have obtained democracy, liberty and justice."

Strife, famine, anarchy and civil war are the

hallmarks of Black Africa, and racism against non-Blacks is widely encouraged and institutionalized. Article 27 of the *Liberian Constitution*, for instance, declares that "only persons who are Negro or of Negro descent shall qualify by birth or by naturalization to be citizens of Liberia."

Free elections in the countries north of South Africa are non-existent, and the usual mode of changing governments in Black-ruled Africa is through violent revolution. In some cases, the deposed ruler is actually cooked and eaten by cannibals. A case in point is Major General Ironyi of Nigeria, who was actually eaten by the victorious tribe following his overthrow.

Toward the end of 1985, the Catholic daily *Munno*, reported on conditions in Uganda, "The soldiers are once again on the rampage, shooting and knifing civilians, abducting women and young girls and taking turns to rape them." According to Amnesty International, atrocities in Uganda routinely involve raping women and "crushing or pulling testicles off men."

The Republic of South Africa has by far the best human rights record on the African continent. Yet the "human rights" zealots in the Free World have chosen to ignore glaring abuses of real human rights in the rest of Africa and have concentrated on South Africa. As a result of this persistent criticism and pressure, the South African Government has resolved to abolish apartheid.

Genuine Reform

Is the internal reform process real? The South African people have often reminded the world that they are an independent, sovereign nation, asserting that their sins, whatever they may be, are not ours. Yet they are also sensitive to Free World criticism, and they have accordingly dismantled the most objectionable laws that have become associated with the concept of Separate Development (apartheid), including pass laws, laws forbidding interracial marriage, and restrictive housing laws. In recent times, nearly every phase of South African life has been integrated, from the work place to the sports stadium.

The first major constitutional step toward a form of "power sharing" was made in 1984 with the adoption of a new Constitution. This "New Dispensation" provided for a tricameral legislature, with Whites, Coloreds, and Asians each having their own house of parliament. Although not yet finalized, plans are currently being made to include Blacks in the evolving federation structure.

So genuine are these changes that a major political realignment has occurred in South Africa. Conservative South Africans, who had traditionally provided the chief grassroots support for the ruling Nationalist Party, now form the chief opposition to the government. On the other hand, South African White liberals and leftists, who were formerly the government's main critics, are now the most vocal supporters of the reform program.

The reform program in South Africa is certainly genuine. But it has also made South Africa vulnerable to attack. The philosopher Alexis de Tocqueville once observed: "Experience shows that the most dangerous moment for a bad government is usually that point at which it begins to reform itself." This is also true for good governments, when they undergo reform in the face of charges and accusations that they are "bad" governments. Such a government undergoing reform in response to pressure and coercion is vulnerable because its action is widely perceived as a sign of weakness and as an admission of past wrong-doing. Not only has the Free World utilized South Africa's reform process as the means to increase coercive tactics, but internal subversive groups have seized the opportunity to launch an unprecedented and bloody wave of revolution within South Africa.

The Soviet Union

Does the Soviet Union have designs on South Africa? Leonid Brezhnev stated in 1973: "Our aim is to gain control of the two great treasure houses on which the West depends—the energy treasure house of the Persian Gulf and the minerals treasure house of central and southern Africa."

In his book, *Strategy and Economics*, Soviet Major-General A. N. Lagovskiy stressed the same theme, noting that America's dependency on certain strategic materials from abroad constituted a "weak link" in the U.S. defense strategy for the Free World. The Soviet authority candidly stated that it is a top priority in the Kremlin and its satellites to deprive the Free World, especially the United States, of key raw materials necessary for the survival of the industrialized Western economies.

"The Republic of South Africa has by far the best human rights record on the African continent."

Not only are the Soviets moving rapidly to surround the strategic Middle East, but they are also moving rapidly to conquer all of southern Africa. Angola, Mozambique, and Zimbabwe are already in the hands of puppet dictators loyal to World Communism. There are also numerous Communist-bloc combat troops stationed in southern Africa, including some 40,000 Cuban troops in Angola alone. As a consequence of these ominous developments, South Africa finds herself completely flanked by hostile Marxist states, and the final battle for the control of southern Africa has already begun.

Testifying before the Subcommittee on Mines and Mining in the House of Representatives in September 1980, Alexander Haig stated: "Should future trends, especially in southern Africa, result in alignment with Moscow of this critical resource area, then the USSR will control as much as 90 percent of several key minerals for which no substitutes have been developed, and the loss of which could bring the severest consequences to the existing economic and security framework of the Free World."

Revolutionary Groups

What are the main anti-apartheid revolutionary groups in South Africa, and who are their leaders? Of the many revolutionary groups operating against the Republic of South Africa, two predominate—the African National Congress (ANC) and the United Democratic Front (UDF). Since the former has been officially banned by the government for its open advocacy and employment of violence, the ANC's main headquarters is located in Lusaka, the capital of Marxist Zambia. Situated next to the golf course of Zambian President Kenneth Kaunda's palace are the buildings where ANC officials meet guests, supporters, and admirers. Yet the real action takes place in the bombproof multi-story underground structure that houses the ANC's National Executive Committee and the Soviet case officers. Within the confines of that elaborate shelter, ANC-Soviet personnel map out their "Active Measures" campaign against the Republic of South Africa.

Although the original purpose of the ANC, which was founded in 1912, is rather obscure, ample documentation exists proving that it is now totally dominated and controlled by the South African Communist Party (SACP), which in turn is controlled by the Kremlin. In his official history of the South African Communist Party, Michael Harmel, writing under the pseudonym A. Lerumo, stated:

> Today the ANC has been so thoroughly infiltrated and taken over by the SACP that the two are virtually synonymous. . . . Joint planning by the USSR, ANC and SACP of the strategy to be used against South Africa is coordinated in Moscow where there has recently been increasing pressure on the ANC to provide proof that it is capable of "intensifying the struggle."

In November 1982, the U.S. Senate Subcommittee on Security and Terrorism issued a report, entitled *Soviet, East German and Cuban Involvement in Fomenting Terrorism in Southern Africa*. Among those who testified before the Subcommittee was Bartholomew Hlapane, a former member of the Central Committee of the SACP and of the National Executive Committee of the ANC. Hlapane, it should be noted, paid with his life for daring to tell the truth about the African National Congress. Shortly after giving his testimony before the Subcommittee, he was gunned down by an ANC assassin armed with a Soviet AK-47 assault rifle.

Hlapane testified: "No major decision could be taken by the ANC without the concurrence and approval of the Central Committee of the SACP. Most major developments were in fact initiated by the Central Committee." He added: "The military wing of the ANC, also known as *Umkhonto we Sizwe*, was the brainchild of the SACP, and, after the decision to create it had been taken, Joe Slovo and J. B. Marks were sent by the Central Committee of the SACP to Moscow to organize arms and ammunition and to raise funds for *Umkhonto we Sizwe*." Joe Slovo, a White South African and a Colonel in the Soviet KGB, is a member of the National Executive Committee of the ANC and of the Central Committee of the SACP.

Death and Violence for South Africa

The acting head of the ANC is Oliver Tambo, who has repeatedly promised death and violence for South Africa. Although there is no firm evidence that Tambo is an official member of the SACP, he serves, along with two other top ANC leaders, Alfred Nzo and Yusuf Dadoo, on the Presidential Committee of the World Peace Council, a well-known Soviet front organization. Tambo has also attended official meetings of various Communist Parties around the world, and has even addressed some of those meetings to praise the goals of the world Communist movement.

"The Soviets . . . are . . . moving rapidly to conquer all of southern Africa."

At the 60th anniversary celebration of the South African Communist party, held on July 30, 1981, Tambo stated: "Members of the ANC fully understand why both the ANC and the SACP are two hands in the same body, why they are two pillars of our revolution." That same year, Tambo also stated: "The relationship with the South African Communist Party is not an accident of history—the SACP has been an integral part of the struggle of the African people. . . . Ours is not merely a paper alliance . . . it is a living organism that has grown out of struggle. . . ."

Thus, by Tambo's own admission there is a definite link between the Communists and his own ANC. On January 23, 1987, to quell concerns about the weapons that the ANC receives from the Soviet Union, Tambo stated: "Because we are getting arms from them for free does not mean we are mortgaging ourselves." If the ANC really is *not* mortgaging itself to the Soviets, it can only be because it has already done so.

Of course, the symbolic leader and "martyr" of the ANC is Nelson Mandela, who has been serving a life sentence in prison since 1964 for plotting the violent overthrow of the South African Government. When brought to trial in 1964, Mandela confessed to writing books "on guerrilla warfare and military training" and admitted that he "planned violence." Placed in evidence at the trial were documents in his own handwriting bearing such titles as *Dialectical Materialism* and *How To Be A Good Communist.*

In one document, Mandela wrote: "As in Cuba, the general uprising must be sparked off by organized and well-prepared guerrilla operations. . . . " In another, he wrote: "We Communist Party members are the most advanced revolutionaries in modern history. . . . " And in still another: "The people of South Africa, led by the South African Communist Party, will destroy capitalist society and build in its place socialism. . . . "

"The struggle is not Black versus White, but Black and White versus Red."

For the past few years, the South African Government has offered to release Nelson Mandela if only he would pledge to refrain from violence. Mandela has thus far refused to take that pledge. While he stays in prison, by his own choice, his wife Winnie serves as his mouthpiece and carries on with his revolutionary work.

Disturbing Evidence

Is the ANC a tool of the Communist Conspiracy? The U.S. Senate Subcommittee on Security and Terrorism, which investigated both the ANC and SWAPO (a terrorist group attacking South West Africa/Namibia), stated in its November 1982 report:

> The evidence received by the Subcommittee is deeply disturbing. It suggests strongly that the original purposes of the ANC and SWAPO have been subverted, and that the Soviets and their allies have achieved alarmingly effective control over them. The demonstrated activities of these organizations, moreover, cannot easily be reconciled with the goal of liberation or the promotion of freedom. The evidence has thus served to illustrate once again the Soviet Union's support for terrorism under the guise of aiding struggles for national liberation. It is past time to bring these facts to the attention of our policymakers, the American people, and the world at large.

The report also concluded:

> The findings of the Subcommittee appear particularly relevant at a time when SWAPO and the ANC are being touted as the sole legitimate political forces and representatives of the people of Namibia and South Africa, respectively. Cuba, Vietnam, Nicaragua, and Iran are glaring and tragic reminders of our failure to fully comprehend and appreciate the motives, ideologies and interrelationships of those who sought political power under the guise of national liberation. These situations also serve as graphic examples of the

terrible price which others have paid for our previous mistakes.

A Front for the ANC

Does the UDF provide an alternative to the ANC? The United Democratic Front (UDF) was launched in August 1983 during an emotion-filled multi-racial rally at Cape Town. Although the UDF claims to be a nonviolent alternative to the violent ANC and to represent some 700 anti-apartheid groups, it is clearly an internal front for the banned ANC. The UDF was in fact launched amidst chants of "Tambo! Tambo!" The delegates at the founding meeting elected three well-known ANC supporters—Archie Gumede, Oscar Mpetha, and Albertina Sisulu—as UDF Presidents. Among the 14 people elected as UDF Patrons were Nelson Mandela, Dennis Goldberg, Goven Mbeki and Walter Sisulu, all of whom are serving life sentences in prison for their terrorist activities.

Thabo Mbeki, head of the ANC's Department of Information and Publicity, commented on the formation of the UDF: "The formation of the UDF is a very significant development. . . . This raises our struggle to a higher level." Writing in the Council on Foreign Relations journal *Foreign Affairs,* Dr. Thomas G. Karis, a supporter of the ANC and clearly no friend of South Africa, hailed the launching of the UDF as "the best organized display of support for the ANC in almost a quarter of a century."

The current leader of the UDF is Dr. Allan Boesak, President of the World Alliance of Reformed Churches. Dr. Boesak spearheaded the UDF's first major drive by sponsoring the "One Million Signatures" campaign, ostensibly to gain support for the UDF, but in reality to gain recruits for the ANC. The campaign was exposed by the prestigious South African journal, *The Aida Parker Newsletter,* which termed it "One Million Signatures for Communism." Regarding his own views, Dr. Boesak has stated: "I do not expect we will have the sort of classic Marxist textbook revolution people talk about. What we will have . . . is something of a Lebanon situation."

Rounding out the anti-apartheid forces is the outspoken Anglican Bishop Desmond Tutu, who has publicly expressed his fondness for socialism. In 1979, for instance, Tutu declared: "I am a socialist—I detest capitalism. Capitalism is exploitive and I cannot stand that." In February 1984, he claimed that "we will not have security and peace until we have justice, and we will not have that without the participation of the premier black liberation group, the ANC." In November of that year, he predicted that, "if the Russians were to come to South Africa today, then most blacks who reject Communism as atheistic and materialistic would welcome them as saviors. Anything would be better than apartheid." And in July 1986, in response to a speech by President Reagan on South Africa, the clergyman and Nobel Peace Prize recipient stated: "I am quite angry. I think the West, for my part, can go to hell."

The *Freedom Charter*

What are these anti-apartheid revolutionary groups fighting for? What the anti-apartheid revolutionary groups claim they are fighting *against* has always been far better understood than what they are fighting *for*. To clarify their position, the subversive groups formed the Congress of the People, which convened at Klipton, near Johannesburg, to adopt a so-called *Freedom Charter* on June 25 and 26, 1955. This *Freedom Charter* is still officially endorsed by the ANC and the UDF, and therefore offers further insight into the nature of the internal South African revolution.

The *Freedom Charter* promised a utopia for South Africa: "The People Shall Share the Country's Wealth!" "There Shall Be Work and Security!" "There Shall Be Houses, Security and Comfort!" "There Shall Be Peace and Friendship!" The method of bringing this worker's paradise to South Africa was spelled out in detail. "The national wealth of our country, the heritage of all South Africans, shall be restored to the people," by confiscation. "The mineral wealth beneath the soil, the banks and monopoly industries shall be transferred to the ownership of the people as a whole," as Karl Marx advocated. "All other industry and trade shall be controlled to assist the well-being of the people," as the basic tenets of scientific socialism dictate. This *Freedom Charter* sounds as if it had been written by Communists because it *was* written by Communists. In testimony before the U.S. Subcommittee on Security and Terrorism, former ANC and SACP executive member Bartholomew Hlapane said: "It is a document I came to know about, just having been drafted by Joe Slovo at the request of the Central Committee and finally approved by the Central Committee of the Communist Party."

Terrorist Methods

By what methods are the anti-apartheid groups "liberating" the South African people? The revolutionary forces of "national liberation" within South Africa are trying to "liberate" the non-White peoples by waging a systematic campaign of terrorism in the Black townships and by murdering the very peoples they claim to be liberating. Dominating the scene in that country are assassinations and intimidation of Black policemen and democratically-elected local Black officials, firebombings of Black-owned businesses, boycotts and strikes enforced by coercion, calls for nonpayment of rent, and the establishment of revolutionary Marxist "People's Committees" and "People's Courts." The struggle is not Black versus White, but Black and White versus Red.

Black-on-Black civil war has gripped virtually every Black community in South Africa. At Crossroads, near Cape Town, decent Blacks have organized "vigilante" groups to defend themselves from crazed ANC-UDF mobs, and thousands of homes have been burned in pitched battles, leaving some 200,000 Blacks homeless. In Durban, Zulu Chief Gatsha Buthelezi's Inkatha members are openly battling the ANC-UDF Marxist "comrades." And in Soweto, one resident recently told a *Newsweek* reporter that "Soweto is in a state of civil war. It's no longer news to wake up in the morning and see bodies in the streets and the front yards." It was in response to the breakdown of law and order, in fact, that the South African government imposed a state of national emergency.

Especially significant is the growing number of public executions of decent moderate Blacks with the technique of "necklacing." This technique calls for ANC-UDF radicals to place a rubber tire around a shackled victim's neck. The tire is then filled with gasoline and set on fire. As the victim is engulfed in flames, the radicals gather around to taunt him with a callousness that defies human understanding.

Necklacing is a savage form of torture and murder. Yet, Winnie Mandela has boldly proclaimed: "[W]ith our boxes of matches and our necklaces, we shall liberate this country."

US Policy

Whose side is our government on? In many respects, this is by far the most important aspect of the South African crisis. Within the U.S. State Department, White House, and Congress, there is considerable disagreement over foreign policy toward South Africa. The disagreement, however, is largely confined to differences of opinion over how best to apply coercive pressure on the South African Government and assist the ANC-UDF forces.

"It was in response to the breakdown of law and order . . . that the South African government imposed a state of national emergency."

Major shifts in U.S. foreign policy are usually first presented in *Foreign Affairs*, which is published by the Council on Foreign Relations. In 1980, Dr. Chester Crocker authored an article for that journal entitled, "South Africa: Strategy for Change." Crocker presented the strategy for inducing South Africa to undergo its reform process. Upon assuming the position of Assistant Secretary of State for African Affairs in the Reagan Administration, Crocker carried out this strategy under the name

"Constructive Engagement." The result has been to render South Africa more vulnerable to internal and external attack.

Despite the conservative image surrounding "Constructive Engagement," Crocker is on record as endorsing the ANC radicals, saying that they qualified "in a generic sense" as a group of freedom fighters. Even President Reagan has taken a stand on South Africa that has won the approval of Andrew Young. In an open letter to Bishop Desmond Tutu in mid-1986, Andrew Young stated: "For Ronald Reagan to recognize the need to un-ban Black political leadership and release Nelson Mandela is an important commitment."

"The Republic of South Africa is under attack by subversive forces that are . . . torturing and murdering the very peoples they claim to be liberating."

The recent radical shift in U.S. foreign policy toward South Africa was signaled by the appearance of a 1984 article in *Foreign Affairs* by Dr. Thomas G. Karis. Karis praised the ANC and the UDF and concluded by declaring that the U.S. Government would like to see a South African Government led "by individuals like Frederick van Zyl Slabbert, the late Steve Biko, Desmond Tutu, Oliver Tambo and Nelson Mandela."

Orwellian Perversity

The logical extension of this attitude was the passage of tough sanctions against South Africa by Congress in the fall of 1986. The proper phrase to describe the sanctions bill was ironically provided by Crocker himself, who told the Senate Subcommittee on African Affairs on September 26, 1984:

> We fail to see how waging economic warfare against the Government of South Africa can advance our goals or serve the interests of either the American people or the citizens of all races in South Africa. . . . There is an Orwellian perversity in proposing such measures in the name of liberal and humanitarian goals.

There was indeed an "Orwellian perversity" in the Anti-Apartheid Act, the official name of the 1986 sanctions bill. Among other things, the law called for U.S. funding of anti-apartheid South African groups; termination of U.S. military cooperation with South Africa; pressure on Western allies to apply similar punitive measures; the "unbanning" of terrorist organizations such as the ANC; and the release of all "political prisoners," with Nelson Mandela mentioned by name.

In his remarks on the Senate floor in opposition to the sanctions bill, Senator Jesse Helms noted that the measure "is not about segregation. It is not

about the sharing of power, it is about the transfer of power . . . to a small minority elite. That elite is the Communist Party of South Africa." Helms continued:

> The intent of the new legislation is to recognize the Communist movement of South Africa as the legitimate and preferred successor to the present government of South Africa. The bill itself gives preference in almost every respect only to those opponents of the government and those groups that are deeply committed to the Communist Party of South Africa, an organization funded and controlled by the Soviet Union. The non-Communist leaders of the Blacks and non-Whites are treated as though they do not exist.

The Senator from North Carolina asked: "Why is it that the only persons mentioned by name in the bill are Communists? Why is it that the only parties referenced are precisely those parties which are under the total control and support of the international Communist movement?" Helms summarized the matter by stating frankly that the measure "is a bill for Communist rule" in the Republic of South Africa.

In Favor of South Africa

How do the facts add up? South Africa is a close friend and time-tested ally of the United States and, because of her geographic position and valuable mineral deposits, is strategically important to the survival of the Free World. South Africa has by far the best human rights record on the African continent. It is undergoing a genuine reform process, a process that has rendered that country more vulnerable to internal and external attack.

The Republic of South Africa is under attack by subversive forces that are clearly under the total control of Moscow. Those revolutionary forces are torturing and murdering the very peoples they claim to be liberating. Most important of all is the incontrovertible fact that our government is supporting those revolutionary forces.

Warren L. McFerran is the author of the book, The Betrayal of Southern Africa: The Story of Rhodesia and South Africa.

"The situation in South Africa is now deteriorating, not by the day or the month, but by the hour."

A Black Takeover in South Africa Is Inevitable

Colm Foy

Soweto is a place without a name. The minority government which rules South Africa, supposedly in the name of the "Free World," has never seen fit to grant this township, home to two million people, the dignity of a real name. Instead, it is known simply as South West Township—SoWeTo.

Yet Soweto is a symbol. Like Sharpeville before it, the excesses of the South African forces of "Law and Order" ensured that Soweto would be remembered as the site of resistance clumsily and viciously repressed. In June 1976, school students engaged in vigorous protests against the apartheid government's decision to enforce the teaching of Afrikaans as the main language in schools. For young African people this policy was anathema since it attempted to force them to accept the culture of their oppressors as their own—with all that this would imply for permanently relegating non-white people to the status of second-class citizens.

In the 1976 rebellion, over 600 people were killed by the apartheid state and countless others injured. Nevertheless, Afrikaner power had been given a tremendous shock and things were never quite the same again.

Every year since 1976, June 16 has been commemorated by those seeking freedom and a multi-racial society in South Africa both as a day of sadness and a symbol of hope. For white South Africa, nothing is quite as chilling as the slogan of the African National Congress (ANC): "Don't mourn, mobilize!" For this has become an article of faith for the majority population. It is their passionate reply to the ruthless intimidation of the apartheid state and their avowal that no amount of murder, torture or hardship can break their spirit and determination to fight for freedom to the bitter end.

So it was that the South African authorities did all in their power to prevent [the] tenth commemoration of the Soweto uprising. On June 12, [1986] a nationwide state of emergency was introduced, covering the whole of the national territory. The security forces were given even greater and more frightening powers than they had had during the previous state of emergency, covering specified areas only and introduced in the wake of rising protest towards the end of [1985]. Throughout the country, black townships were battened down tight by rings of police and soldiers who allowed only residents through. Thousands of people from the churches, the trade unions and the two-million-strong United Democratic Front (UDF) were arrested. Their names and whereabouts were kept secret.

All Gatherings Banned

All attempts to "remember Soweto" were banned, and even church services the day before the anniversary—a Sunday—were carefully monitored, disrupted or simply prevented. In at least three cases, entire congregations of worshippers were detained, though later the government spokesman announced that a "concession" had been made when children under ten years of age were released. Everyone else was held "for trying to hold an illegal gathering" (not difficult to charge since *all* gatherings had been banned). In spite of this, however, the churches refused to be silenced. Encouraged by their congregations, all the denominations managed to hold some sort of service in which the name of Soweto and the tragic events of a decade ago were mentioned.

On the anniversary itself, the population effectively managed to outmanoeuvre the state which, in its simple-mindedness, had assumed that the commemoration would be marked with demonstrations and marches. Instead, the people reacted in a way to which the forces of apartheid

Colm Foy, "South Africa: The Point of No Return," *AfricAsiA*, July 1986. Reprinted with permission.

could not respond: they did nothing. Literally that. In the biggest strike Africa has ever seen, millions of people, in places virtually the entire working population, simply stayed at home. They did not go to work, they did not go shopping, only rarely did they go to church. Police and army vehicles patrolling the empty streets could find no demonstrators to fire upon, no meetings to disrupt, no crowds to use their ample supplies of tear gas on.

Instead, they were reduced to breaking down doors to seek out "trouble-makers" and swell the ranks of the already teeming prisons. Where incidents did occur, the security forces acted with their characteristic ruthlessness and killed several people, while in occasional outbursts of anger, local people turned on police informers and punished them with the now-familiar horrendous "necklace" a burning tyre placed around the neck.

Restricting the Press

This form of punishment, revolting even to the nationalist movement's strongest supporters, has become one of the main props of the state propaganda machine. Photographs of its administration, whenever they can be found, are exploited ruthlessly by the regime as evidence of the need to control "mob rule" and to reinforce the power of the white state. Other photographs, however, are not so welcome. Part of the rules governing the state of emergency placed the most severe restrictions yet on both the local and international press. As the Pretoria regime has seen its international image plummet to new depths—in spite of a spirited rearguard action by President Ronald Reagan and Prime Minister Margaret Thatcher—it has increasingly tried to muzzle the press. Initially, photographers and cameramen were prohibited from entering "trouble spots" without the express, and rarely given, permission of the security police. President P.W. Botha (considered by Reagan as the "Great Reformer") justified this measure on grounds that the "presence of the press in potential trouble spots incites rioting and civil disorder. There are even proven cases [not cited] when the press has encouraged rioting. . . ."

In the latest state of emergency, however, these restrictions were tightened even further and the state intended that only its own statements would form the basis of the day's news from South Africa. Apart from banning reporters from any even remotely likely scenes of unrest, the apartheid authorities prohibited journalists from publishing "any statements calling for strikes, boycotts or any other form of resistance to the government," and reintroduced total censorship of the names of all detained persons. Two local newspapers, the courageous *Weekly Mail* and the *Sowetan*, had their offices invaded and their issues destroyed.

The situation led to some ridiculous incidents. At the daily briefings by the misnamed "Information Bureau," journalists tried to evade the crackdown by asking leading questions which the government spokesman was clearly ill-equipped to handle. In reply to a question asking whether the government's decision not to allow statements by ministers and officials to be quoted amounted to a ban on such quotes, the spokesman's reply was, "I want to stress that there is no ban. It is merely that such statements will not be allowed to be published." The press corps collapsed with bitter laughter.

"The response of the nationalist organizations and the liberation movement has been to step up the call for sanctions and to increase the armed struggle."

While there was some comedy in the situation for the press, there was also tragedy. The government had clearly decided it had endured enough of press freedom and was going to teach journalists a lesson. One of the sore points has been the coverage of the incidents at the Crossroads squatter camp outside Cape Town, where state-supported "vigilantes" have been engaged in open warfare with young activists known as "the comrades." Crossroads has been a thorn in the side of apartheid ever since it was identified internationally as exemplifying everything which was wrong with the South African system.

Running Sore

Thousands of people live in this squalid settlement illegally, preferring it, with all its hardships, to a new location far from the city and their places of work. They have tenaciously resisted being moved, and the recent growth in black militancy has reinforced their stand. With Crossroads' "special relationship" to the outside world, the South African authorities have been hampered in using the violent methods they usually employ to force black people to do as they are told, and the place has remained a running sore on the Group Areas Act landscape.

Pretoria's answer has been to foment what the authorities cynically call "black on black" violence between the vigilantes and the comrades, ensuring that in the battles between the two groups, Crossroads would be burned and its people faced with no alternative but to move. On their own, the vigilantes would have had no hope of overcoming the enormous popularity of the young militants, so the apartheid authorities tipped the balance by giving firearms to their surrogates. What followed was a systematic destruction of the shanty town, with all areas that came under control of the vigilantes being set on fire. Some 70,000 people lost their fragile homes as a result.

It was at this site that the authorities chose to teach the press its lesson. While filming scenes of the fighting, a cameraman working for the American CBS network, John De'Ath, was suddenly surrounded by a group of vigilantes. After a brief discussion amongst themselves in which the apparent deciding factor was that they had been "told to hit the press," they attacked De'Ath and beat him to death.

The main question for the outside world is whether or not to impose mandatory economic sanctions. In order to work, such economic measures would need to be all-embracing and to be adopted by all countries, especially South Africa's main trading partners: the United States, Japan, Britain, West Germany and Switzerland. Such sanctions would end new investments, exports from South Africa, its imports of raw materials and technology, and cut transport links and all contacts which help the economy to prosper. The effect would be to bring about an economic crisis in the country which would not only be felt by the business community but also by the white population generally. Since the claimed "strength" of the South African economy is largely a myth—as demonstrated by the current financial crisis, even in the absence of effective sanctions—the apartheid regime would soon find itself deserted, even by its supporters, and forced to negotiate with the majority's leaders.

Blocking Sanctions

London, Washington and, following the lead of the Thatcher government, Bonn, have so far blocked every international effort to get sanctions imposed. The British Conservative government, while citing potential damage to the black South African population as its excuse for not allowing sanctions, is locked into the White House's irrational southern African policy, which sees white South Africa as a "Western ally" and fears the arrival of majority rule as a "victory for communism." Even so, London has other things to take into consideration. As head of its own Commonwealth, the British government has come under increasing pressure from other Commonwealth countries to fall in with world opinion and adopt sanctions. At [the 1985] Commonwealth summit in Nassau, Ms. Thatcher managed to gain time by proposing the establishment of the so-called Eminent Persons Group (EPG) of respected Commonwealth leaders who would try to work out a basis for negotiation between the nationalist forces and the Pretoria government.

This was always a forlorn hope, but the EPG was completely sabotaged when the apartheid regime launched a series of attacks on supposed ANC bases in Zimbabwe, Zambia and Botswana at the end of

the EPG's fact-finding tour, when the group was still in the region. This proof of Pretoria's intransigence was the final straw for the EPG's spokesman, former Australian Prime Minister Malcolm Fraser, who declared to the world's press that "millions may die in the worst bloodbath since the Second World War," if the West did not step in and impose punitive sanctions immediately. These conclusions from what was effectively the stubborn British prime minister's own creation still failed to move her, and as South Africa continued to experience the agony of growing civil war, she responded only to her own party's extreme right wing and heeded only the bland and cynical statements of the U.S. president.

Meanwhile, Reagan was having his own problems in "holding the South African line." On June 19, [1986] the U.S. House of Representatives, in a surprise move, unanimously approved a resolution calling for a virtually total trade boycott of the apartheid regime. Though unlikely to get through the Senate—which is controlled by the president's Republican party—and certain to be vetoed by Reagan himself, the resolution reflected the deep sense of urgency felt by members of Congress and their shock at the administration's refusal to act against a regime which had not only murdered and maimed thousands of its own citizens, but which had also engineered the murder of a journalist working for a U.S. television station.

"Death . . . has become so much a part of our daily life that it can no longer serve as a deterrent, discouraging struggle. We must steel ourselves for war."

Even the Reagan administration has been caught off guard by the latest outrages of the South African government. Despite the "special relationship" between Washington and Pretoria, U.S. Assistant Secretary for African Affairs Chester Crocker has been unable to gain even minimal information on the approximately 4,000 detainees, some of whom include people the United States had identified as potential allies. As a result, the Reagan administration has been forced to concede that it is "being kept in the dark" by its friends in Pretoria.

These friends, praised by the White House as defenders of Western interests, forced a new bill through the President's council on June 20, [1986] allowing for an almost permanent state of emergency. The bill, which even the tame, so-called "tri-cameral" parliament supposedly representing Indians, "Coloureds" and whites had refused to enact, gives the government authority to detain people, without trial, for 180 days—as compared with 14 under the current state of emergency. It also gives the security forces virtually unlimited powers in designated "unrest areas." The bill turns the country into a *de jure* as well as a *de facto* police state.

Increasing the Armed Struggle

The response of the nationalist organizations and the liberation movement has been to step up the call for sanctions and to increase the armed struggle. A number of bomb attacks during the state of emergency, one of which breached an oil pipeline—of deep symbolic importance in this oil-starved country—demonstrated that the ANC has the potential to inflict heavy damage on the economy and on the morale of the National Party government's supporters. On sanctions, ANC President Oliver Tambo said that they "are a weapon that the international community can and must use against the racist regime—a weapon that can weaken Pretoria's capacity to maintain its aggressive posture. . . . Sanctions will not and cannot be expected in themselves to bring down the apartheid system. They are not an alternative to struggle by the South African and the Namibian people, but an important complement to it. The effect of sanctions, properly implemented, will be to limit the scope, scale and duration of the war that is now raging in southern Africa."

As for the internal South Africa opposition, the regime moved against 119 organizations on June 21, [1986] banning them in certain areas and forbidding their leaders to be quoted. This move, which was not unexpected, in fact recognizes the strength particularly of the UDF which the state hopes will effectively be muzzled. It may, however, be too late. For the UDF's leaders are already well known—it numbers Bishop Desmond Tutu and the Reverend Allan Boesak among its patrons—and it will be almost impossible to silence them without putting them in prison, which itself would cause a fresh outcry.

The situation in South Africa is now deteriorating, not by the day or the month, but by the hour. Renewed repression no longer represents the strength of the regime but, rather, its weakness, and, though democracy may still be a long way off, progress towards it is irreversible. That said, the road ahead will involve violence, made worse by the British and U.S. refusal to impose sanctions and their vetoing of the latest anti-apartheid resolutions in the United Nations Security Council in June [1986]. President Tambo, speaking at the UN conference on sanctions, held in Paris, painted a grim scenario. "Death," he said, "which has become our daily bread in South Africa, has become so much a part of our daily life that it can no longer serve as a deterrent, discouraging struggle. We must steel ourselves for war, with all the consequences that implies." The people of nameless Soweto already know what that means.

Colm Foy is the assistant editor of AfricAsia, *a monthly magazine of news, opinion, and analysis on Africa and Asia.*

"Americans who confine their study . . . to items contained on the nightly television news can be forgiven for assuming that a black takeover is near."

viewpoint **154**

A Black Takeover in South Africa Will Fail

Frank J. Parker

"Seven blacks and two whites died today in war-torn South Africa." Americans who confine their study of the subject to items contained on the nightly television news can be forgiven for assuming that a black takeover is near. Four factors rarely discussed in depth in the popular media argue to the incorrectness of such an assessment: 1) the strength of the South African military and police; 2) the paralyzing divisiveness in the black community; 3) the white backlash; and 4) the negative consequences of sanctions.

Military Supremacy

Since 1910, first as part of the British Empire and then as an independent nation, South Africa has been self-governing. The roots of white domination are planted deep and cannot be extracted without enormous counterforce being applied. When released by the South African Government, nightly news clips on U.S. television show the one or two places in South Africa where violence has erupted that particular day. They do not show the 10,000 other spots kept quiet by Government control.

South African police and military are well-trained, amply equipped, battle-hardened and determined. Only in the last quality can their opponents match them. At least in the short run, when angry mobs fight armies, the latter always win—regardless of the justice of the complaints of the former.

Even sadder, from the perspective of reaching peace in South Africa, is that nearly a majority of the police and more than that among the military are black themselves. Given the bitterness of the struggle, they have become pariahs among their own people—subject to certain death if caught. Such outcasts will fight for their white masters to the very end.

Frank J. Parker, "South Africa Hemorrhages," *America*, January 10, 1987. Reprinted with permission.

One element rarely mentioned is that South Africa possesses the capacity to manufacture or obtain tactical nuclear weapons deliverable from air or land. In fact, it may have tested one such device in 1979. Cornered rats fight, and the teeth possessed by South Africa are as sharp as those of any except the world superpowers.

Black Turmoil

Because the white power-structure still dominates, frustrated blacks have turned to killing other frustrated blacks in large numbers. As a result, the revolutionary effort is divided and diluted in a fashion reminiscent of that in Lebanon. Even to list all the factions is a political scientist's dream. Three main blocks have emerged: A.N.C.-U.D.F.; P.A.C.-A.Z.A.P.O.; and Inkatha.

The African National Congress (A.N.C.) has been engaged in the liberation struggle for three-quarters of a century. Since Sharpeville in 1960, the A.N.C. has had to direct these efforts from outside the country. Inside the country, the United Democratic Front (U.D.F.) has emerged as A.N.C.'s internal link. In the short run at least, both groups proclaim the need for a multiracial "one man-one vote" government structure. Even before the recent Government-proclaimed state of emergency, cooperation between the two groups had been intermittent. The unexpected emergence of savagely militant teen-age township dwellers, who call themselves the "comrades," has weakened markedly the leadership authority of the U.D.F. The "comrades" have been involved in many of the horrific burning-rubber-tire assassinations of fellow blacks, known as necklace killings.

Under circumstances like these, the A.N.C. would have difficulty in establishing predominance even if it were not divided internally. Oliver Tambo and other long-time leaders disagree frequently with their younger associates. The South African

Communist Party, a part of the A.N.C., frequently has its own agenda. In addition, when Nelson Mandela eventually is released from prison, he undoubtedly will claim a large share of the leadership role. Even without the threat from the P.A.C.-A.Z.A.P.O. and Inkatha, the A.N.C. is a troubled organization.

Weakened Coalition

The coalition of the Azanian Peoples Organization (A.Z.A.P.O.) and the Pan-Africanist Congress (P.A.C.) is mainly one of convenience. Both groups are xenophobic black organizations who believe that the only role for whites is to swim in the sea. No compromise of any sort is foreseen. Both groups have been left behind in world opinion and do not have the international support that the A.N.C.-U.D.F. has attracted. As a result, enticing the "comrades" to their side has become a major undertaking. Like the A.N.C., the P.A.C. is a banned, exiled organization. Its noncooperation with the A.N.C. is historic and largely tribal in origin. A.Z.A.P.O. is a more recent urban phenomenon whose dispute with the U.D.F. is philosophic. The only time the P.A.C. and A.Z.A.P.O. join together is when engaged in armed skirmishes against A.N.C.-U.D.F. supporters.

Bloody as the A.N.C.-U.D.F. battles against P.A.C.-A.Z.A.P.O. have been in the townships, they pale in comparison to the battles both these coalitions have had (sometimes joint efforts) with Inkatha, the political arm of the Zulu nation. Led by Chief Gatsha Buthelezi, Inkatha has for many years gone its own way, seeking what it believes is best for its own people. Even though Chief Buthelezi still expresses support for Nelson Mandela, relations with the A.N.C. have been poor habitually, and currently are worse than ever. Chief Buthelezi has been severely criticized for opposing sanctions and for allowing the Kwa-Zulu homeland to participate in the Pretoria Government's now thoroughly discredited racially constructed federation policies.

"The revolutionary effort is divided and diluted in a fashion reminiscent of that in Lebanon."

Labor leaders, religious leaders and those speaking for the Indian and mixed-race communities also play important roles in opposition to the Government. Their cooperation with the nonwhite political coalitions is uneven at best and is an added complication in the attempt to have all those who seek change speak and act in unison. In detaining most of these leaders during the current state of emergency, the Pretoria regime may have unwittingly forged a unity among them that heretofore has been lacking. If true peace ever is to come to South Africa, something must bring all opposition elements together. The latest statistics from the U.S. State Department South Africa Special Working Group, covering November 1984 to November 1986, estimate that between 2,000 and 2,200 blacks have died—and more than one-third of these in black-against-black violence.

White Backlash

Disagreement within the white community is less violent but ideologically is becoming as deep. The policies of President Pieter Willem Botha are the point of controversy. Though the rest of the world finds it difficult to believe, the mainstream white South Africans believe that President Botha has moved too quickly—not too slowly—in dismantling apartheid.

The National Party currently is in its 38th year of power in South Africa. Faced with the ongoing racial crisis, the strains in the party are starting to show. General elections are not due until 1989. Unless President Botha dies, resigns or loses the support of his parliamentary majority in the interim, he should remain in power until then. The recent military attacks on neighboring countries and the state of emergency declared days before the 10th anniversary of the beginning of the Soweto riots (June 1976) were aimed at least as much at placating white criticism as in counteracting nonwhite pressure.

Without doubt, the political center in white South Africa is shifting to the right. How far this political shift will go and what its consequences might be remain to be seen. In the last year, the extreme right wing has become a very frightening group indeed, as Eugene Terre'Blanche and his Afrikaner Resistance Movement (A.W.B.) become increasingly popular.

Eugene Terre'Blanche used to be a bodyguard to the state president. Afterwards he formed a stormtrooper-like military organization that calls for the violent suppression of all dissent. Lately, hints have been made that the A.W.B. would attempt a military coup against the Botha Government if that were the only way available to quell nonwhite revolt. Mr. Terre'Blanche is a mesmerizing orator who frequently employs Old Testament quotes such as: "When thou dost go out to war against thy enemies, never be daunted by the sight of horsemen and chariots, and a host greater than thy own arrayed against thee; the Lord thy God, who rescued thee from Egypt, fights on thy side" (Deut. 20:1-2). Every other Afrikaner politician pays attention to Mr. Terre'Blanche and governs his own conduct accordingly.

The Ayatollah of the North

Presumably, the rightward swing of the pendulum will halt before it reaches the A.W.B. It could well carry as far as Andries Treurnicht, the leader of the Conservative Party. For those hoping that South Africa will negotiate, this is entirely too far. In 1982, Mr. Treurnicht, who then was a minister in the Botha cabinet, and 17 other National Party M.P.'s formed their own party as a protest against liberalizing trends initiated by President Botha, most notably the introduction of limited Governmental authority for Indian and mixed-race South Africans. This extremely intelligent former head of the Broederbond and leader of the Dutch Reformed Church at one time carried the nickname "the ayatollah of the north." His attitude toward compromise and negotiation can be guessed.

"Is the turmoil in South Africa almost over? Definitely not. It may just be beginning."

With the mainstream of the National Party gravitating toward the hard-line, President Botha, by necessity, is making accommodating gestures toward the main opposition Progressive Federal Party. Since for the most part this party is made up of English-speaking liberals (in white South Africa, "liberal" and "one man-one vote" are not necessarily synonymous terms), President Botha can only be hoping that, in a direct confrontation with the Conservatives, the "Progs" will have nowhere to go but to his side. The outcome is much in doubt. Military and police support could be crucial. Indications are that their loyalties are as divided as are everyone else's in white South Africa. It is not beyond the range of possibilities that the army might stage a coup. What would happen then is anyone's guess.

Sanctions as Savior

In their frustration at the slow pace of reform, opponents of apartheid both within and outside South Africa have seized upon economic sanctions as the only solution. Since the Congressional override of President Reagan's veto, the United States has taken the lead in sanctions imposition. Whether such a view is correct is highly questionable. The pros and cons have been debated endlessly and do not need repetition. What has been discussed only rarely, however, and does need mentioning, is that the South African Government has not been sitting counting daisies while the discussion about sanctions has been taking place. The South African Government has taken advantage of the fast-disappearing American presence to tighten controls and further stifle internal dissent. Additional press-censorship has been enacted and critical foreign journalists deported; detention of Government

opponents has risen alarmingly as have attacks on neighboring countries suspected of harboring A.N.C. forces. Huge stockpiles of oil have been amassed. Coal-to-oil conversion technology has been perfected. With French assistance, nuclear power stations have been constructed. Internal railroad systems have been improved. Legislation making it extremely difficult and costly for foreign corporations to repatriate profits has been enacted. Agreements with clandestine middlemen have been arranged.

In Rhodesia, which is landlocked and one-fifth the size of South Africa, it took 15 years for sanctions to play a part in bringing that white minority regime to an end. Even the British Foreign Secretary who oversaw the Rhodesian sanctions, Dr. David Owen, has been quoted as doubting they would work in South Africa. In his opinion, too many greedy corporations will step around them.

While fighting in Namibia and guarding its borders against A.N.C. incursions, South Africa has demonstrated its clear military superiority over its black neighboring countries. Its economic hegemony is equally as strong. If South Africa took retaliatory action and shut its borders as a reaction to sanctions, its neighbors' main source of imports and their exporting route to the sea would vanish. Would the overseas supporters of sanctions pick up the resulting bills? Such an action seems unlikely.

Finally, economic sanctions enhance the siege mentality that has been building in South Africa. As the economy has weakened, the appeal of the right has strengthened. Easy assumptions that sanctions will bring South Africa to its knees may not prove correct. If the United States and Great Britain go along with broadly based sanctions and they do not succeed, it is hard to see what bargaining chips they will have left.

Is the turmoil in South Africa almost over? Definitely not. It may just be beginning.

Frank J. Parker is the author of South Africa: Lost Opportunities *and professor of management at Boston College, Chestnut Hill, Massachusetts.*

"The ANC is controlled by the South African Communist Party, and the SACP is, in turn, controlled by the Soviet Union."

The African National Congress Is Communist

Donald S. McAlvany

Since the Soviet Union, the United Nations, the United States, the World Council of Churches, the U.S. State Department (led by George Shultz and Chester Crocker), the world media, and a growing number of U.S. Congressmen and Senators are working for a new South African government headed by the African National Congress, it might be helpful to analyze just what the ANC is, what it stands for, and who controls and directs it. Is it just a black nationalist group dedicated to greater political and human rights for South African Blacks? Is it a "genuine freedom fighter organization," as it is portrayed by the State Department? Or is it something more?

Historical Background

The African National Congress (ANC) was founded in 1912 to provide political, social, and economic advancement for Blacks. (In some ways, it was similar to the U.S. NAACP.) However, the Communist International, at its sixth Congress in 1928, had its own thoughts about the future of the ANC. That Congress resolved that "the CPSA [Communist Party of South Africa] should pay particular attention to the ANC. Our aim should be to transform the ANC into a fighting nationalist revolutionary organization . . . ." By the late 1940s, known Communists had infiltrated its leadership. According to the *African Communist* Number 87, Fourth Quarter 1981, the mouthpiece of the South African Communist Party (SACP), the catalyst of this "ideological leap forward was the 1948 militants in the ANC Youth League—led by men like Tambo, Sisulu and Mandela, and supported by leading Communists in the ANC leadership like Kotane and Mofatsnyana."

In 1955, the Freedom Charter was drafted and

Donald McAlvany, "The African National Congress," *McAlvany Intelligence Advisor*, July 1986. Reprinted with permission.

became the rallying platform for the revolution. When Bartholomew Hlapane, former SACP and ANC executive member, testified before Senator Jeremiah Denton's (R-AL) Senate Subcommittee on Security and Terrorism in 1982, he said, "It [the Freedom Charter] is a document I came to know about, just having been drafted by Joe Slovo at the request of the Central Committee and finally approved by the Central Committee of the Communist Party." Joe Slovo is the chairman of the SACP, a member of the National Executive Committee of the ANC, second-in-command of the military wing of the ANC, and a colonel in the KGB. Bartholomew Hlapane was assassinated by the ANC at his home in Soweto on December 16, 1983. In the introduction to the book *South African Communists Speak, 1915-1980*, Dr. Yusuf M. Dadoo, former national chairman of the SACP said, "The Freedom Charter has become the immediate program of the national liberation alliance and the short term program of our [Communist] Party."

The Freedom Charter says, "The mineral wealth beneath the soil, the banks, and monopoly industry shall be transferred to the ownership of the people. . . . The land shall be shared among those who work it." Nelson Mandela wrote an article in 1956, later quoted in the August 1985 edition of *Sechaba* (the ANC magazine):

> It is true that in demanding the nationalization of the banks, the gold mines and the land, the Charter strikes a fatal blow at the financial and gold mining monopolies and farming interests. . . . But such a step is imperative because the realization of the Charter is inconceivable, in fact it is impossible, unless and until these monopolies are smashed and the national wealth of the country turned over to the people.

In March 1960, the ANC and another liberation group, the Pan African Congress, were banned, but new underground organizations took their place. Umkhonto We Sizwe (Spear of the Nation) was established in 1961 by Nelson Mandela and other

ANC leaders for sabotage operations in preparation for the commencement of guerrilla warfare. During the first half of 1962, Mandela toured Africa to obtain financial support for Umkhonto; during this tour he underwent training in Algeria and arranged for Umkhonto recruits to undergo similar training.

ANC Hierarchy

In 1963, the hierarchy of the ANC was arrested at Rivonia (near Johannesburg); in the treason trials that followed, several articles and documents in Nelson Mandela's own handwriting were submitted to the court. One article was entitled, "How To Be A Good Communist"; another, "Dialectical Materialism." In another document, entitled "Political Economy," Mandela wrote: "We communist party members are the most advanced revolutionaries in modern history. . . ." In another Mandela article, entitled "Operation Mayebuya," he stated, "As in Cuba, the general uprising must be sparked off by organized and well prepared guerrilla operations during the course of which the masses of the people will be drawn in and armed."

And still another 18-page document in Mandela's handwriting was submitted as evidence. In it Mandela said:

> The people of South Africa, led by the South African Communist Party, will destroy capitalist society and build in its place socialism. . . . The transition from capitalism to socialism and the liberation of the working class from the yoke cannot be effected by ·slow changes or by reforms as reactionaries and liberals often advise, but by revolution. One must . . . be a revolutionary and not a reformist.

Mandela admitted his guilt, and he and seven others were jailed for life.

During the ensuing years, the main focus of the ANC's actions was building up its position overseas. With the active assistance of the United Nations, the Soviet Union and its allies, and some Western governments and organizations, the ANC made steady progress in achieving greater international support and recognition. In 1974, the United Nations declared the ANC to be the "authentic representative of the overwhelming majority of the peoples of South Africa." The UN, besides lending political and moral support to the ANC, channeled $20 million to the ANC in 1984. The Soviet Union, its allies and front organizations, such as the World Peace Council, also extended massive assistance to the ANC.

Policy of Violence

From the late 1970s up through the present, the ANC has gradually escalated its armed stuggle. In 1983, it killed 19 South Africans of all races in a car bomb explosion in Pretoria. In June 1985, the ANC reconfirmed its policy of indiscriminate violence at a conference described by Oliver Tambo, President of the ANC, as a "council of war." At that conference,

its leadership decided that a distinction would no longer be made between civilian and government targets. In the words of Oliver Tambo: "The distinction between 'soft' and 'hard' targets is going to disappear in an intensified confrontation, in an escalating conflict."

A resolution, entitled "The South African Question," adopted by the Executive Committee of the Communist International in the Soviet Union in 1928, stated:

> The party should pay particular attention to the embryonic national organizations among the natives, such as the African National Congress. Our aim should be to transform the African National Congress into a fighting nationalist revolutionary organization . . . developing systematically the leadership of the workers and the Communist Party in this organization.

During subsequent years, the SACP continued its policy of infiltrating the ANC. This process accelerated after 1950, when the SACP was banned and when large numbers of Communists had to find an alternative organization through which to pursue their objectives. In 1982 testimony before the Denton Senate Commission, Bartholomew Hlapane said, "It is a standing rule that members of the South African Communist Party must belong to a mass organization such as the African National Congress or the South African Congress of Trade Unions. The idea was to get members to infiltrate such organizations, to undermine the leadership, and ultimately gain control of these organizations."

"It is a standing rule that members of the South African Communist Party must belong to a mass organization such as the African National Congress."

Over the years the relationship between the ANC and the SACP grew to the point where Oliver Tambo was able to tell the SACP on July 30, 1981, during its 60th anniversary celebrations, that when the ANC spoke, "it was not so much as a guest invited to address a foreign organization. Rather we speak of and to our own." In September 1985, the monthly ANC publication *Sechaba* stated that, "The members of the ANC fully understand why both the ANC and the SACP are two hands in the same body, why they are two pillars of our revolution." Today, 23 out of 30 of the members of the National Executive Committee of the African National Congress are either members and/or active supporters of the South African Communist Party.

The ANC is controlled by the South African Communist Party, and the SACP is, in turn, controlled by the Soviet Union. (Remember, its leader, Joe Slovo, is a colonel in the KGB.) The ANC clearly aligns itself with the Soviet Union in global policies. In the January 1984 edition of *Sechaba*, Alfred Nzo, Secretary General of the ANC and a vice-president of the Soviet front, the World Peace Council, declared, "The ANC has been a consistent champion of the cause of world peace, and voices its full support for recent Soviet peace initiatives." In the March 1984 issue of the same publication, Oliver Tambo said, "We therefore have an international obligation to be active in the struggle to defeat the counter-offensive that the imperialists, led by the Reagan Administration of the United States, have launched."

"If an [African National Congress] dominated government were to come to power, it would be based on Marxist/Leninist principles and subservient to the Soviet Union."

It is highly significant that at funerals of members of the UDF (United Democratic Front—the internal wing of the ANC), the Soviet flag is always given pride of place at the head of the procession. Behind it is the ANC flag. UDF banners then follow in subordinate positions. This clearly indicates that if an ANC/UDF-dominated government were to come to power, it would be based on Marxist/Leninist principles and subservient to the Soviet Union.

Soviet revolutionary theory accords a central role to "national liberation movements" in Third World countries. In terms of Soviet theory, Third World countries cannot move directly to the phase of a Communist revolution. They must first pass through the phase of "national liberation." During this phase, a broad national front should be created comprising a coalition of all "progressive elements" (i.e., liberals, churchmen, students) and workers under the leadership of the "vanguard party." In the case of South Africa, the "vanguard party" during the national liberation phase is the ANC.

The Second Phase

Once the "national liberation" has been achieved and the "national democracy" has been established, the second phase of the revolution takes place under the leadership of the "vanguard party" of the workers, i.e., the SACP. During this phase, liberal and democratic elements in the former national front are dispensed with prior to the establishment of the "people's democracy" or Communist state. The SACP clearly subscribes to the two-phase theory of revolution. In the publication, *The African Communist*, Number 87, Fourth Quarter 1981, the SACP states that its immediate aim is to "win the

objectives of the national democratic revolution, more particularly to win national liberation for all the black oppressed and to destroy the economic and political power of the ruling class." The same publication went on to say that the SACP's strategic aim is to "destroy the system of capitalist exploitation in South Africa and to replace it with a socialist system in which the ownership of the means of production will be socialized and the whole economy organized to serve the interest of the people."

The ANC also subscribes in recent publications to the doctrine of the two-phase revolution. The first phase is the "liberation under the banner of the Freedom Charter." The second phase is the establishment of the "people's democracy." The ANC publication, *Sechaba*, published in East Germany, mentions in its September 1985 edition that, "We in the ANC know that a nationalist struggle and the socialist struggle are not one and the same thing, and they do not belong to the same historical period. The two represent two distinct categories of the revolution." The same publication goes on to say: "[T]he chief content of the present phase of our revolution is the national liberation of the black people. It is impossible for South Africa to make the advance to socialism before the national liberation of the black oppressed nation."

Other Examples

The two-phase revolution has been practiced successfully in other countries:

• *Vietnam:* In Vietnam there was a national front, the FLN, which included non-Communists such as academics, Buddhists, Catholics and students. However, as soon as the "national liberation" had been achieved, the vanguard element of the front came to the fore and quickly eliminated its former democratic and liberal allies in the front. Many went to re-education camps, many fled, and many were killed.

• *Cuba:* In Cuba, there was also a broad front known as the July 26 Movement, including many democrats opposed to the Batista regime. At this stage of the revolution Fidel Castro promised his liberal allies that he would lead the country to genuine democracy with free elections. However, once he had seized power, many of his former non-Communist allies were imprisoned, exiled, or executed.

• *Nicaragua:* The same scenario was played out in Nicaragua after the success of the National Liberation Front in overthrowing the Somoza regime. Once again, the vanguard party, in this case the Sandinistas, seized power and began to eliminate the influence of its erstwhile democratic and liberal allies.

In the Fourth Quarter 1981 issue of *The African Communist*, Sol Dubula explains why it is correct that the ANC, and not the SACP, should lead the liberation alliance during the first phase of the revolution. "This is exactly the way the party (SACP) exercises its leading and vanguard role. . . . This is the way the Vietnamese Communists exercised their vanguard role in relation to the FLN during the liberation struggle, and it is also the way in which the early Cuban Communists related to Fidel Castro's July 26 Movement."

A Terrorist Organization

The ANC is part of the international terrorist network. The May 1986 *ADL Bulletin*, published by the Anti-Defamation League of B'nai B'rith (which can hardly be called pro-South Africa, pro-apartheid, conservative or racist—it is known to be very liberal), documents in great detail the close ANC working relationship with the Palestine Liberation Organization. In the article, authors Nathan Perlmutter and David Evanier describe how "The ANC is a strident supporter of the PLO. In September 1980, Oliver Tambo spoke in Paris at an International Conference on Solidarity with the Struggle of the Namibian People, sponsored by the World Peace Council, a Soviet front. He said, 'I would like to assure our comrades in the liberation struggles . . . and the PLO . . . that their struggle is ours.'"

The PLO Ambassador to Zimbabwe, Ali Halemeh, said recently: "It is necessary for the PLO and the liberation movements in southern Africa to work together on their struggles and their plight, because we are convinced that the collapse of the South African system will lead to the destruction of the Zionist state in the Middle East."

Jeremiah Denton's Senate Subcommittee has established that ANC terrorists were being trained by PLO terrorists in various locations across Africa, including Libya, and in the Soviet Union (i.e., at the Prvalnye Camp), East Germany and Angola. The ANC is dependent for its arms and support exclusively on the Soviet Union and other East bloc countries. It uses PLO communications facilities in Zimbabwe. The ANC is headquartered in Lusaka, Zambia with terrorist bases in Zambia, Botswana and Zimbabwe. In 1982, when Israeli troops raided PLO camps in Lebanon, they uncovered documentary evidence of PLO and Libyan coordination of terrorist activities throughout southern Africa. This past April, the ANC, Pan African Congress, SWAPO (Southwest Africa Peoples Organization) and the PLO met in the Libyan capital to discuss "1986 as the crucial year in the fall of Pretoria."

An Appeal to Arms

On December 1, 1985, Joe Modise of the ANC made the following appeal on Radio Freedom (the ANC radio service): "Our people must organize

themselves into groups, manufacture traditional weapons which must be used against the enemy. After arming themselves in this manner, our people must begin to identify collaborators and enemy agents and kill them. The puppets in the tri-cameral Parliament and the Bantustans must be destroyed." On May 4, 1986, Radio Freedom broadcast the following message to South Africa: "Let's take all our weapons, both rudimentary and sophisticated, our necklaces, our grenades, our machine guns, our AK47s, our limpet mines and everything we can get—let us fight the vigilantes, the police and the army."

On February 18, 1985, Radio Freedom broadcast the following appeal: "Enemy property must be petrol bombed, or attacked in any possible way. Enemy collaborators must also be isolated and attacked." (Over the past year, there have been 193 separate ANC terrorist attacks against civilian targets in South Africa, not including the murder of over 600 moderate blacks since September 1984, mostly by the necklace method.) On January 20, 1985, Radio Freedom said: "Puppets [i.e., freely elected Black town councilors] were killed, their houses burned, many were forced to resign and are still resigning today." On October 7, 1985, the Voice of Freedom, broadcasting from Zimbabwe, said: "The strategy of burning sellouts of the system seems to have paid out well in the ultimate end."

"The ANC is part of the international terrorist network."

During a meeting at California State University on October 10, 1985, ANC spokesman Alosi Moloi, justified this policy of violence as follows, "Among us we have people who have openly collaborated with the enemy. You have to eliminate one to save hundreds of others." His colleague, Tim Ngubane told the same meeting that, "We want to make the death of a collaborator so grotesque that people will never think of it." This is called "operation intimidation": intimidate the masses by the brutal murder of moderate supporters of the government as examples and the masses can be completely controlled by terror. This was one of Lenin's primary revolutionary tactics, and has been used in every Communist revolution since 1917.

Death by Necklace

Black moderate town councilors, mayors, police, or those accused by the revolutionary "comrades" of collaboration with the enemy are tried by peoples revolution courts, held by ANC or UDF (the internal wing of the ANC) revolutionaries. The following revolutionary justice is then meted out:

(1) The terrified victim is captured by his (her) executioners. Frequently his hands are hacked off as a deterrent to resistance. Barbed wire is otherwise used to tie the helpless victim's wrists together.

(2) The tire is placed over the shoulders and filled with petrol or diesel. (The latter has been found to stick to the skin when it burns.)

(3) The fuel is ignited with a match. Exhibiting boxes of matches is one of the ways the Comrades create respect or fear in the townships. The victim is usually forced to light his own necklace.

(4) The fuel ignites the tire, which rapidly attains a temperature of 400°C to 500°C.

(5) As the tire burns, great clouds of black smoke spiral upwards. Various short-chain hydrocarbon type fumes are released which reach a temperature of 300°C. Inhaled, they destroy the lining of the throat and lungs.

(6) The rubber melts and the molten rubber runs down the neck and torso, burning as it goes, deeper and deeper into flesh and tissue. The tire cannot be removed by others, such as family, at this point; neither can the fire be doused with water. The victim is now a living corpse.

(7) The victim may take up to 20 minutes to die. While he endures this agony, the Comrades stand about laughing and ridiculing him. Often members of his family are encouraged to attempt to save him. The Comrades know that this cannot be done. The molten rubber is similar to boiling tar and cannot be separated from the scorched flesh.

(8) In the first six months of 1986, the year in which the Comrades have promised to free the people of South Africa, 350 Blacks died in this way (172 between March 1st and June 5th). Between September and December of last year, 250 Blacks were necklaced, for a six-month total of about 600.

Hiding the Truth

These were living souls, human beings brutally butchered in the name of liberation, revolution and human rights. And the United States and Western press continue to hide these atrocities from their readers and create impressions that the violence and deaths in South Africa are being perpetrated by the "hated apartheid regime."

Necklacing is only part of the horror. Fire has destroyed 1,714 black businesses, 4,435 houses, 28 churches, and 54 halls. On Sunday, July 6th, Bishop Mokoena, the moderate black leader of the Reformed United Independent Churches of South Africa (an evangelical denomination with 4.5 million black members), was supposed to be preaching in his church near [Johannesburg]. He took ill and the assistant pastor took his place in the pulpit. ANC cadres entered the church, mistook the pastor for Bishop Mokoena, and shot him dead. Now do you understand what Winnie Mandela, the darling of the U.S. media and liberal U.S. Congressmen and

Senators, meant when she said, "with our boxes of matches and our necklaces, we shall liberate this country." The purpose of the necklace is not just to kill, but to terrorize the bystanders into obeying the revolutionary Comrades instantly and unquestioningly, to intimidate the frightened black masses into surrender. This is liberation ANC style!

Using South African Liberals

A document issued by the South African Communist Party to its cells in May 1986, entitled "SACP Directive Discussion Document," describes how SACP and ANC members need to have a uniform approach to negotiations and to working with white South African liberals. It should be noted that one of the most liberal, naive, appeasement-oriented groups in South Africa, in addition to the universities, certain church organizations, and the Progessive Federal Party, is composed of certain white South African businessmen (mostly *Englikaaners*) who seem to believe in the inevitability of an ANC victory and seem eager to negotiate "the best peace possible" with the ANC.

"The ANC is dependent for its arms and support exclusively on the Soviet Union and other East bloc countries."

The highest profile of these is Gavin Relly, Chairman of Harry Oppenheimer's Anglo-American Corporation. Many of these naive, liberal businessmen believe that they can continue to function and profit under an ANC government. On July 6th, eight South African business and industrial leaders, led by Relly, called for the South African government to release Nelson Mandela and to legalize and begin negotiations with the ANC. Relly said, "I have always taken the view that whether one likes the ANC or not . . . it constitutes an important factor in the South African setup."

Gordon Waddell, head of Johannesburg Consolidated Investments said, "We cannot start to find a solution unless Mandela is part of the process." And Southern Life Insurance Chief Neil Chapman said, "There can be no meaningful decision on South Africa without Mandela's release and the unbanning of the ANC." This, in spite of Mandela's, the ANC's, and SACP's promises to nationalize all mining companies, mineral resources, farms, and businesses.

The May 1986 SACP document talks about the revolution and the necessity of using white South African liberals to help further their objectives. On page 13, the document, in referring to the liberal bourgeoisie, said: "A serious revolutionary movement always tries to divide the enemy and to broaden the base of opposition . . . a continuing political readjustment in the ruling power block which favors its liberal bourgeoisie wing would undoubtedly create better objective conditions for the continuing struggle by the revolutionary forces to achieve the aims of the national democratic revolution . . . . We are justified in helping by all means (including talks) to advance the process of breaking the cohesion and unity of the ruling class." It is called "divide and conquer."

Negotiation and Revolution

On negotiations, the document said, "We must not mechanically dig in our heels against any future possibility of negotiations. We must remember that virtually all revolutionary struggles in the post-war period (Algeria, Vietnam, Angola, Mozambique, etc.) reached their final climax at the negotiating table. But the question of negotiations usually arrives at a time of a major revolutionary climax involving the transfer of power based on the massive strength of the people's offensive. . . . The main thrust of our present strategy remains a revolutionary seizure of power."

This document seems to be preparing SACP and ANC members for closer cooperation with South African liberals and for approaching negotiations. The leadership, anticipating the negotiation/final climax phase of the revolution described in the document above, must be trying to prepare their people so as not to appear to be "collaborating" with or "selling out" to the enemy.

George Shultz, Chester Crocker, and the U.S. State Department are leading the chorus for Mandela's release and for the South African government to negotiate a new government with the ANC. Our intelligence services and the State Department know and understand the information in this newsletter (and much more). Why then is the State Department pushing for an ANC government in Pretoria? One gets a real sense of deja vu when one remembers the U.S. betrayal of the Shah, Somoza, Ian Smith, Batista, and Marcos. But this time the stakes are the highest ever.

Donald S. McAlvany is editor of the McAlvany Intelligence Advisor, *co-editor of the* African Intelligence Digest, *and Chairman of the Council on Southern Africa.*

viewpoint**156**

The African National Congress Is Not Communist

Thomas G. Karis

In a free election in South Africa, the now-outlawed African National Congress could possibly win three-fourths of the black vote as well as some white votes. No such election is in sight, but the popularity of the ANC poses a challenge for U.S. policy. Since one of the ANC's allies is the pro-Soviet South African Communist Party, there is apprehension that the Communist Party dominates or controls the ANC. This issue has become so contentious that the October 1986 U.S. Anti-Apartheid Act, which imposes sanctions on South Africa, also directs the president to report to Congress about "the extent to which communists have infiltrated" black South African politics. As the conflict in South Africa intensifies and becomes more violent, the issue of who the ANC is and what it stands for will preoccupy U.S. policy.

This essay argues that focusing on the role of communism or the Communist Party risks misunderstanding the nature of the ANC. Although some of the ANC's support is only symbolic, and its capacity to control events in South Africa is weak, its strength lies in its stature as a national movement rather than a party. Most students of South African black politics do not believe that the ANC is dominated or controlled by the South African Communist Party. Their key premise, grounded in South African history, is that non-Communist African leaders work with Communists for their common end of opposing white domination.

A Unified Opposition

From its formation in 1912 by a group of African nationalists, the ANC has been the standard-bearer of the African's quest for equality and full political rights. It has sought to unify all opponents of white domination. After five decades of peaceful protest,

the ANC was outlawed in 1960, forcing its leadership into exile and its cadres underground. But open support for the ANC since its resurgence in the late 1970s has been defiant and nationwide, cutting across classes and ethnic groups and bridging the racial divide. Its goal is a democratic, nonracial and undivided South Africa, and its economic program is moderate and pragmatic.

In contrast, the South African Communist Party, founded in 1921 and outlawed in 1950, is a clandestine Marxist-Leninist party, claiming to be tightly controlled and highly disciplined. Its membership, undoubtedly very small, is almost entirely secret; its program is rigidly ideological and pro-Moscow. It responds primarily to its own elitist perception of the interests of the working class, although African nationalism has influenced the party. Beginning in the late 1920s, a few African Communists joined the ANC, some later becoming major figures in it. They are there today, valued and trusted by nationalists as comrades in a common struggle.

The allegation of outright Communist control over the ANC cannot be substantiated, and estimating the degree of Communist influence in the ANC is nearly as difficult. Though the Communists' ideological convictions and long-range agenda distinguish them from many in the ANC, at this stage of the struggle for national liberation Communists and non-Communists in the ANC have no significant differences on policy or strategy. Furthermore, the Communists and the ANC share an anti-imperialist stance, condemnation of many aspects of U.S. foreign policy, and embrace of all who support the ANC. . . .

One reason for the difficulty in assessing Communist influence in ANC decision-making is the absence of significant differences in policy or strategy during the current stage of the struggle for national liberation. Another reason is the nature of

Thomas G. Karis, "South African Liberation: The Communist Factor." Reprinted by permission of FOREIGN AFFAIRS, Winter 1986/87. Copyright 1986 by the Council on Foreign Relations, Inc.

influence that arises from personal friendship and shared experience. Influence, furthermore, is a two-way street—although anti-Communists often assume that only Communists can exert it effectively. Walter Sisulu, former secretary-general of the ANC who is now, with Mandela, in prison for life, would say to friends about critics who assumed that Communists would dominate any collaboration: cannot these people see that *we* might be using the Communists?

When asked about Communist domination, Oliver Tambo, clearly not a Communist, said: "It is often suggested that the ANC is controlled by the Communist Party . . . by Communists. Well, I have been long enough in the ANC to know that that has never been true."

Another ANC spokesman has pointed out that "at the peak of the civil rights struggle in the United States, [Martin Luther] King was called a Communist." The occasion for his remark was a meeting in Lusaka, Zambia, on August 23, 1986, between a delegation of Rev. Jesse Jackson's Rainbow Coalition, which was visiting the Front Line States, and a delegation of 17 ANC leaders, a majority of them members of the National Executive Committee. The meeting was unprecedented; said Alfred Nzo, the secretary-general, "for some of us, today is like a dream." In a spirit of solidarity rather than skepticism, a Jackson delegate and former activist in the civil rights movement asked the first question: how should he deal with the Communist issue when he returned home?

Pallo Jordan, a member of the National Executive Committee in his early forties who has lived in the United States, and who is not considered a Communist, gave a spirited reply. It was "absurd," he said, to assume that Communists are "smarter and cleverer than anybody else." (There were as many "geniuses and fools" among non-Communists as among Communists, he had said earlier in private conversation.) To assume that ANC members who were not Communists can be dominated now or in the future was "an insult." Africans who were Marxist-Leninists were not exempt from apartheid and had been welcomed as members of the ANC since the 1920s along with everyone else opposed to racism. "If this makes people in Washington uncomfortable, too bad."

Few Communist Members

Unlike speculation about influence, inquiry into the number of Communists in the National Executive Committee has the appeal of statistical objectivity, the assumption being that the number correlates with influence. Indeed, if it were true that the committee was dominated numerically by Communists, the question of influence and manipulation would become irrelevant. A further reason for interest in the composition of the committee is the presence of whites and Indians.

One suspects that this interest may resemble a habitual racist assumption of white South Africans: that when Africans engage in complex activity, whites or Indians must be manipulating them behind the scenes.

The London *Economist* of July 26, 1986, declared that the ANC's 30-member National Executive Committee contained at least ten "members" of the South African Communist Party "and perhaps as many as 14 or 15." That such a judgment has become commonplace illustrates how an assertion can take on authenticity through repetition, even if based only on flimsy evidence. Senator Jeremiah Denton's (R-Ala.) Subcommittee on Security and Terrorism began the process in 1982 with assertions and information that were provided by South African intelligence and contained major inaccuracies.

"Focusing on the role of communism or the Communist Party risks misunderstanding the nature of the ANC."

In June 1986 the South African government distributed a booklet listing 23 members of the ANC executive committee as "members" and/or "active supporters of the SACP." In the same month, Congressman Dan Burton (R-Ind.) listed in the *Congressional Record* the names of 19 who were "members" of the party, adding that "we believe that as many as 25 of the 30 are Communists." His information had been "compiled from South African intelligence and other sources" by Senator Denton's staff. Two months later, Senator Jesse Helms (R-N.C.) announced that William Casey, [former] director of Central Intelligence, had declassified at his request "the biographies of the Communist members of the Executive Committee."

In my view, the CIA biographies do not substantiate the conclusion that all or even more than three of the 18 men profiled are "Communists." Three men in these biographies are publicly known as members of the Communist Party: Joe Slovo, 60, the party chairman, and, as chief of staff, the third-ranking officer of the ANC's military wing; Steve Dlamini, who was imprisoned on Robben Island and later tortured, and Dan Tloome. Dlamini and Tloome, both in their seventies, are well-known stalwarts of trade unionism, the Communist Party and the ANC. Other members of the executive committee may also be party members; many almost certainly are not. Definitive proof most likely will not be forthcoming, though accusations with insufficient evidence are just as likely to continue.

But more important are the attitudes of current key ANC leaders toward the Communist Party, its thinking and its aims. The three top officials of the ANC are all in their sixties and veteran activists. Oliver Tambo, 68, the president, has been in the ANC forefront for some 40 years. He is a lawyer, an African nationalist, a practicing Christian, and a man of widely respected integrity, who is committed to Western forms of political democracy. It is difficult to think of any major African leader less interested than Tambo in personal power.

Other Key Leaders

Another top ANC leader is Thomas Nkobi, an African nationalist who has not been prominent as a political spokesman. Perhaps because he succeeded Moses Kotane, a Communist, as treasurer general, there has been speculation about his possible relationship to the Communist Party, but his biography was not among those submitted by the CIA to Senator Helms.

The third top ANC official is the secretary-general, Alfred Nzo. The CIA describes him as "a self-avowed Communist" although he has never made such an avowal. In conversation with me on June 27, 1986, he emphatically denied being a member, saying he was "an African nationalist." This characterization is consistent with his public record and reputation. Another major ANC leader, although not among the top three, is Joe Modise, who is in his early fifties. He is commander of the military wing and has a reputation as a man of action who talks little of politics. His biography is among the CIA 18, but it is devoid of any facts that would justify a supposition about orientation toward the Communist Party.

Communist Party membership is kept strictly secret except for the chairman and general secretary and a few well-known members. Determining who is a member is complicated by the fact that some members of the pre-1950 legal party did not join the post-1953 clandestine party, and others have since dropped out. ANC leaders do not seem to talk among themselves about the identity of party members; it does not appear to be of particular interest. Joe Slovo has said that "a speculative numbers game is being played . . . to spot the Communists" in the National Executive Committee, a practice that the writer does not publicly indulge in. When asked about the number of Communists on the executive committee, Oliver Tambo said, "I have never counted how many, but they all owe their primary allegiance to the ANC and that's all that matters to me."

Whether or not Nelson Mandela differs from Tambo regarding cooperation with Communists and the ANC's more militant evolution has been a matter of speculation among government officials considering his release from prison. A long-standing friend of Mandela who consulted with him told me that Mandela dramatically emphasized his relationship to Tambo in order to remove any doubts about their unity when he replied to President Botha's offer of conditional freedom. Speaking of "my greatest friend and comrade for nearly fifty years," Mandela said of Tambo in a statement read to a mass rally in Soweto, "there is no difference between his views and mine."

Nzo's CIA biography, more than any other, epitomizes the pro-Soviet charge that is levied against the ANC. Nzo, it says, is "the ANC's contact point with the Soviet Union"; he is a vice-president of the World Peace Council; and a high Soviet official has presented him with an award. These facts are not proof of party membership but obviously they indicate appreciation of the Soviet Union and points of agreement. Furthermore, Nzo expressed some typical ANC positions in a speech at the 65th anniversary meeting of the South African Communist Party on July 30, 1986, in London, where he extended "fraternal greetings." He condemned "the bellicose policies of international imperialism, first and foremost American imperialism," and cited conflicts or struggles in which the ANC opposed U.S. policy: the Vietnam War, Palestinian liberation, Nicaragua, El Salvador, Afghanistan, Mozambique and Angola. And he condemned the invasion of Grenada and attacks on Libya.

> "The allegation of outright Communist control over the ANC cannot be substantiated."

Nzo does not make judgments about internal Soviet policy, but he praises assistance from the Soviet Union, a praise that appears genuine and not, as one analyst has said, the currency with which Soviet arms are purchased. In his single-minded pursuit of nationalist goals, Nzo has no problem in accepting the embrace of all who support the ANC, not only the Soviet Union and its allies but also the Nonaligned Movement, the Organization of African Unity [OAU], the Palestine Liberation Organization and "many countries in Western Europe." In his speech at the Communist Party meeting, he praised "capitalists [who] . . . act against the apartheid regime" and Churchill, Roosevelt and de Gaulle, "who emerged as giants" in the fight against Nazism.

Varied Sources of Assistance

Nzo's eclectic reach is reflected in the sources of financial and material aid received by the ANC. Nearly all of its military support comes from the Soviet bloc through the OAU. The kinds of assistance received from governments, anti-apartheid groups, churches and the United Nations are extraordinarily varied and fluctuating. The ANC has particularly sought aid from Western countries, which it says has increased in recent years. In response to an inquiry in October 1986, the ANC's Lusaka office stated that probably more than half of its total aid now comes from Western and Third World governments and private donors, and from China.

The ANC has sympathetic relations with social democratic parties, the Socialist International and anti-apartheid groups in the United States such as the Free South Africa Movement and the American Friends Service Committee. In Lusaka in August 1986, Rev. Jesse Jackson pledged that his Rainbow Coalition would campaign for humanitarian and educational aid for the ANC, and announced an initial gift of $10,000.

"It is often suggested that the ANC is controlled by the Communist Party. . . . Well, I have been long enough in the ANC to know that that has never been true."

The ANC's radical anti-imperialist stance and rhetoric are hardly surprising in the light of the history of U.S. and Western complicity in bolstering the South African regime. What is surprising is the fact that the ANC continues to look to the United States for understanding and solidarity, and hopes for incremental pressure on South Africa by the U.S. government. Despite much of its rhetoric, the ANC historically, politically and culturally is more attuned to the United States and the West than it is to the Soviet bloc. Criticism of U.S. policies does not mean that the ANC accepts the Soviet Union's political system as a model or that an ANC-led government would be aligned with the Soviet Union. Despite the typically cold shoulder shown to Alfred Nzo in Washington in mid-1986, unlike receptions in Moscow, Oliver Tambo stands ready to meet with Secretary of State George Shultz, even though the United States may be sharing intelligence on the ANC with the South African government.

Thomas G. Karis is professor emeritus of political science at the City College of the City University of New York and senior research fellow of the Ralph Bunche Institute on the United Nations at the Graduate School of the City University.

US Policy Can Effect Peaceful Change in South Africa

Chester A. Crocker

Thank you for your hospitality and for the opportunity to discuss with you our policy toward Southern Africa. In the six years that I've been responsible for this policy arena there have been periods when we made real progress toward our goals of strengthened peace and stability, with democratic government and respect for individual human rights in all the countries of a region of critical importance to the United States. There have been other periods when these goals have seemed more distant as proponents of violence and extremism held the upper hand. We are currently in one of these seasons of uncertainty about the future of Southern Africa, and any assessment we draw about the future must be sober.

First let me say a word about the debate we have just come through over our policy toward South Africa. That debate was hard fought and doubtless left some bruised feelings on both sides. It was not, however, a debate about the fundamental objectives of our policy. This is best illustrated by the fact that the policy objectives set forth in the Comprehensive Anti-apartheid Act of 1986 parallel closely the goals set forth by President Reagan, Secretary Shultz and other senior officials of this Administration.

Our major difference with the Congress concerned the mix of policy instruments most likely to move South Africa toward the early end of apartheid and its replacement by a new, truly democratic South Africa with effective protection for the rights of majorities, minorities, and individuals. We forthrightly stated our conviction that the adoption of indiscriminate, punitive sanctions would not help achieve our objectives. Majorities in both houses of Congress did not agree. Those sanctions are now the law of the land, and we are implementing them. At

Chester A. Crocker, "U.S. Policy Toward Southern Africa: Peaceful Settlement and Coexistence," a speech delivered to the Detroit Economic Club on December 1, 1986.

the same time, Americans on both sides of this debate are coming to realize that sanctions do not amount to an effective policy toward South Africa. As Secretary Shultz said at the swearing-in of our new Ambassador to South Africa Ed Perkins, "it is time to raise our eyes once again to the horizon and move ahead."

A Turbulent Horizon

Unfortunately, the horizon in South Africa and the region is turbulent with storm clouds of violence and polarized confrontation. In response to international sanctions, the South African Government has retreated further into a self-imposed laager of repression and anti-American sentiment. The policy presence in black townships and restrictions on press freedom have helped keep scenes of violence off our evening news telecasts. But the cycle of repression and violent resistance continues. In recent days we have seen further forced removals of blacks and new detentions of anti-apartheid activists, including prominent churchmen. In both the black and white communities, extremist voices dominate the debate, and moderates are having to shout to be heard.

Tensions between South Africa and her neighbors have also risen dramatically. South African military spokesmen have openly threatened Mozambique and Botswana with armed retaliation unless these countries satisfy Pretoria that they are taking effective steps to halt cross-border guerrilla operations against South Africa. For its part, Mozambique has threatened action against neighboring Malawi unless that country halts alleged assistance to the RENAMO insurgency against the Maputo Government. Zambia and Zimbabwe are considering possible economic sanctions of their own against Pretoria knowing that such moves only invite potentially severe South African retaliation. In Angola, a civil war fueled by Soviet arms and Cuban troops drags on, even though military victory is clearly beyond the reach of either side.

Against this bleak backdrop, questions have arisen about our ability to make a positive contribution to peace, stability and democracy in Southern Africa. The South African Government has responded to the Congressional imposition of sanctions by imposing something of a chill in our bilateral relationship. This is perhaps best exemplified by Pretoria's attacks on our economic assistance program in South Africa.

All Americans can be proud of the contribution our aid program is making to assist South Africans disadvantaged by apartheid to develop essential skills and experience. In the fiscal year . . . [1986], approximately $20.3 million was dispersed to individuals and institutions committed to non-violence and democracy. Our aid has helped fund scholarships for students to study in the US, training of black entrepreneurs and trade unionists, and community-based projects in the areas of child care, youth activities, and legal advice.

Our aid program in South Africa—initiated during this Administration with bipartisan support in Congress—exemplifies the search for alternatives to violence and polarized confrontation that is at the heart of our policy toward South Africa and the region. We have been active partners with those in South Africa and the region who want to turn away from a mindless descent into violence and toward peaceful options for constructive change.

A Constructive American Approach

This constructive American approach is also exemplified in the activities of American businesses in South Africa. American firms have made an important positive contribution in South Africa by challenging the apartheid system and by spending over $200 million outside the work place to provide scholarships, training, non-racial housing and other benefits to black employees. While we understand the reasons why some American firms have withdrawn from South Africa, we applaud the determination of others to stay. These firms are in the forefront of American efforts to remain positively involved in the search for a better future in South Africa, and their honorable contribution deserves to be recognized by all Americans. Indeed it was so recognized—explicitly and eloquently—in recent legislation passed by Congress.

Despite the grim realities of the present situation in South Africa, we remain hopeful that the contending parties will come to their senses and recognize that the path of violence and confrontation is a dead end street. Earlier [in 1986], the Commonwealth's Eminent Persons' Group seemed to be making progress in convincing both the South African Government and its black opposition that constructive change can occur only through negotiations. There seemed also to be a growing

recognition on all sides that no party can be allowed to dictate in advance the agenda or outcome of the negotiations and that all South Africans will have to have confidence that their fundamental interests and rights would be protected.

At the heart of the EPG initiative was an effort to convince the parties to begin the essential process of confidence building by taking limited, but important steps that could be reciprocated by the other side. The EPG effort eventually collapsed following the May 19 South African Defense Forces raids on ANC installations in Zimbabwe, Zambia, and Botswana. However, the EPG's effort to help the parties undertake these so-called matching commitments is a positive and important legacy for the future. That approach has *not* run its course; indeed, it has barely been tested.

"The search for alternatives to violence and polarized confrontation . . . is at the heart of our policy toward South Africa."

President Reagan and other Western leaders have publicly called on the South African Government to do its part to get negotiations started by ending the state of emergency, releasing Nelson Mandela and other political prisoners, unbanning political parties including the ANC, and setting a timetable for appealing apartheid laws. If the South African Government were to take these steps, it would be entitled to expect from its opposition a firm commitment to cease violence and enter negotiations.

While the immediate prospect for negotiations is not bright, we have seen some signs that the parties remain open to discussion of the idea of matching commitments. In our contacts with both the South African Government and its opponents, we have made clear that the US will not uncritically endorse the demands of any of the contending parties. We are, however, ready now to explore seriously with each of the parties the contribution it can and should make in the interest of a negotiated settlement. In a word, the diplomatic option is open and our good offices are available.

We have no illusions about the near-term prospects for progress. External parties, however well-intentioned, cannot help solve South Africa's crisis unless South Africans themselves are prepared to take risks for peace. They cannot demand guarantees in advance of the precise outcome of a process that must, inevitably, entail compromise and accommodation of interests. We intend to challenge the South African Government, the ANC and other black opposition groups, and the Frontline States to do their part to help create a framework for negotiations that might provide real hope for a lasting resolution of South Africa's crisis.

Alternatives to Confrontation

We will also continue to support efforts by South Africa and her neighbors to work out alternatives to confrontation, and cross-border violence. The urgent need for practical steps in this direction is nowhere more evident than in the current tense relations between South Africa and Mozambique. These countries are still officially party to the Nkomati Accord which commits each signatory not to aid insurgent movements on the territory of the other party. Following its signature in 1984, the Nkomati Accord *did* lead to a reduction of tension and enhanced security for both South Africa and Mozambique.

In recent months, the Government of Mozambique has alleged that South Africa has resumed and increased assistance to the Mozambican insurgent movement RENAMO. For its part, South Africa rejects the claim and warns Mozambique against harboring guerrillas of the African National Congress. In our view renewed cross-border violence or threats of violence, and intervention in neighboring countries, cannot resolve South Africa's problems and may well exacerbate them. Instead, we urged both parties to fulfill strictly their obligations under Nkomati and handle their compliance concerns through a direct security dialogue. The US played a significant role in the negotiation of Nkomati, and we stand ready to assist the parties in revitalizing it. But the primary impetus must come from the countries that stand to benefit most from Nkomati—South Africa and Mozambique.

We have watched with growing concern as tensions have escalated between Mozambique and Malawi. These tensions arise from conflicting claims about Malawi's relationship with RENAMO and its position on the insurgency in Mozambique. We firmly believe that the interests of neither Mozambique nor Malawi would be served by confrontation. The two countries have agreed to establish a joint commission to address mutual security concerns. This is a potentially positive development and we urge that this commission be activated immediately.

In Angola also, we are convinced that there is potential for accommodation rather than violent confrontation. We continue to seek a diplomatic resolution of the conflict in Angola that would provide for Namibian independence and withdrawal of all foreign forces—South African and Cuban—from that country. We believe that the gap between South Africa and Angola on a timetable for the withdrawal of Cuban forces is bridgeable. We have made clear to all the parties our readiness to help

bring this negotiation to a successful conclusion.

We had hoped that South Africa's conditional agreement to begin implementation of UN Security Council Resolution 435—the Namibian Independence plan—on August 1, 1986 would prompt the Government of Angola to reply constructively to our ideas on a Cuban withdrawal schedule. Unfortunately, no such response was forthcoming from Luanda and the August 1 opportunity was lost. We nevertheless believe that this peace process remains the one way out of a long and bloody civil war for the Angolan parties. Our invitation to the Government of Angola to resume these negotiations remains on the table, and we urge that they take it up.

> "We intend to challenge the South African Government, the ANC and other black opposition groups . . . to do their part to help create a framework for negotiations that might provide real hope for a lasting resolution."

Although reconciliation among contending Angolan parties is an issue only Angolans themselves can resolve, we believe that it must occur if there is to be real peace in that country. Our support for UNITA [the National Union for the Total Independence of Angola] underscores our conviction that it is a legitimate nationalist movement which must participate in any serious effort at reconciliation among Angolans. We have made clear that we do not expect any Angolan party to commit political suicide, nor do we have an American plan for Angola's political future. We will continue to work actively toward the day when they can do so free of external military presence from any quarter.

Practical Objectives

As we consider opportunities for accommodation among contending parties in southern Africa, our focus should be on practical objectives that would redound to the benefit of all. In our view, the re-vitalization of regional transportation routes disrupted by armed conflict would be especially welcome. The US supports African efforts to reach practical arrangements among all the affected parties that could lead to re-opening of these transportation routes, many of which have been closed for years.

The US has made clear its determination to support the efforts of southern African countries to deal with the economic consequences of the region's political crisis. President Reagan has stated that he will propose to Congress a new program of assistance to the black-ruled states of southern Africa in the critical areas of trade, transportation, and support for economic reform. We are now working to prepare the details of this program. As we move forward, it will be essential to consult and coordinate our efforts with the countries in the region and our Allies and friends. Despite the budgetary stringencies of the Gramm-Rudman era, we are determined to fulfill the President's pledge to propose a good program and to see it approved by Congress.

In his recent send-off for our new Ambassador in Pretoria, Secretary Shultz said that, in southern Africa as in other areas of policy, we must ask "not only what we want, but how, practically we can get from here to there." I have tried to underscore for you today our conviction that American goals in southern Africa will not be achieved if the entire region slides into endemic violence. That is what could happen if we simply opt to disengage when the going gets tough. Such a course can only produce chaos and an increase in Soviet influence, since Moscow's strong suit is the promise of arms, advisors, and military solutions.

By contrast, the US role must continue to be to roll up our sleeves and work for negotiated solutions and a peaceful change. We favor this course because it is right. We are—as someone once said—a nation of builders, not destroyers. But we also believe it is practical because the peoples of southern Africa have visions of a positive future for their beloved region. They nurture the hope that their children will enjoy a future of dignity, liberty, peace, and prosperity. They too want to be builders. All Americans are united in their desire to help achieve these objectives. This is the basis of an American consensus on southern Africa that will last long beyond the current pessimism in the region and our own tactical debates of the moment. It is a consensus worth preserving and nurturing because it is worthy of the best traditions of the American people.

An Active US Role

And what does this mean in practice? I submit it means an active role: the maintenance of an active AID [Agency for International Development] role in South Africa and the region to support black advancement and educational development; it means our diplomacy is ready and willing to play a catalytic role—opening channels, floating ideas—between the South African government, Front-Line states, ANC and other major black groups; it means a sustained regional role between South Africa and its neighbors on behalf of peaceful settlement and coexistence; and above all, it means that the West as a whole maintains its presence and influence via all available channels to support its hopes for a brighter future for all the peoples of this troubled yet strategically important region.

Chester A. Crocker is the US assistant secretary of state for African Affairs.

"Using quiet diplomacy to influence the South African government . . . simply has not worked."

US Policy for Peaceful Change Has Failed

Milfred C. Fierce

Some years ago a British scholar, Richard William Johnson, wrote a book entitled *How Long Will South Africa Survive?* Few astute observers of the South African scene in 1987 are prepared to attempt a reply to such a vexing question. More precisely, the question is, How long will the system of apartheid and white minority control over the black majority survive? Many suggest that a large part of the reason the Afrikaner-dominated National Party government of South Africa has survived as long as it has is U.S. foreign policy toward the Republic. I believe that U.S. policy has been found wanting since the National Party came to power in 1948—for almost four decades that include the administrations of Truman, Eisenhower, Kennedy, Johnson, Nixon, Ford, Carter and Reagan.

In some cases there was no discernible policy; in others, the policy appeared to be ill-conceived, poorly informed, and wrong in its misreading of the evolving situation in the region. In still other cases the policy appeared to have good intentions but was, in the final analysis, ineffective. No administration policy has drawn as much criticism as President Reagan's policy of "constructive engagement."

The Reagan approach—using quiet diplomacy to influence the South African government and move it away from apartheid and toward negotiation with the acknowledged leadership of the black majority for a new political order in South Africa—simply has not worked. Nor has the policy brought Namibia any closer to independence than it was in 1980 when Ronald Reagan was elected president. Critics do not quarrel as much with the idea of constructive engagement as with the absence of results, i.e., "too many carrots and too few sticks."

Despite the "modest reforms" of the Botha

government, they fall far short of satisfying the political aspirations of the black majority. Such measures as recognizing black and multiracial labor unions, freeholds or 100-year leaseholds for urban Africans, restoration of citizenship for so-called Homeland Africans, tempering influx control restrictions, repeal of mixed-marriage and immorality laws, and the adoption of a new constitution (which included coloreds and Indians in a new tricameral Parliament but excluded Africans altogether) might be considered significant advances for Afrikaners. They might even have been considered important by some Africans four years ago; now, however, they aggregate to little more than a rearrangement of the deck chairs on the *Titanic*.

Anger and Hostility

Among black South Africans the policy of constructive engagement provokes great anger and hostility. They cannot understand how the Reagan administration can promise assistance to the Savimbi-Unita faction contesting the government in Angola, how the United States government can provide considerable military aid to the Contra rebels fighting the Sandinista government in Nicaragua, how retaliation against Libya can be swift and decisive, how action against Ferdinand Marcos in the Philippines and Jean Claude Duvalier in Haiti can be unequivocal, and, at the same time, how the United States government can be so patient, some would say apologetic, with the Botha regime, not have regular consultations with the African National Congress (ANC), and not receive ANC leadership at all in Washington.

Black South Africans are further agitated by U.S. vetoes of UN resolutions condemning South Africa for behaving like the "rogue elephant" of Southern Africa, violating the borders of its neighbors with impunity. Black South Africans feel that U.S. long-term interests in Southern Africa and South Africa

Milfred C. Fierce, "U.S. Foreign Policy and South Africa," *Social Education*, February 1987. Reprinted from *Social Education* with permission of the National Council for the Social Studies.

are not well served by such an approach. I agree. The policy of constructive engagement has encouraged a view in the Botha government that the price to be paid to the U.S. and its Western allies will not be so high that it must accelerate the pace and direction of change. Therefore, a stronger incentive to get on the road toward a more democratic South Africa has been missing.

In 1981 the Study Commission on U.S. Policy Toward Southern Africa published its report entitled *South Africa: Time Running Out (SATRO)*. This 500-page book contains a lengthy background section on South African history and its people, the system of apartheid and the state of civil liberties, the South African economy, black and white politics, and the Republic's relations with its neighbors and the international community. It is still the best single-volume study dealing with South Africa. The centerpiece of *SATRO* is the final section on policy. Presented here is an invaluable policy framework for analyzing the range of complex issues involved in foreign policy. The policy framework is the creation of the Study Commission. It was developed to analyze policy toward South Africa but can be used to analyze foreign policy elsewhere—for example, in Central America, the Middle East, Poland, or South Korea. For the sophisticated analyst, it can also be used with domestic policy.

> "To declare that the situation in South Africa has deteriorated and is uncertain is to state, or restate, the obvious."

The commission began by cataloguing U.S. interests in Southern Africa. There was no special priority order. An assessment was then made of the situation in South Africa (1979-1981) and the probable range of future events (not predictions) in order to establish a context for making and executing the policy. The next step was to develop a set of objectives based on the U.S. national interests in the region and in South Africa in particular.

Opposing Apartheid

The commission determined that there would be five (others might decide there are more or fewer) and that the most important among them was to demonstrate the fundamental and continuing opposition of the United States government and people to the system of apartheid. In many ways the success of the policy would rest on the degree and extent to which Objective 1 was achieved because later action could be misunderstood and *bona fides* questioned without strong and regular signals of opposition to the repugnant system of apartheid. A series of actions was recommended for

each objective, to be put in place immediately and not withdrawn until apartheid was eliminated. Some of the actions for Objective 1 included sanctions already adopted by the private sector and the U.S. government and other actions that could, if employed, be a forceful influence on the South African government—for example, a freeze on new investment and expansion of various embargoes already in place to cover U.S. subsidiaries.

It is important to realize that the policy framework is highly integrated in nature and that all elements are designed to operate in unison. The commission noted that the greatest invitation to communism in Southern Africa was white intransigence in South Africa. It concluded with an observation that stronger measures might be warranted if the situation worsened. I believe that the findings and recommendations of the Study Commission remain valid in 1987. I also believe the situation in South Africa has grown worse.

To declare that the situation in South Africa has deteriorated and is uncertain is to state, or restate, the obvious. More than two years of unrest have brought the country to its most desperate crisis in the history of the Republic. This appears to have left the government adrift, rudderless, with no clear vision of the future—which path should be taken or what must be done.

There are unprecedented divisions within the ranks of Afrikanerdom. The economy, although still structurally sound, continues to experience its worst recession in 50 years. The South African Rand reached an all-time low of 35 cents in mid-June of 1986. Has South Africa reached the proverbial slippery slope? No one can say; that is part of the uncertainty. The landscape is littered with doomsday forecasts regarding South Africa. So far they have been proven wrong. The clock has been stuck at five minutes to midnight since the Sharpeville Massacre in 1960 which killed 67 Africans (most of them shot in the back) and wounded 186 during a peaceful protest against South Africa's pass laws. This time, however, could be different.

Supporting Sanctions

I support tough, selected, sharply focused multilateral, diplomatic-coercive economic and other sanctions (that assume no moral high ground) against South Africa with clearly stated objectives and with a time-triggering mechanism.

I believe it is appropriate that the United States government has taken the lead because all South Africans care most about what Americans think and do. This is so because Americans have the strongest convictions about the immorality of apartheid and are most annoyed by it, because such an initiative is most consistent with overall U.S. traditions and values, and because the U.S. leads the West. The U.S. should now make an unrelenting commitment to bring allies along (the United Kingdom, West Germany, Japan, France and others). U.S. leadership here is also the best way to protect our long-term interest in the country and in the region.

The escalation of black unrest inside South Africa has unleashed a dramatic and significant increase in U.S. public awareness and interest in what is happening in South Africa and what role the U.S. private sector and government are playing. University campuses are involved, the churches are mobilized, municipalities and local governments are acting, and civil rights groups and others are protesting and criticizing U.S. policy. In October 1986, Congress adopted a sanctions package over the president's veto that restricts loans to the South African public and private sector, bans new investment, bans the importation of South African coal, steel, iron, uranium, agricultural products, sugar and textiles, and eliminates landing rights in the U.S. for South African aircraft.

"In order for the kind of political change to take place in South Africa that will satisfy the black majority . . . there is a need for inducements and pressures both internally and externally."

U.S. government and private assistance for the education and training of black South Africans is growing. In addition, Edward Perkins has been named the first black U.S. Ambassador to South Africa. The U.S. public has not been so aroused since the Vietnam years.

The Need for Outside Pressure

In order for the kind of political change to take place in South Africa that will satisfy the black majority and avert a bloody race war, there is a need for inducements and pressures both internally and externally. I propose using the commission's policy framework and a selection of further sanctions and actions to be put in place right away by business and government and to remain in place until (1) the system of apartheid is eliminated; (2) the ban is lifted on ANC and PAC, and Nelson Mandela and other political prisoners are released; (3) the South African government announces its clear, public and unequivocal intention to begin a process of negotiation for a new political order with the leaders of all population groups and releases a timetable for the promulgation of a new constitution.

One further sanction I propose is the denial of U.S. and other foreign capital. In the words of Malcolm Fraser, cochair of the Commonwealth Eminent Persons Group (EPG), the intention here is "not to bring South Africa to its knees but to its senses.". . .

A range of further sanctions with "bite" could also be employed against South Africa in an effort to influence the government. Although space limitations do not permit a full exposition here, literature on sanctions against South Africa is plentiful.

Sanctions and More

Economic sanctions will hurt black South Africans and the frontline states. They will hurt whites, too. Whether or not they will force the South African government to end apartheid; to release political prisoners; to unban ANC, PAC and other organizations; and to begin negotiating for a radical reformation of South African society cannot be forecast. Such sanctions *alone* probably will not do so. When combined with internal and other pressures, they might succeed. A[n] *Economist* editorial sums up the sanctions dilemma.

> Sanctions have a dismal record. They are a legitimate way of expressing distaste or despair, but they rarely change the things that cause those feelings. They can all too often be evaded. They sometimes stiffen the backs of the sanctioned and spawn dissent among the sanctioners. Once applied, they are embarrassing to remove if they turn out not to have worked. *Yet they remain one of the few extensions of diplomacy available to Governments short of war.* (Emphasis added.)

Now that sanctions against South Africa have been passed by the U.S., the European Community, the Commonwealth, other groupings, and individual nations, the hope is that they will eventually help reduce the slow descent into race-civil war with the resulting massive loss of life and destruction of property that have already begun.

Paradoxically, general strikes, black consumer boycotts, and similar action inside South Africa could render international economic sanctions irrelevant. The next three years, 1987-1990, could determine the realities for South Africa and its people in the 21st century. The highest priority for U.S. foreign policy toward South Africa in the short term, and eventually for the long term, is to take whatever action is required for the majority inside South Africa to know consistently and clearly that the U.S. government and people, speaking with one voice, have aligned themselves with the 30 million blacks who will ultimately be in the best position to protect U.S. interests in the country and in the Southern Africa region.

Milfred C. Fierce is professor and chair of the Department of African Studies at Brooklyn College in New York, consultant for the Ford Foundation Southern Africa Study Group, and former research director of the Study Commission on US Policy.

"Sanctions represent the only hope of bringing the apartheid regime to the negotiating table."

Sanctions Can End Apartheid in South Africa

William Minter

Far from heralding a new national consensus, America's recent economic sanctions against South Africa, imposed over President Ronald Reagan's veto, are likely to touch off new controversy about U.S. policy toward the apartheid regime. Sanctions, after all, are no longer simply a hypothetical option, but the centerpiece of U.S. policy toward South Africa. And they will be judged according to actual results. Consequently, Americans are going to need realistic standards to evaluate these measures.

So far, the country is off to a discouraging start. The various sides of the sanctions debate have rarely acknowledged the wide variety of sanctions that can be imposed. And they seem unaware that sanctions can seek many different objectives and achieve many different results—direct and indirect, positive and negative, short- and long-term. Further, neither supporters nor opponents of sanctions have explained whether their views depend on certain degrees of international compliance.

Most important, the views of both sides reflect hidden assumptions that are at best highly dubious. Although many vehemently deny it, most sanctions opponents believe that the South African government either should or will survive indefinitely to preside over needed change. Many supporters of limited sanctions seem confident that partial measures will persuade Pretoria not only to abolish the apartheid philosophy of rigid racial separation, but also to dismantle voluntarily the century-old socioeconomic order of white privilege. And some supporters of comprehensive sanctions often appear certain that such measures can produce dramatic results quickly.

Benefits of Sanctions

Thus the United States can expect the new sanctions debate to be dominated by the slogans and

half-truths that have filled the air so far—especially opponents' assertions that sanctions never work and that sanctions and diplomacy are mutually exclusive. But a look at what is known about the history of economic sanctions and about South Africa's politics, economy, and society produces some surprising conclusions. First, sanctions have achieved important successes in various situations. Second, comprehensive sanctions stand a good chance of encouraging fundamental change in South Africa—though not right away. Moreover, unless Americans want to go to war against apartheid, such sanctions represent the only hope of bringing the apartheid regime to the negotiating table. Third, in the short term, tough sanctions will indeed hurt black South Africans, but they probably will hurt whites more. And the costs to the black population will be far outweighed by the long-term gains.

In a 1965 memorandum on sanctions and the South African economy, the CIA, without making any detailed economic projections, catalogued South Africa's economic strengths and chided many "Afro-Asian" countries for refusing to admit that "boycotts simply do not work." But even those who frequently voice these adages ignore them when convenient. In Western Europe, general opposition to sanctions is strong. All the same, Great Britain adopted sanctions against Argentina during the war over the Falkland Islands (Islas Malvinas) in 1982. And during peacetime, France imposed sanctions on New Zealand to recover French agents who had bombed the vessel *Rainbow Warrior* and its crew of antinuclear activists. Although American politicians appear ready to impose sanctions against leftist regimes on a moment's notice, the sanctions-never-work thesis always takes on new life in the South African case.

Such selective use of the maxim is easily exposed as hypocritical. But more important, successful cases of sanctions are easy to find, even when the goal is

William Minter, "South Africa: Straight Talk on Sanctions." Reprinted with permission from FOREIGN POLICY 65 (Winter 1986-87). Copyright 1986 by the Carnegie Endowment for International Peace.

the difficult one of overthrowing a government. U.S. sanctions against Salvador Allende Gossens's Chile were a major factor leading to his government's overthrow in 1973. U.S. and, to a lesser extent, British sanctions helped oust Idi Amin of Uganda in 1979, and South Africa itself used sanctions to provoke a coup in Lesotho in January 1986.

Studies on Sanctions

The two weightiest academic analyses of sanctions in recent years—the Columbia University political scientist David Baldwin's subtly argued *Economic Statecraft* and a massive study by the Washington-based Institute of International Economics (IIE)—both conclude that sanctions sometimes work and sometimes do not. Baldwin notes that previous studies often centered on impossibly narrow definitions of "success." They tended to consider sanctions a success only if they worked immediately and directly achieved their announced goal. These studies neglected indirect effects, the long-term toll, and the fact that the stated objective might not be the only or even the most important one.

Measured by such standards, almost any kind of political action—war, diplomacy, foreign aid, propaganda—can be labeled a failure. Yet if judged realistically—in terms of making a significant contribution to certain goals—sanctions probably have as good a record as any alternative strategy. The IIE study, for example, cites a 36 per cent success rate for 103 cases studied, including Chile, Rhodesia (now Zimbabwe), Uganda, and Iran, where American pressures helped topple the regime of Mohammed Mossadegh in 1953.

"Successful cases of sanctions are easy to find, even when the goal is the difficult one of overthrowing a government."

Opponents of South Africa sanctions like to argue that sanctions failed in Rhodesia, a former British colony where a white minority regime defied London's entreaties to pave the way for black majority rule. It is true that in 1966, then British Prime Minister Harold Wilson predicted a Rhodesian collapse in "weeks, not months," and that black rule did not come until 1980. Further, in the years immediately following the imposition of sanctions in 1966, Rhodesia's economy grew and even became more self-reliant. In the long run, however, sanctions exacted major economic costs and represented a constant drain on the white regime—especially after the rise of oil prices and the escalation of guerrilla warfare in the 1970s. According to white business leaders, sanctions did indeed bite, and hampered the

counterinsurgency. Moreover, these measures signaled the regime's moral isolation, giving legitimacy and encouragement to its opponents.

Their success is all the more remarkable since the British government did not, for most of the period, share the basic African and U.N. goal of near-term majority rule, but rather pursued the more limited objective of gaining white approval for the principle of eventual majority rule. And the major Western powers tolerated sanctions violations by South Africa, Portugal, and even their own oil companies. After 1971, Congress permitted open U.S. sanctions-busting by approving the importation of Rhodesian chrome. Without sanctions, the war would probably have continued for many more years. With stronger enforcement of sanctions, Zimbabwe could have been independent much sooner.

Defining Apartheid

With regard to South Africa specifically, as opposed to sanctions generally, the dispute over economic pressure is muddied by a big definitional problem: What exactly is apartheid? Even conservative Western politicians now claim to agree that "apartheid is repugnant." If apartheid is defined merely as the explicit ideology of rigid racial separation that was tagged as introduced in 1948 by Afrikaner nationalists, its defenders are indeed now largely confined to the far-right opposition to South Africa's ruling National party.

But if apartheid is taken to mean the essentials of the system that has reserved political rights and economic privilege for whites in South Africa for more than a century, then it must be recognized as firmly entrenched, albeit challenged as never before. And it is bolstered by a multitude of ties to supposed opponents overseas. Inside South Africa, moreover, not only the regime and the Afrikaner community benefit from the existing order, but the entire white population and a small number of blacks as well.

As a result, a return to the pre-1948 status quo or to the limited reforms proposed since then by the opposition parties of English-speaking whites would do little to satisfy black grievances. Eliminating apartheid in any sense meaningful enough to meet essential black aspirations and democratic values involves less a shift in policy than a transition to a totally new sociopolitical order. The minimum black agenda would deny whites not only political and economic dominance, but also veto power over the rate of change. The most appropriate American parallel—if one exists—is not the modern civil rights movement but the abolition of slavery and the Civil War.

Yet sanctions opponents who trust persuasion and "constructive engagement," the Reagan administration's strategy of seeking change through quiet diplomacy, tend to focus on eliminating apartheid in the narrow sense. In fact, South African President P.W. Botha's regime might take such steps or even move further toward power sharing—although without additional pressures the pace will probably be too slow. But Botha knows that abolishing apartheid, broadly defined, would entail ending the dominance of any white political party. And for the National party regime this would be political suicide.

Abolishing Apartheid

As a government "reform," therefore, apartheid's abolition is a contradiction in terms, impossible to achieve by sanctions or any other means. But if a new order is improbable through government-led reform, all who seek such change still need to ask how it can be achieved with the least possible human suffering.

South African white liberals have long counseled patience, arguing that black rights can be won gradually. When South African blacks protested in London against the white dominance about to be ratified by the 1910 Union constitution, they were told to place their hopes in the Cape province's decision to give the vote to a few educated blacks and in the eventual spread of liberal ideas. Following World War II, blacks were asked to await the liberalizing effects of industrialization. After the Soweto uprising of 1976 was suppressed, they were offered mainly the trickle-down morality of nondiscrimination codes adopted by foreign businesses.

The South Africa Foundation, established by the country's business leaders in 1959 with the encouragement of the former government information chief Piet Meiring, has since then urged the outside world to forgo coercive pressures and encourage white-led reform. Reagan's constructive-engagement strategists are only the latest of a host of foreign sympathizers with white South Africa to be mesmerized by the same broken record. No Western country truly interested in ending apartheid in the fullest sense can avoid taking sanctions seriously.

Political Effects

Disentangling the political effects of economic sanctions is highly complicated. Economic projections of any kind are uncertain enough. In general, however, analysts tend to underestimate the effects of sanctions by concentrating on symbolic short-term rather than substantive long-term consequences and by stressing the isolated effects of single measures rather than cumulative impact, and the interaction of sanctions with other factors influencing economic and political confidence.

The stress on the short term is congenial to sanctions advocates, who want a quick solution and who have an interest in short-term results, as well as

to opponents eager to debunk the whole idea as soon as possible. Quoted in the January 7, 1986, issue of the *New York Times*, Desmond Tutu, the Anglican archbishop of Cape Town, claimed that comprehensive sanctions could end apartheid in "next to no time." But other, more cautious Tutu statements suggest that he knows better. In the short run, sanctions are undoubtedly likely to produce defiance rather than surrender.

The South African economy has substantial short-term resilience. Additionally, even comprehensive measures adopted under mandatory U.N. provisions and implemented by South Africa's major trading partners would be subject to leakage. The world market price of South Africa's major exports—gold, platinum, and diamonds—would probably increase, providing extra revenues to cover the costs of evading sanctions. The more likely scenario of partial sanctions adopted step by step, reluctantly, with delays and deliberate loopholes, provides even more leeway for evasion and compensatory action.

"No Western country truly interested in ending apartheid in the fullest sense can avoid taking sanctions seriously."

But the 30-year record also shows that for the near future there is no alternative way, short of Western military action, to induce the apartheid regime to negotiate its surrender. Partly because important short-term results are so improbable, many sanctions proponents have understandably stressed the symbolic benefits of economic pressure. Symbolism, however, has its limits. Unless the goal of helping to topple apartheid is no longer taken seriously, Americans must look at the long-term as well as the short-term impact of their actions.

Sanctions and Negotiations

Genuine despair—and crocodile tears—over the gloomy short-term outlook for sanctions have caused some to place their hopes in negotiations instead. In fact, the Reagan administration claims to oppose tough sanctions largely for fear that they will undercut diplomacy—either by using up Washington's leverage all at once or by fatally antagonizing Pretoria.

But even though comprehensive sanctions are indeed likely to provoke short-term defiance, the dichotomy set up in the South African case between sanctions and negotiations is false. It wrongly implies that the parties are close to conceding the essential points in dispute. In South Africa today the basic will to reach a solution is missing, and talk about negotiations has become in effect a ploy to fend off the escalation of pressure while the conflict continues to fester or escalate.

The success of British mediation in ending the Rhodesian civil war inspired the architects of constructive engagement, among others, to envisage parallel prospects for Namibia or even for reform in South Africa. But then Rhodesian Prime Minister Ian Smith's white minority regime went beyond promises and began negotiating seriously only in 1979, as the toll taken by sanctions and guerrilla warfare mounted. Pretoria has never been and is not today weak enough to prefer concessions—even on regional issues—to intransigence and stalemate. In particular, South Africa has declared nonnegotiable the core black demand of a unified, nonracial state with universal franchise, and shows no sign of changing this position.

"Only after the regime is weakened by sanctions and other factors . . . is it likely to begin serious bargaining."

Negotiations will be essential at some stage. But sanctions will surely help bring them about. Only after the regime is weakened by sanctions and other factors—internal strife, boycotts, and strikes—is it likely to begin serious bargaining. Although a small minority of whites support a nonracial society, most whites—English-speaking as well as Afrikaner—are likely to accept such a risky future only when the consequences of refusal seem even riskier. Today, the time for negotiations may be nearer than it was 2 years ago, before the escalation of internal protest and initial steps toward international sanctions. But it is not yet imminent. Without comprehensive sanctions, the time is likely to be pushed back further, as the bitter toll of violence mounts. . . .

If the best the future can bring is an indefinite stalemate on the model of Northern Ireland or Lebanon, then it may be logical to continue the Western dance of delay. If, however, the moral and demographic weight of the antiapartheid forces is considered certain to prevail, Americans must explore how sanctions may contribute to minimizing bloodshed and to preventing the emergence of a despotic, anti-Western black government.

Sanctions opponents frequently insist that such measures are sure to hurt blacks, whether they are South Africans left unemployed as foreign companies pull out or the populations of neighboring countries hit by spin-off effects and South African retaliation. Those who use this argument—particularly South African officials and the white business establishment—seem to sport dubious credentials for expressing concern about black welfare.

Yet ad hominem arguments aside, the disagreement over the impact of sanctions rests on distinctions between short- and long-term effects. Sanctions supporters rarely contest predictions of short-term hardships, but counter that blacks will accept temporary suffering to bring an end to their long-term misery.

But even in the medium term, the consequences of sanctions for blacks are not as clear as is commonly assumed. All told, during this period serious sanctions will probably make white as well as black lives harder. And even discounting the potential payoff of ending apartheid, there are possible benefits rarely considered in the debate.

Take the potential disinvestment of a U.S. firm from ownership of a factory. If simple closure resulted, unemployment, of course, would rise right away. But chances are that white unemployment would increase proportionately more than black, since the white-black ratio in capital- and skill-intensive U.S. subsidiaries is far higher than in the work force as a whole. If, as is more likely, the factory were sold to South Africans, and imported inputs and capital made more costly by sanctions, the plant might be forced over time into more labor-intensive operations, thus increasing black employment. . . .

Forcing Whites To Act

Nor will the end costs of sanctions necessarily fall most heavily on blacks. Clearly, the white government will try harder to offset the difficulties for its own constituency. But Pretoria's capacity to extract economic concessions from blacks is increasingly under challenge, as is shown most dramatically by the escalating rent strikes in the government-controlled black townships. Both internal and external considerations are forcing the South African government into efforts to win over at least a portion of blacks. A wholesale assault against black living standards can only undermine the reform side of the government's strategy.

But it may also be harder to make further cuts in black welfare as opposed to white. The vast majority of rural Africans are already living on the margin. Moreover, the militant black trade union movement, which now endorses sanctions, is on the offensive despite high unemployment, while white-dominated unions are losing influence. And the luxury in which the white business and professional classes live gives ample scope for reductions in living standards. Proportionately, it is they who may be hurt most by sanctions.

William Minter is a contributing editor of Africa News Service and the author of King Solomon's Mines Revisited: Western Interests and the Burdened History of Southern Africa.

"Evidence is already accumulating that sanctions will not bring white South Africa to the negotiating table."

viewpoint 160

Sanctions Will Not End Apartheid in South Africa

Fleur de Villiers

The international crusade for punitive sanctions against South Africa has won its first major victory—and claimed its first victims. The overwhelming vote by Congress to override President Reagan's veto of the Lugar bill was pre-eminently a victory for the African National Congress and its acolytes who have campaigned for sanctions in the callous, if mistaken, belief that they will shorten the fuse on revolution in South Africa. It was a victory for those who needed to rally the Democratic party and public opinion on one of the few issues where, because of the conspicuous failure of constructive engagement, the Reagan administration appeared weak and vulnerable. But for those who have supported sanctions because they believed or were persuaded that there was no viable alternative, it has been a victory for the politics of fatigue, frustration, and failure.

In the final days of the 99th Congress, a slogan finally left the streets, the pickets, and the campuses and became a policy. Once again, and once again with the best will in the world, the United States has committed itself to folly, based on a fundamental misperception of the world beyond its borders. If sanctions begin to bite, there will be victims—the black South Africans and their families who will lose their livelihood, and possibly their lives. But the successful passage of the Lugar bill has already claimed some prominent victims. President Reagan, suffering his first major foreign policy defeat, is the most obvious, for the administration has now finally and permanently lost control over U.S. policy towards Pretoria.

The sanctioneers in Congress will not be long content with the first *tranche* of anti-Pretoria measures. Following the time-honored foreign policy

principle that if at first you don't succeed, fail, fail again, further and more heroic doses of the same medicine will certainly be demanded and applied until all hope of internal reform in Pretoria is smothered, white attitudes harden under external threat, and polarization becomes terminal. And if the Lugar bill has emasculated White House control over this area of foreign policy, it has by the same token claimed another victim in the Department of State which, in the last few months before the Senate vote, was reduced to a desperate attempt at damage limitation, trying to synchronize sanctions with Britain and stiffen Bonn's spine, thus keeping punitive measures to the minimum with which President Reagan could live, however uncomfortably. In the end, its efforts were in vain. Reagan was torpedoed, not by Chancellor Kohl or Mrs. Thatcher but by American legislators. Washington having broken ranks with its two major allies, it is now inevitable that Thatcher and Kohl, however reluctantly and against their own material interest, will be compelled eventually to bring their measures into line with those of the U.S. Congress. . . .

Sanctions Will Not Work

Evidence is already accumulating that sanctions will not bring white South Africa to the negotiating table. Instead, at a unique moment in history when the forces for change within were beginning to outweigh the forces of reaction, sanctions have begun to tip the scales the other way.

It was predictable that President Botha's utterances over the past few months would for the first time draw the bottom line on reform. The equation which the government has made and which the electorate is making in growing numbers is a false one, but it is nonetheless persuasive to people who see their security threatened. It is this: reform was respectable when it was generated by pressures within South Africa itself. It ceased to be politically attractive

Fleur de Villiers, "Changing South Africa—A Choice of Weapons," *The National Interest*, Winter 1986/87. Reprinted with permission.

when it could be portrayed by the far right as a concession to external demands. So the left has achieved its first objective. The stumbling process of relatively peaceful change is being halted, an already fractured society is being further and perhaps terminally polarized.

Thus have sanctions and the threat of sanctions as a means of producing an atmosphere conducive to a negotiated peace in South Africa already failed. South African business, which for the past few years has been at the cutting edge of the reform process, now sees itself as the undeserving first victim of the sanctioneers, and its attention is being diverted from pushing for further and more fundamental change to the immediate, politically safer and more absorbing challenge of sanctions-busting. The growing voices of dissent from the moderate center within the white electorate, and within the governing party, which were being heard early in 1986, have been stilled as white South Africans rally once again round the flag of national unity—a phenomenon that observers believe will be dramatically demonstrated during the general election, which will probably be held early in 1987.

The Effects of Sanctions

Far from bringing white South Africa to the conference table, sanctions will have precisely the opposite effect. But let there be no doubt about what they will achieve. They will not stop South African exports from reaching the outside world—albeit at a premium. Sanctioneers may reflect ruefully on the fact that it was the United Nations arms embargo that not only made South Africa almost self-reliant in arms production but taught it the art of sanctions-busting (today it is one of the world's major arms exporters). By the same token, sanctions will lead to import substitution in South Africa, which will in turn produce a brief, but confidence-building boost to its flagging economy. They will lead to a loss of jobs in the sanctioning countries. They will lead to a substantial increase in black unemployment in South Africa—already running at 60 percent in some areas—and a consequent increase in deprivation and human suffering.

"Far from bringing white South Africa to the conference table, sanctions will have precisely the opposite effect."

One of the most frequently quoted justifications for sanctions is that they are not merely the chosen weapon of the ANC, but have been demanded by Archbishop Desmond Tutu and other black leaders within South Africa itself. The argument appears unanswerable: if black South Africans demand

sanctions, who are we to deny them their suffering? It is difficult to answer without being accused of an *ad hominem* attack on the Archbishop of Cape Town, but it must be said that those who call most stridently for sanctions are not those who will lose their daily bread if they are applied. They are churchmen, trade union and party officials, all guaranteed a secure living. They are the ''comrades,'' school children sustained by their parents. In an article published by the Center for Applied Social Sciences at the University of Natal (August 1986), Professor Lawrence Schlemmer meticulously examined every survey of black South African opinion on the issue of divestment, boycott, and sanctions, and discovered that

> only a minority of around one quarter or less of blacks in major metropolitan areas would support total disinvestment or full economic boycotts. Their reasons, as my surveys and others have shown, are simply that they would not wish to endure collective economic punishment in the sanctions process . . . it is certainly true that a majority of black spokespeople, members of the middle class intelligentsia, students and clergymen support sanctions. This is not surprising since their interests are political rather than economic. They would undoubtedly benefit from an economic collapse if it means a consequent collapse of the South African government—an unlikely outcome.

Professor Schlemmer is not a supporter of the South African government, but South Africa's leading psephologist, a past president of the South African Institute of Race Relations, and a man with unimpeachable liberal credentials.

A Third World Basket Case

Should they succeed and lead to economic collapse, sanctions will reduce the only successful industrial economy in Africa to yet another Third World basket case, dependent on a massive injection of Western aid to save not only South Africa itself, but the network of surrounding states, which are critically dependent on migrant workers' remittances for much if not all of their GDP [Gross Domestic Product] and on trade with and through South Africa to keep their tottering economies alive. Sanctions do not have to be effective or universal to collapse those fragile economies—as studies by those states' own governments have shown. Recent confidential estimates by Zimbabwe have shown that it is 85 percent dependent on trade with or through South Africa. African leaders who call loudly for sanctions admit privately that ''they will kill us,'' that hopes to reduce dependence on South Africa by upgrading the Beira and Tanzara rail links are expensive pipedreams, and that no amount of Western aid is going to help them pay for their rhetoric. Which is why it is becoming ever more doubtful whether Zimbabwe or Zambia will actually live up to their rhetoric and apply the sanctions they seek from the West. Other ''Frontline states'' such as Mozambique and Botswana have already said that sanctions are a luxury they cannot afford.

With the South African problem now firmly ensconced in the domestic political arena in Britain, the United States, and Europe, it is not enough, however, to point out that sanctions are at best a means that will not achieve the desired end and, at worst, are a prescription for political and economic disaster. One has to suggest a viable alternative—and there is one at hand. It has already been dubbed a Marshall Aid Plan for South Africa—a title that is probably unhelpful and confusing, especially as Jesse Jackson has since hijacked the phrase to denote a rescue operation for the Frontline states that has no hope of success. But whatever it is called, it could be said to represent a variation of "constructive engagement"—with one important difference.

> *"Sanctions are at best a means that will not achieve the desired end and, at worst, are a prescription for political and economic disaster."*

Constructive engagement sought to engage the South African government. A Marshall Plan instead pushes Pretoria to the periphery and seeks constructive engagement with the South African people themselves, both black and white. It accepts that the only successful pressures for change are those generated within South Africa which have the willing support of the majority of whites, and it seeks to increase those pressures by offering whites (if not the government) an alternative to isolation, and blacks an alternative to deprivation.

Unlike sanctions which, whether total or partial, effectively deprive the West of any further leverage over an isolated and increasingly intransigent Pretoria government, this sort of aid will require continuing commitment, concern, and involvement. For those who see morality as a fit base and purpose of foreign policy, it should therefore have a greater appeal than sanctions, which seek to solve a problem by turning a collective back on it. . . .

Negotiation Instead of Isolation

There is a substantial element within the National party that is deeply disenchanted with the government's inability to grasp the nettle of further, fundamental political reform. Powerful voices in the Afrikaner community were raised early in 1986, urging the creation of a multiracial transitional government of national unity. But internal disaffection does not flourish under external threat.

If, instead of threatening isolation, the world were to offer a viable alternative, making acceptance of this kind of help and investment the price of South Africa's readmission to the international community, and if Pretoria were to reject it, the tide of white opinion could swing against a recalcitrant government and against all those who would prefer isolation to negotiation. A Marshall Plan could thus become the catalyst that would create the conditions for real negotiation between South Africa's polarized communities. A program of aid such as this will doubtless be attacked by the left as offering disguised help to Pretoria to shore up the apartheid regime. If properly packaged and presented as a diplomatic offensive and alternative to sanctions, it could achieve the exact opposite. Moreover, as an attempt to provide a climate in which moderation can flourish and moderate black and white South Africans find each other and their path to a democratic government, it is essential that its proponents ignore attacks from both the extreme left and the extreme right—neither of which favors moderation or democracy.

In answering these charges, however, it is important to point out that the plan does not embody a new principle. That principle is already enshrined—under the rubric of aid to the victims of apartheid—in the Lugar bill, in Commonwealth resolutions, and in statements by the EEC Council of Ministers. The amounts—$40 million a year in economic aid in the Lugar bill for "disadvantaged South Africans" and considerably less in EEC aid—are derisory. But the principle has been accepted and the funds represent a start. The total bill would also represent a fraction of the billions of dollars that would have to be poured into South Africa once sanctions and their political effects reduced it to an economic wasteland. But because of the way in which the Lugar aid is packaged and presented—as conscience money and an apologetic excuse for not going further down the sanctions road—it has been overlooked by the media and the public.

An Alternative to Sanctions

If it were removed from the sanctions package and presented separately, a positive, coherent, and well-publicized aid policy would not merely recapture the moral high ground from the sanctions lobby but win support from growing numbers of people who are beginning to realize that sanctions are a high-cost formula for disaster, and who are desperately casting around for an alternative.

The final objection is that the international tide of opinion has swung so far behind punitive sanctions that a plan such as this will be dismissed as too little too late. That is a counsel of despair. If support cannot be won for a policy that offers not decreasing leverage, but greater influence, challenge rather than destruction, then the West will have to live with the consequences of its impatience. Its desire to get South Africa off its conscience and the international menu, whatever the cost, could eventually involve

the positioning of peacekeeping forces in the
Frontline states and the Lebanonization of South
Africa. To borrow Sir Geoffrey Howe's phrase, it
should not require a quantum leap of the
imagination to realize that there is a better way.

Fleur de Villiers is assistant editor of the Sunday Times
*in Johannesburg. She is researching a book on South
Africa while on sabbatical as a visiting fellow at the
International Institute for Strategic Studies in London.*

"The Nicaraguan revolution has taken on the tasks that other oppressed peoples have assumed in order to attain a better life."

The Sandinistas Have Improved Nicaraguans' Lives

Gary Ruchwarger

Nicaraguans call their revolution the "Popular Sandinista Revolution." The anti-imperialist struggle of General Augusto Cesar Sandino and his army of peasants, workers, and artisans in the 1920s and 1930s has served as an important source of identity and historical experience for the contemporary revolutionary process.

Nevertheless, the Sandinista revolution can be compared with the major social revolutions of modern history. In its own unique way, rooted in the country's particular history and social structures, the Nicaraguan revolution has taken on the tasks that other oppressed peoples have assumed in order to attain a better life: the battle against imperialist domination; the construction of a sovereign nation-state; the eradication of hunger, ignorance, backwardness, and exploitation; the recognition of human dignity; and the conscious participation of the people in the creation of their own future as a nation. . . .

Contra War

Since the first inauguration of Ronald Reagan, the Sandinista revolution has confronted an escalating counterrevolutionary war, a well-funded and elaborately-planned war of attrition. In the words of CRIES, a Central America think tank based in Nicaragua, "The military war against Nicaragua is not merely designed to destroy the army; rather its principal aim, in the long run, is to waste and drain the limited resources of the Nicaraguan economy."

Indeed, the U.S.-orchestrated counterrevolutionary war combines military attacks with economic sabotage, political assaults, and psychological pressures. Carrying the insidious label of "low intensity war," the imperialist onslaught has forced the Sandinista revolution to concentrate nearly all its

Gary Ruchwarger, "The Revolution at Age Seven," *Against the Current*, January/February 1987. Reprinted with permission.

human and material resources on the interrelated activities of defense and production. The twin pillars in the Sandinistas' struggle against U.S. aggression, defense and production have become the rallying cry of Nicaragua's popular sectors.

Strengthening the Country

As the revolution makes its way through its eighth year, the three centers of revolutionary power—the Sandinista National Liberation Front (FSLN), the revolutionary state, and the Sandinista mass organizations—are expanding their efforts to strengthen the country's defense system and increase the levels of economic output.

Party, state, and mass organization efforts to strengthen Nicaragua's military defense have borne fruit in the last two years. Bolstered by the military service law passed in September 1983, the Sandinista army launched an offensive against the contras in December 1984. Newly-formed "irregular fighting battalions," made up of draftees, continually pursued detected contra units in search and destroy missions that by late 1985 made it impossible for the contras to launch any effective attacks.

In early 1985 the Sandinista military began to employ MI-8 and MI-24 Soviet helicopters which allow the army's battalions to deploy themselves faster than the contras can flee the ground. The helicopters also give the army the advantage of air fire support. With the addition of some 25,000 draftees between February 1984 and February 1986 the Sandinista army grew in strength to some 62,000 soldiers.

Backed by newly-formed army reserve units drawn mainly from recently demobilized draftees, the Sandinista army killed 2,745 contra troops and captured 300 more during the first six months of 1986. Ministry of Defense officials increasingly employ the phrase "the strategic defeat of the contras" when analyzing the status of the war.

On August 2, 1986, the Sandinista army's chief of staff Joaquin Cuadra, reported that during the first half of the year the revolution's armed forces prevented the contras from penetrating their targeted territories and accomplishing their political-military plans. Although admitting that the infusion of 100 million dollars would improve the contra army in a tactical sense, Cuadra insisted that the contras' strategic defeat could not be reversed.

The Cost of War

The Sandinistas have paid a tremendous price for their military gains. Since 1980 the U.S. war against Nicaragua has claimed 12,000 victims, with more than 4,000 killed, 4,500 wounded, 3,000 kidnapped, and 120,000 displaced from the war zones. Moreover, economists calculate that the total direct and indirect costs of the war surpass $2 billion—more than the country's annual gross national product. The war's direct costs, estimated at $601 million, are greater than two years of exports.

Aware that the contras' recent reverses will not deter the U.S. from continuing its aggression, Sandinista leaders are preparing the Nicaraguan people for an extended war. In opening his speech on the revolution's seventh anniversary, President Daniel Ortega confessed that he would have preferred "to speak of the aggression as a thing of the past, and to dedicate this anniversary speech to production, health and education." But he admitted that "the aggression is present, is not disappearing, and threatens to increase."

"The Sandinista revolution . . . seeks to develop the institutions of participatory democracy."

In the short term, there does not appear to be any possibility of a compromise between the United States and Nicaragua. The continuing war has both positive and negative consequences for the revolutionary process. As time passes the revolution is consolidating its popular base of support and institutionalizing its political and social transformations. The ongoing threat of U.S. aggression has strengthened national unity and popular support for the Sandinista regime. In addition, the army and civilian militias are gaining more combat experience and the system of national defense is attaining greater efficiency.

However, the prolongation of the war and U.S. economic sabotage will severely damage the country, draining scarce economic resources and interrupting development plans. The loss of human lives will continue as will the destruction of homes, farms and economic infrastructure. Indeed, the war has already

thrown the country into an economic recession from which it will take years to recover.

The Task of Nation-Building

In most Latin American countries the local bourgeoisie confronted the process of state-building during the first half of the nineteenth century, as part of their project of integrating their economies into the international market.

Nicaragua's pre-1979 capitalist state was a product of North American military invasions and U.S. political influence exerted on the country through the Somoza dictatorship. For four decades the dominated classes acquiesced to their subordination to a dictatorial state which was itself subordinated.

The anti-imperialist struggles of Sandino and the FSLN challenged this neo-colonial project. The Sandinista revolution faces the task of establishing a modern and sovereign nation-state employing a revolutionary bloc of social forces composed principally of the working masses. The painstaking creation of a new state by the popular sectors has set the stage for the genuine realization of Nicaragua's national sovereignty, but now as an aspect of a larger popular project, a revolutionary process comprising radical social transformations.

The task of state-building is obviously arduous and problematic:

> It implies taking responsibility for the effective spatial integration of the national territory; the creation of an effective administrative apparatus; the institutionalization of a new type of army based upon the principle of arming the people; the creation of an autonomous judiciary in a country without a genuine judicial tradition; the development of ideological and institutional mechanisms capable of integrating the entire population in a project that is for the first time really national.

Like Frelimo in Mozambique and the MPLA in Angola, the FSLN guides the state-building process in Nicaragua. This raises the complex issue of the relationship between the state and the political organization that leads the revolutionary process and establishes the new state. The FSLN's conception of the state is quite explicit:

> The state is nothing more than an instrument of the people to make the revolution, an instrument of the motive forces of change, the workers and peasants, which provides a means for breaking the obstacles that the revolution encounters, and the manner in which we use the state to break these obstacles will determine the extent to which we serve these motive forces....Whoever does not understand that the state is nothing more than a means and not an end, who believes that our people must be spectators while the state acts as the source of all initiatives, want consciously or unconsciously to introduce our state within a reactionary mould.

Although the FSLN rules the state due to its dominance of the executive branch of government and its majority in the National Assembly, the party avoids replacing the state:

The Sandinista Front has as its mission to assure and guarantee that the state functions as an executive and administrative entity; therefore, its mission is to confer on the state a political line, give it eyes by which to orient itself, without tying its hands and feet because this could cause the state to lose its executive character and complicate the party's leadership mission.

A Non-Partisan Government

Obviously in practice matters have been more complicated. The fact that a political organization exercises hegemony in the tasks of nation-building makes these tasks themselves appear to be partisan. Consequently, the revolution's opponents charge that both the state's institutions and the state's objectives are inherently partisan. They claim to oppose the FSLN in the name of a "nation" that transcends partisan matters. The conservative opposition characterizes the Sandinista Popular Army as an "armed party" and criticizes the military service law as a device to recruit young people into the army solely to defend the interests of the ruling party.

Contradictory Notions

The Sandinistas and their opponents hold contradictory underlying notions of what constitutes the nation. For the conservative parties, the nation is the property of the ruling classes and the neo-colonial state. For the FSLN, the nation belongs to the people and is institutionalized in the revolutionary state. As Harris and Vilas comment:

> Even though the present situation is one in which the tasks of nation-building are being undertaken by a party—the FSLN—these tasks do not lose their national character as a result of this circumstance. On the contrary, it is precisely the national character of the tasks being carried out by this revolutionary organization that give the FSLN its national content and authority. The struggle of this revolutionary organization has rescued the title of the nation for the popular masses.

During the course of 1986 the battle over what constitutes the nation has been waged in the debate over the new Nicaraguan constitution. The constitutional process entered its final stage in September [1986] when the Special Constitutional Commission submitted the final draft to the National Assembly for debate, revision, and final approval. In the FSLN's view, the ratification of the Carta Magna . . . will mark the ultimate step in the institutionalization of representative democracy. . . .

Achieving Representative Democracy

It is common for revolutionary parties to reject representative democracy as incapable of implementing a social revolution. In recent years revolutionaries have pointed to the tragic failure of representative democracy under Allende's Popular Unity Government of 1970-73 in Chile. Moreover, victorious social revolutions, while often introducing measures to democratize social and economic decision-making, seldom allow the direct participation of the people in the major political decisions of society. These revolutions have created extremely centralized political systems, with a range of mediating institutions, in which the most important state functions are outside the direct influence of the people.

"Despite what many foreign observers believe, the Sandinista revolution is not a socialist revolution nor is it undergoing a transition to socialism."

In backing the constitutional process and the November 1984 national elections, the Sandinistas have attempted to institutionalize the revolutionary state and democratize the revolutionary process at a time when the revolution's long-range economic and social goals have still not been clearly defined. The FSLN's linkage of *revolutionary political legitimacy* with the *procedures of representative democracy* will contribute to the debate over revolution and representative democracy and could influence other societies where social revolutions are occurring.

While the Sandinista revolution continues to consolidate the process of representative democracy, it also seeks to develop the institutions of participatory democracy—the Sandinista mass organizations. There are five principal Sandinista mass organizations: the Sandinista Defense Committees (CDS), the National Union of Farmers and Ranchers (UNAG), the Sandinista Workers' Federation (CST), the Rural Workers' Association (ATC) and the Luisa Amanda Espinosa Association of Nicaraguan Women (AMNLAE). These organizations are called Sandinista because they recognize the FSLN as the guiding political force in the country.

Three of the five mass organizations are class-based, that is, they represent specific socio-economic groups in Nicaraguan society. The Union of Farmers and Ranchers represents a large proportion of the country's peasants, the Rural Workers' Association represents most of the agricultural workers on both private and state farms, and the Sandinista Workers' Federation represents the overwhelming majority of Nicaragua's industrial workers. The Nicaraguan Women's Association, on the other hand, is open to all women regardless of socio-economic status.

Finally, the Sandinista Defense Committees are made up of people who live in the same neighborhood. Although neither the women's organization nor the neighborhood associations are class-based institutions, the overwhelming majority of activists in these two mass organizations are peasants, workers, artisans and poor merchants. Consequently, they share many concerns with the strictly class-based popular organizations.

The mass organizations have demonstrated their power to the extent that they have been able to win some of the demands of their membership and influence certain revolutionary policies. Thus the neighborhood committees have gained land and housing for thousands of barrio residents, the farmworkers' union has won permanent employment and better working conditions for its members, the peasants' union has attained loan cancellations and higher prices for its members' products, the women's association has pushed through child-support legislation and raised the status of women at the workplace, and the industrial workers' union has fought for health and safety improvements and participates partially in economic management.

The mass organizations have made significant advances in democratizing their internal structures. All the grassroots organizations employ democratic procedures to choose their leaders and assess their behavior in office; but they have not yet implemented fixed terms of office.

"Revolutionary policies are mainly designed to meet the demands of the popular classes—the peasantry, the workers, the artisans, the semi-proletariat, and segments of the petty-bourgeoisie."

However, lack of full political equality within the popular organizations is a major problem. Due to the "double shift" and unequal access to education, many women are unable to fully participate in the life of the grassroots organizations. Inequality within these organizations also stems from educational differences among members. The vast majority of popular association leaders possess sufficient formal education to write reports and conduct meetings. The mass organizations must constantly work to increase the capacities of their least educated members and afford them access to leadership positions.

The mass organizations are organizationally and financially independent of the FSLN. While they tend to follow Sandinista policies, the popular associations sometimes forcefully oppose the party in the interests of their constituencies. And although the grassroots organizations work hand-in-hand with state institutions, they also closely monitor the government, blowing the whistle on corruption and mismanagement.

Generally, the Sandinistas have promoted the

autonomous development of the mass organizations, feeling that their independence strengthens the revolutionary process. However, when the grassroots organizations pursue a path that contradicts the FSLN's attempt to maintain national unity, the Sandinistas withdraw their support. . . .

Participation of the People

Although lack of space precludes an adequate discussion of the mass organizations' key role in the Sandinista revolution, there is no question that they have become an important axis of power in Nicaraguan politics. No revolutionary policy can be implemented without the massive participation of popular association activists, and most political, social, and economic measures are introduced only after the mass organizations have been included in the planning phase.

Nevertheless, the power of the popular associations remains circumscribed for three basic reasons. The Nicaraguan mass organizations, like their counterparts in other societies that possess the most meager resources of capital, technology, and skilled personnel face tremendous obstacles in developing their capacity to act as a counterweight to state and party organs. They inevitably have to compete with these power centers amid this situation of scarcity.

Second, to the extent that they subordinate their tasks to those set by party policy and mobilize their constituencies only to fulfill state goals, the popular associations will be unable to realize their full potential to influence the revolutionary process. Finally, the power of the mass organizations is limited to the extent that they lack full representation throughout the various levels of the state apparatus; their representation on some bodies is merely token.

Despite what many foreign observers believe, the Sandinista revolution is not a socialist revolution nor is it undergoing a transition to socialism. Nevertheless, the fact that the Sandinistas are not progressively socializing both the forces and relations of production does not mean that Nicaragua is experiencing a "bourgeois democratic" revolution. Although it is not planning to eliminate the bourgeoisie, the Sandinista revolution has stripped the capitalist class of its political power and severely curtailed its economic influence.

The FSLN has created a popular, democratic, and anti-imperialist regime, introducing forms of both participatory and representative democracy in both the state sector and civil society. Revolutionary policies are mainly designed to meet the demands of the popular classes—the peasantry, the workers, the artisans, the semi-proletariat, and segments of the petty-bourgeoisie.

As Harris and Vilas contend: "The Sandinista revolution can most accurately be characterized as a revolution of national liberation directed against imperialist domination as manifested in its contemporary neo-colonial and dependent capitalist form."

The revolution's principal goal is to convert Nicaragua into a modern nation-state that is politically, economically, and culturally free of foreign domination. For this reason the FSLN leadership stresses the need for national unity and the continuation of a multi-class alliance in pursuit of a common project of national reconstruction. In the current period of reconstruction the class contradictions within the revolutionary bloc of political forces are of less importance than the gains that the revolution derives from unity.

At the same time, however, the attempt to promote national unity has led to heavy economic costs that have fallen mainly on the popular masses—particularly the salaried workers. Through mid-1986, the Sandinista leadership has appealed to the political understanding of the masses and attempted to persuade the bourgeoisie to participate in economic development. The question may be raised of how much longer the Sandinistas can ask working people—repeatedly termed the "motor force" of the revolution—to withstand the economic consequences of their deteriorating real income, while at the same time similar sacrifices are not demanded from the capitalists. Yet the level of political and administrative development of the new state—the shortage of cadres and the lack of adequate planning apparatus—preclude any substantial and rapid expansion of the state sector.

The Vanguard of the Workers

Characterizing the Sandinista revolution as a revolution of national liberation does not mean that the FSLN rejects socialism or that the revolution will not lead Nicaragua towards a future transition to socialism. Indeed, on May Day 1982 Tomas Borge asserted: "The Sandinista Front is the vanguard of the workers and peasants. . . . is the living instrument of the revolutionary classes, is the guide leading toward a new society."

Nevertheless, for the time being the revolution faces the primary tasks of establishing Nicaragua's national independence and developing popular democracy. Once these priorities have been achieved, the transition to socialism will be an option.

Gary Ruchwarger is co-director of the Programa de Estudios de Participacion Popular (PEPP) and is writing a book on the Sandinista National Liberation Front (FSLN).

"Nicaragua is a tragedy that never should have happened."

viewpoint 162

The Sandinistas Have Harmed Nicaraguans' Lives

J.H. Ingraham

It is hard to imagine a more idyllic setting. Viewed from my seventh-floor window in the Hotel Internacional, Managua lies bathed in moonlight, breathing tranquility. The air is soft and sweet, and the haunting strains of a Latin love song drift up from a Mariachi band playing somewhere below. With a sigh I turn away, thinking of the reality that is present-day Nicaragua.

That reality is scarcely known to most Americans. Although never in history has a people been so bombarded with "news," it is safe to say that misinformation, obfuscation and omissions have left Americans with little knowledge and less understanding of what is actually happening in the world around them.

A Catholic Church humiliated and silenced, a press debased into an instrument of propaganda, an impoverished people lacking basic necessities while a ruling elite lives in luxury, fraudulent elections, neighbor spying on neighbor, jail terms for fabricated "infractions," 5,000 political prisoners—Nicaragua is a tragedy that never should have happened. It is also well on its way toward becoming a Soviet bastion in the Western Hemisphere, a threat to the security of all Central America and ultimately the United States.

A Story of Human Frailty

How all this came about is a story of human frailty—a combination of ignorance, naiveté, treachery, bitterness and hate. I think of past history as I talk with anti-Sandinista Nicaraguans, many of whom did their bit to bring about the present catastrophe. I am struck with wonder at how they could have expected Daniel Ortega's Marxist dictatorship to turn out differently. Yet, in the face of 65 years of Communist performance, many

Nicaraguans, blinded by bitterness and by hatred of Somoza, so thought—or convinced themselves.

Seated in our well-fortified embassy, I ask Ambassador Harry Bergold if the Sandinistas were Communists from the start. He replies that "the original intellectual formation of the Sandinista leaders was Marxist-Leninist. Although their goals were apparent from the start, most people were focusing on getting rid of Somoza rather than on the qualities of the emerging Sandinista leadership."

I recall that, starting in the early 1960s, the Sandinista guerrilla incursions and terrorist attacks were made possible by Communist backing. Trained, armed and equipped by the Soviet bloc through Cuba, Libya, the PLO and Panama, their knowledge of tactics and weaponry was first-rate. Well-known as all of this was to Nicaraguans, the consensus among them was that the Sandinistas could be dealt with later; one could always negotiate or make deals. If worse came to worst, the people could "rise up" and demand a democratic process.

That this was the point of view of the various political parties, the private business sector, the press, the upper class, and the Catholic Church is a matter of record. Nursing their animosity against Somoza, these people were early sympathizers with the Sandinistas, seeing their armed might as the only power capable of destroying their old enemy. Contemplating this past naiveté, I am unprepared for the incredible courage of these same people in remaining on the scene today and refusing to surrender the last vestiges of freedom in their native land.

A Game of Pretense

For there is still a little room in which to maneuver in Nicaragua. A certain degree of pluralism exists, simply because conditions are so bad that the revolution has had to stop and defend itself. This defense takes the form of a game of

J.H. Ingraham, "Reality in Nicaragua," *The New American*, March 24, 1986. Reprinted with permission.

massive pretense; of pretending the press is free by allowing the publication of *La Prensa* although every word is censored; of pretending there is freedom of religion by allowing the Catholic Church to exist although severely circumscribed; of pretending there is freedom of association, although every move is spied upon; of pretending there is freedom of speech, although "counter-revolutionary" talk is punished by a jail term.

So, too, in order to pretend the economy is working, a nominally "private" sector that produces about half the GNP is allowed to function. Thus it is possible to talk to people who represent business and professional associations, chambers of commerce and industry, and growers' associations. For their protection, it is not possible to name them here. All tell a tale of the tightening of the screws on the economy that has caused production to plummet and has reduced per capita income from $800 or $900 under Somoza to $500 today, As one grower dourly puts it, "The government tells you what to grow, how much to grow, when to sell, where to sell, to whom to sell, and at what price to sell."

Another adds wryly, "Under Somoza we could grow as much as we liked and get the best price on the free market. At that time the exchange rate was 7 to 1; now it's officially 760 or 1200 on the black market."

The sad tale of suffocating controls continues: "Wages are set by a national system of 28 categories with promotion by permission of the Labor Ministry, destroying incentive to work and putting a straightjacket on upward mobility. All foreign trade is a government monopoly. A new monetary law compels everyone to deposit all cash in the government banks, with all transactions handled by checks. Businessmen are even told how much petty cash they can have on hand. Unemployment is high and last year the inflation rate was 300 percent. It used to take three days to earn enough to buy a shirt—now it takes a month and the quality is much poorer." The speaker, a grower, hesitates as if reluctant to think the next thought.

"Overriding everything is fear," he continues, "even fear of one's family. We can't use the law to defend ourselves—if they want to get you, they get you. I have had a jail term myself. The best one can do is keep a low profile and break up one's family by sending the children to school in another country."

"That's true," another businessman says. "I've sent my kids to school in the States because this isn't my war and I'm not having them killed."

Not Their War

I leave, stunned by their courage in the face of such odds and pondering their culpability. Not their war? No class hated Somoza more, or did more to undercut him at the time of the Communist

advance, than these business and professional people. It was not the campesinos, whom Somoza greatly benefitted in order to lock in their majority vote, but the upper class which came in conflict with him economically. It has been estimated that Somoza had a financial interest in about one-third of the industries in the country; much of the profit went into his pocket. Whether his financing of these industries was bad for the country as a whole has never been rationally discussed, but clearly his transgressions were of a different order than those of the Sandinistas today.

"The sad tale of suffocating controls continues."

Even though the GNP was growing, the standard of living rising, and seventy percent of the market lay outside Somoza's interest, the upper class understandably wanted a bigger slice of the pie. Their fatal mistake lay in the method they chose; in believing they could use the Sandinistas for their own purpose and still come out on top. It is a mistake that has often been made. One who made it was the popular and charismatic Jorge Salazar, president of the Union of Nicaraguan Agricultural Producers, who at first worked with the Sandinistas but soon planned a farmers' uprising against them. No sooner had the Sandinistas gotten wind of this than Salazar was gunned down in 1980. It was already too late.

Depressing as it is to contemplate the fact that intelligent, educated people could have once been so naive about the nature of Communism, what can be said about Americans who, in the face of the evidence, still cling to an even more simple-minded viewpoint? It is easy to pick them out at the Hotel Internacional. Church groups, peace groups, "human rights" groups, liberal political types, NBC and CBS personnel bustling importantly through the lobby. Once every week, about 2000 protesters appear at the gates of the U.S. Embassy, harassing the arriving employees and excoriating the Reagan Administration's support for the Contras. They are all Americans. According to embassy estimates, only ten percent of Americans visiting Nicaragua are anti-Communist.

Also much in evidence at the hotel—the only luxury spot in the country—are East Germans, Cubans, PLO types, Libyans and others from the Soviet bloc. The Sandinistas make sure the food and service are excellent. While there are shortages of all basics for the Nicaraguan people, the hotel's buffets and dessert tables can only be described as lavish.

Suffering perhaps most acutely for its naiveté is the Catholic Church. Here the opposition to Somoza was based on a combination of the economic illiteracy of the Jesuit priests, many of whom actually viewed Communism as the savior of the poor, and Cardinal Obando y Bravo's personal antagonism toward Somoza. This hostility had its roots in the 1972 earthquake that devastated Managua and resulted in hundreds of millions of dollars worth of aid being poured into the country. The Cardinal wanted this aid channeled through the churches. Somoza opposed this and kept control over it himself. Thereafter the Cardinal's hand was against Somoza. At the time of the Sandinista terrorist attack on the Castillo Christmas party in 1974, in which many were killed and 45 held hostage, the Sandinistas asked for Cardinal (then Bishop) Obando as negotiator. Obando proved so openly sympathetic to the terrorists that he had to be replaced by Papal Nuncio Monsignor Gabriel Montalvo before progress could be made. Interestingly, one of the criminals let out of jail in the final trade was Daniel Ortega. In 1979, a few days after the Sandinistas assumed control, Cardinal Obando celebrated a victory mass in front of the old cathedral.

That Somoza kept hands off the religious functions of the Church is a matter of record; in no way were these circumscribed. This was so even though Somoza was well aware that many Jesuits taught Communism and indoctrinated upper-class children, many of whom turned against their own families, thus bringing about one of the most heartrending aspects of the revolution. Although many of these Jesuits were from the U.S. or Spain, Somoza imposed but few legal sanctions against them, deporting only twelve Spanish Communists during his nine years in office.

"Things are much worse now materially—and infinitely worse in the area of human rights."

Today, however, a far different story is told by Monsignor Carballo, vicar of the Archdiocese of Managua. This is the same Monsignor who was trapped into going to a parishioner's home where he was set upon, stripped naked, then photographed by TV cameras in a compromising position with a woman. He is youngish, with coal black hair. He speaks forcefully in Spanish:

"Beginning in 1982 our radio broadcasts were censored; we could no longer reach our people with the truth. In 1983, after the Pope's visit, live Mass on TV and radio was prohibited. In 1984, a German archbishop sent us mobile radio equipment but it was confiscated. In 1985, our church bulletin was confiscated, the content changed, and then

redistributed—hence, we have had to discontinue publishing. In 1986, our radio station was closed and we now have total suppression of communication. Even church news in *La Prensa* is censored. But the so-called Popular Church, which is completely politicized, is free to utilize all outlets. In this Popular Church, children are baptized in the name of revolutionary heroes."

Effects of Censorship

Monsignor Carballo pauses and contemplates space with somber eyes. "Mass is allowed only on Sunday, prohibited during the week," he continues. "Our Catholic schools are forbidden to mention religion in the classroom; all religious instruction must take place in Sunday school."

How many priests and nuns have gone over to the Popular Church? Monsignor Carballo says it is a small minority. Out of 960 only 60 are pro-Sandinista, although there are other foreign priests unofficially in the country who work with them. It is hard to know if his figures are accurate—he may be downplaying this disgrace.

One feels a sense of deep dismay over the situation of Cardinal Obando and the Catholic Church in Nicaragua. Humiliation and degradation are hard enough to bear. But, when they come partly as a result of one's own mistaken actions, the burden is infinitely worse. I can't help but reflect on the opposition of the Catholic Church to President Marcos in the Philippines. The parallel is striking. In each case the Church became the most formidable voice against the established order and in favor of change of an unknown nature. Looking ahead, there is every indication that Cardinal Jaime Sin of Manila may one day find himself in Cardinal Obando's desperate position. . . .

Most ironic of all, *La Prensa*, the formerly pro-Sandinista influential newspaper which for many years freely published daily diatribes against the Somoza government, is now severely censored and its former editor in exile in Costa Rica. It was the murder of Pedro Joaquin Chamorro, publisher of *La Prensa* and Somoza's archenemy, that was used as the catalyst to start the civil revolution in 1978. Without a shred of evidence, the world press immediately crucified Somoza. Although the murderers were later caught and confessed publicly on TV, this news never went beyond the borders of Nicaragua. I ask anti-somosistas if Somoza had been involved in the death. They answer a little impatiently, "Of course not."

Today *La Prensa* is allowed to publish only at the whim of the government. The only other paper is *Barricada*, the government mouthpiece. Its representative turns out to be a lovely young woman, Sofia Montenegro, who speaks flawlessly and passionately in English.

"We are creating the New Society," she says. "It is

very exciting being a part of this. We can see what we're accomplishing. We started with only thirty journalists and 30,000 copies daily. Now we have acquired experience and established political and ideological influence. We get paper from the Soviets, Sweden, Finland, and Canada and publish 100,000 copies daily. We make enough to cover expenses and reinvest the profit 'for the benefit of the workers,' who now number 250."

She brushes back her long dark hair with a slender hand. "My father and my brother," she continues, "were both killed by the Sandinistas. Before my brother was killed he said to me, 'I love you and I know you love me. But if we meet on the street, shoot.'"

Outside I am surprised to find the sun is still shining and everything looks as before, as I go to the Ministry of Foreign Relations. Nora Astorga is not available, having just been named Ambassador to the United Nations. This is the same Nora Astorga who set a trap for General Reynaldo Perez Vega, number two man in the Guardia Nacional, and participated in his atrocious murder, wherein his eyes were gouged out, his throat cut, his body burned with cigarettes, and his genitals cut off and stuffed in his mouth. Doctors estimated it took General Vega several hours to die.

Orwellian Double-Think

Instead, I talk to an assistant who is in charge of North American affairs. This attractive young man of 26 is Martin Vega, an American citizen born in San Francisco of anti-Somoza Nicaraguan parents and educated through two years of college in California. In 1979, after the take-over, he arrived in Nicaragua where his rhetorical skill has obviously been well rewarded. His talk turns out to be an arresting example of Orwellian double-think. He tells me:

> Emergency powers and restrictions are due only to American opposition—they are not the policy of the party.
> We wouldn't censor La Prensa if it had a measure of social responsibility. The only reason you can allow yellow journals like the Washington Times and New York Post to publish is because you're not at war.
> We consider education not to be neutral. The schools have autonomy to develop their own curricula without interference by government but there must be guidelines. These are not based on Marxism but on Sandinista ideology. It is not our intention to create an ideological system. We have no intention of 'exporting revolution.' Arms for El Salvador's guerrillas were sold to them by corrupt Salvadorean army officials.
> The Contras are supplied and directed by the United States and so are operating outside international law and are no longer considered to be Nicaraguans. Since 1985, we have used better methods against them with helicopters and new rifles supplied by the Soviets. These are defense weapons only, being used to fight a foreign-sponsored invasion.
> About fifty percent of the priests in Nicaragua are from abroad. With these we have been able to go

ahead with social and economic reform. But Obando has placed himself in opposition, thus his position is not objective. We want to eliminate conflict with the Church, but we have to be critical of actions of which we disapprove.

Our foreign debt is $4.5 billion. We owe Western Europe, Canada, certain eastern countries, the socialist bloc. We continue to receive from private U.S. banks.

I ask if Nicaragua is servicing these debts. "In essence," he smiles, "we are symbolically paying back the debt by continuing to talk to the bankers."

"All food is scarce, . . . but this is denied by the government so as not to arouse people."

I am interested in this information about the banks. I remember having asked Ambassador Bergold about the practice of American banks, such as Morgan Guaranty Trust, loaning hundreds of millions of dollars to Soviet-bloc countries which then turn around and loan millions to Nicaragua. The Ambassador replied that in order to stop that, we would have to stop all east-west commerce. The implication was that this is clearly unthinkable.

I ask the young man if he's happy he came to Nicaragua. "Oh, yes!" he replies emphatically. Cold drinks are brought by a servant hovering in the background. I need one. As I drink I wonder about the convolutions of this young Sandinista's mind— not so different, after all, from much of what is being taught in many of our universities and churches.

Although there are armed soldiers in battle fatigues everywhere, it is possible for Americans to walk freely about Managua. I clearly feel that my protection is the imperative need of the Sandinistas for the defeat of aid to the Contras coming up in Congress. Toward this end the Sandinista image abroad must be kept "pure." So it is that I am able to visit an ordinary family in their middle-class home. I look about the bare living room with its vinyl floor, white-washed walls and wooden ceiling. The furniture consists of three unattractive upholstered chairs, three wooden chairs, two small tables, and a radio. A six-armed chandelier boasts only two globes—the other four bulbs are bare.

The mother begins: "No more meat after today. It doesn't exist, even on the black market where we've been getting it. Yet we are exporting it, I don't know where to. All food is scarce, especially dairy products, but this is denied by the government so as not to arouse people. It is prohibited to say things are scarce. Cooking oil and soap are non-existent, beans and rice disappearing. We are allotted one roll of toilet paper per month for four people, but there is none available. I saw a fight in the market today over a small piece of cheese."

Her words cause me to remember how a pregnant woman, waiting silently in the background, had quickly consumed the scraps left on my plate after I had eaten in the marketplace that noon.

The woman continues impassively: "It is not against the law to have small gardens of our own and keep the produce. But we are prohibited from using water in the yard. If we use over a certain amount, we are fined. Here in our neighborhood we haven't as much problem with informers as poorer areas have, but we must still be very careful. All neighborhoods have churches, but they are closed except on weekends. The government created the Popular Church in order to indoctrinate people in liberation theology. It put great pressure on priests in order to change church doctrine to support the State. Most of our native priests are against the Sandinistas. Some have been jailed. One priest who had gone to the U.S. Embassy and reported tortures he had sustained in a previous arrest was arrested again."

The mother's voice trails off as the front door opens and an attractive young woman enters the house. We sit in silence. The mother waits, expressionless. There is talking and laughing in the next room. Finally the door slams again.

"I cannot speak in front of her," the mother explains.

"Who is she?" I ask.

"A friend of my daughter's." Then she continues. "The government pays anyone it can get to come here and demonstrate in front of the U.S. Embassy. They go on TV and say everything is wonderful. But things are much worse now materially—and infinitely worse in the area of human rights.

"There is much unrest and disillusionment among the people. If a free election were held, the Sandinistas would be voted out. But there's so much fear it's impossible to make use of the dissatisfaction. . . .

American Involvement

While many Nicaraguans unwittingly contributed to their own undoing through naiveté, no such innocence can be attributed to the role of the Carter Administration and Congress in bringing the Sandinistas to power. Again, few Americans have any knowledge of this history.

The groundwork was laid when Father Miguel d'Escoto (now a member of the ruling Marxist junta), Father Fernando Cardinal, and a few other Marxist priests made contact with far Left members of Congress, including Clarence Long of Maryland, Edward Koch of New York, David Obey of Wisconsin, and Jim Wright of Texas. An organization known as the Washington Office for Latin America came into being and started a campaign to destabilize Nicaragua based on the emotional, but highly falsified issue of human rights. The Jesuits did their job well, supplying misinformation to liberals and Marxist sympathizers in Congress and the Executive Branch, including the State Department. Opposition to Nicaragua gathered momentum, although all these elements of government knew that the Sandinistas were trained and supported by Castro's Cuba.

One week after Mr. Carter's inauguration in 1977, with pious mouthings about "human rights," he moved to prohibit the sale of arms and ammunition to what was, after all, our staunchest pro-American ally in Latin America. Eventually Carter made it impossible for Nicaragua to buy military supplies anywhere in the world, even using the U.S. Navy to intercept an Israeli ship and force its recall. It was this U.S. embargo that primarily settled the question as to whether the Communists would take control. It was only a matter of time before the Guardia Nacional, which for years had won every skirmish, was rendered helpless.

"Thanks to their superior firepower and Marxist-Leninist discipline, the Sandinistas grabbed full control. It was all over."

While waiting for this to happen, Carter made additional moves to destroy the Nicaraguan economy. Finally isolated economically, and with the Guardia Nacional out of ammunition, the government capitulated in June 1979. It was at this point that the Carter Administration could have proved it was truly interested in "human rights" and installed a democratic process. This, however, is not what happened. The State Department under Cyrus Vance's leadership sent Ambassador Lawrence Pezzullo to Managua to handle final negotiations. With Somoza ready to go into exile on the one proviso that the country not be allowed to go Communist, the procedure of setting up a transitional government without the Sandinistas should have been simple. Pezzullo did indeed give his word that the Sandinistas would be kept out. Yet he then proceeded to establish a five-man junta that contained two Sandinistas—all the power base they needed. Somoza left on July 17th; two days later, thanks to their superior firepower and Marxist-Leninist discipline, the Sandinistas grabbed full control. It was all over.

J.H. Ingraham is a Florida-based free-lance writer and specialist on Central American affairs. She is writing a novel about Nicaragua.

"At the moment there is space to work for pluralism."

Political Pluralism Can Be Achieved in Nicaragua

Tony Jenkins

Nicaragua is a land of myths, where reality does not match perception. President Reagan himself proved the point in his March 16 [1986] speech on television. Afterward, his aides were obliged to scurry around correcting his falsehoods about Sandinista links to drug smuggling, anti-Semitism and Brazilian guerrillas. But one myth that remains firmly rooted in U.S. political circles has yet to be laid to rest; it is the myth that there is a democratic center in Nicaragua.

Perception: the opposition political parties, trade unions, media and church hierarchy are dedicated democrats who have been excluded from power by brutal, communistic repression. Reality: although these groups have undoubtedly been harassed, most of the Sandinistas' domestic opponents are not now, and never have been, good democrats. They have failed as an opposition and they must share a large part of the blame for Nicaragua's continuing agony. Yet, carried along on the rising tide of bipartisan consensus that the Sandinistas are totalitarian and undemocratic, Congress will approve millions of dollars for President Reagan's blood-thirsty "freedom fighters."

It appears that the money will be frozen to give the Sandinistas time to reconsider their repressive ways. But if Congress wants a thriving pluralistic democracy in Nicaragua, it should address the principal conservative opposition group, the Democratic Coordinating Committee (otherwise known as the C.D.N. or the Coordinadora). The Coordinadora should be clearly told to abandon its fantasy of a U.S. invasion or a *contra* victory, to join the domestic political debate and to commit itself to the electoral process.

The Coordinadora has never made a serious effort to attract broad, popular backing for its demands. It has never organized a consistent program of political meetings—even indoor ones, which are legal. Not one of the four parties making up the C.D.N. has conducted a major recruiting drive. Some of them do not even keep records of their membership. As Miriam Arguello, a Coordinadora leader, explained in an interview, "We don't need to, we know the majority of the country already supports us." Yet until recently C.D.N. member parties did not have offices in every department in the country, and Mario Rappaccioli, millionaire boss of the Nicaraguan Conservative Party, said of the other three parties, "They have so few people I could fit them all in a bus."

Sandinista Political Efforts

The contrast between them and the Sandinistas could not be greater. Immediately after Anastasio Somoza fled the country, Sandinista leaders, working sixteen to twenty hours a day, toured the country, galvanizing support, setting up trade unions and mass organizations, forging a popular movement to back their claim to power. The opposition did virtually nothing. Instead, by mid-1980, long before anyone ever raised any complaints of harassment, the right's most popular and charismatic leader, Jorge Salazar, was plotting a coup d'état with anti-Sandinista officers in the army. He met with *contra* leaders in Miami and started smuggling guns. In November 1980 he was killed while being arrested by Nicaraguan police. In the few months before and after Somoza's fall, 20 to 30 percent of the country's businessmen emigrated, taking their expertise and hundreds of millions of dollars and depriving the opposition of their support.

Alfonso Robelo, after Salazar, the only credible leader of the so-called democratic center, also gave up the struggle at an early stage. He was one of two original non-Sandinistas on the five-member

Tony Jenkins, "Nicaragua's Disloyal Opposition," *The Nation*, April 12, 1986. © 1986, *The Nation* magazine/The Nation Company, Inc.

governing junta that ran the country from 1979 to 1985, and the leader of the Nicaraguan Democratic Movement. His positions provided an ideal base from which to organize a democratic opposition, but instead Robelo resigned in April 1980, on the pretext that the Sandinistas had packed the consultative parliament, the Council of State, with their supporters. Opposition leaders now admit that the 25 percent of the seats allocated to them was more than they could then have won in an election. In November 1980, the six delegates from the Superior Council of Private Enterprise, or COSEP, the private businessmen's group, walked out of the Council of State, never to return. And so another platform from which to launch an effective democratic opposition was lost. In June 1982, Robelo joined the *contra* commander Edén Pastora, leaving the Coordinadora leaderless.

What had the Sandinistas done to justify this intransigence? Their treatment of the opposition over the past six years stands in stark contrast to that in El Salvador, Guatemala and even Honduras. In Nicaragua no death squads have been at work, cases of torture have been isolated, political leaders do not disappear, no one receives death threats. Comparatively speaking, Nicaragua has been a beacon of human rights in the region.

A Broad Ideological Choice

In Nicaragua there are ten legal political parties, ranging from the loony left to the rabid right. They all have offices, telephones and vehicles. Managua is studded with party billboards carrying messages like "Conservatism means free trade unions." Opposition leaders attend small political meetings without bodyguards; they don't need them. In their November 1984 elections Nicaraguans were offered a broader ideological choice than Americans were in theirs.

To be sure, the Sandinistas have harassed the opposition: prominent C.D.N. members have been arrested and even jailed, sometimes without benefit of trial. During one invasion scare, Coordinadora leaders were barred from leaving the country. *La Prensa* has been consistently and crudely censored. Opponents have been roughed up by Sandinista mobs and their property has been confiscated. Such incidents are deplorable and have rightly been condemned by human rights organizations, including Amnesty International and Americas Watch. But do they justify abandoning the democratic struggle and joining the *contra* murderers? The abuses have been of civil, not human rights—a fine distinction, but an important one in the regional context.

By the same token, the opposition has rarely challenged Sandinista controls. It has never organized general strikes or regular protest demonstrations. Of course such activities are illegal under the current State of Emergency, but if the

army and death squads have been unable to halt union and protest activity in El Salvador and Guatemala, what explains the passivity in Nicaragua, where the Sandinistas have never used the police or troops to suppress a strike? Perhaps the C.D.N. does not have the support it claims?

Nor has the right offered any alternative program. The C.D.N. does not have a detailed policy on such important issues as health care and land reform, or even on how to end the war. The three most influential voices in the Coordinadora are wealthy businessmen Enrique Bolaños, Ramiro Gurdian and Mario Rappaccioli, who speak for the old conservative landed aristocracy. Rappaccioli is so right-wing that he once said, "all the American media, especially *The Washington Post*, are communist." The C.D.N.'s policy can be summed up in one sentence: Under the Americans everything will be fine. It is not surprising that most Nicaraguans cannot name the C.D.N.'s leaders, or that those leaders are popularly referred to as "the same people who used to make deals with Somoza."

Shortcomings of the Right

The intellectual bankruptcy of the right is reflected in the fact that its generally recognized leader is a cleric, Cardinal Obando y Bravo, and he has been powerless to stop the constant factional squabbling: the Conservative Party has split four times in the past three years. Because it lacked a politician of stature, the Coordinadora was obliged to import Arturo Cruz from Washington as its putative presidential candidate in 1984. That candidacy was nothing more than a propaganda ploy; Rappaccioli has admitted that the C.D.N. voted to boycott the elections before Cruz returned to Managua.

"In their November 1984 elections Nicaraguans were offered a broader ideological choice than Americans were in theirs."

Cruz was an unsuitable leader for several reasons. A dry, uninspiring economist, he is relatively little known in Nicaragua, having spent most of his adult life in the United States. Also, he and his son had been working closely with Edén Pastora long before the elections. But Cruz's worst fault was his own admission, after the polling, that he had accepted money from the Central Intelligence Agency.

Within two days of his arrival in Managua, Cruz revealed that he did not understand democratic struggle: he announced that the sine qua non for C.D.N.'s participation in the elections was negotiations between the Sandinistas and the *contra* leaders. "Many are my friends, I could not participate knowing they could not," he said. The demand for negotiations, as many European diplomats complained, had nothing to do with the mechanics of free and fair elections; it should have been the centerpiece of the C.D.N. campaign platform.

The elections provided the Coordinadora with an opportunity to make up lost ground—a chance for television and radio air time, relaxed censorship and outdoor rallies throughout the country. The Sandinista's control of the government undoubtedly gave their party, the Sandinista National Liberation Front, an unfair advantage in the campaign, but no serious commentator has questioned the honesty of the polling, and the vast majority of the observers accepted the validity of the results. By boycotting the elections, the C.D.N. again rejected the opportunity to participate in a National Assembly and to build up their support.

The Old Political Mentality

One explanation for the C.D.N. boycott is that its leaders are dominated by the old mentality, forged in the days of dealing with Somoza, that political change is achieved in secret meetings in smoke-filled rooms. They have no experience in campaigning for votes. They rely, as Nicaragua's aristocracy always has, on the U.S. Embassy to apply pressure for change. Coordinadora leaders continuously tour European and U.S. capitals; Washington is more the C.D.N.'s constituency than contra-battered Wiwili. Ramiro Gurdian is so proud of the U.S. link that he once boasted in an interview: "Reagan's peace proposals are taken from the Coordinadora. I am going to charge him royalties." That's hardly necessary. The C.D.N. already receives funds from Reagan, as does La Prensa. Both receive thousands of dollars from the National Endowment for Democracy, a group formed by Congress that grants money to anti-communist organizations in foreign countries.

Part of the Coordinadora's problem is that its leaders have never held nationalist views. As Agustin Jarquin, former president of the Social Christian Party, admits, "In Nicaragua there was never a national bourgeoisie." Many politicians on the right were educated in the United States, some have second homes there and speak fluent English, some used to work for American firms and felt their first allegiance was to the United States. They speak Washington's language, which accounts for why such a small group has attracted so much attention in the nation's capital. Yet the C.D.N. is unable to comprehend that U.S. policy is designed to reduce the space for dissidence and opposition in Nicaragua in order to force the Sandinistas to restrict civil liberties, thus providing an excuse for further U.S. aggression.

And the C.D.N. also has links to the contras. Not only are the leaders of the two groups good friends; they meet regularly and have even shared press conferences. Adolfo Calero, leader of the Nicaraguan Democratic Force, once described the Coordinadora, of which he was formerly a senior member, as "my political wing." Significantly, the C.D.N. leaders have never renounced armed opposition by condemning the contra massacres, kidnappings, rapes and economic sabotage; nor has the Catholic hierarchy led by Obando.

Indeed, Obando has always been an implacable opponent of the Sandinistas. Two days before Somoza fell the Cardinal was in Caracas, Venezuela, trying to persuade President Luis Herrera Campins to force the Sandinistas to install two more conservatives on the junta. More than 110 priests, nuns and religious workers suspected of sympathizing with the Sandinistas have been forced out of their jobs. And he has encouraged priests to break the law by preaching against the military draft. Many clerics suspect that he welcomes this confrontation as a way of discrediting the Sandinistas.

"Those who argue that the Sandinistas have used their monopoly of power to harass a weak and useless opposition should remember that more than 60 percent of the economy is in private hands."

But the final failure of the right is its adamant refusal to accept the legitimacy of the revolution and its institutions. In a pluralistic democracy a majority of the political parties must accept the society's fundamental institutions; they may want to change them, but they accept them as a framework in which they must operate. The Nicaraguan right does not. It rejects the executive, the bureaucracy, the legislature, the judiciary, the army, the police force, the education system, the health-care system, the banking system—everything. It refuses to work from within to change them. When given the chance to do so, it boycotts, resigns, runs away. The right is not a loyal opposition, and if Nicaragua is not a working pluralistic democracy that is partly because the leaders of the C.D.N. are such bad democrats.

A Good Opposition

Sergio Ramírez, the Vice President, once said in an interview that the government needs more and better criticism. A good opposition helps bring about good government, and the lack of one has caused the Sandinistas to make some bad mistakes. Moreover, by not helping to build an effective democracy, the C.D.N. has provided the Reagan

Administration with an excuse for backing the *contras* now ravaging the Nicaraguan countryside.

Those who argue that the Sandinistas have used their monopoly of power to harass a weak and useless opposition should remember that more than 60 percent of the economy is in private hands. As long as that situation continues, and there is no evidence that it will change in the near future, the socialist Sandinista government and the conservative pro-U.S. opposition will continue to struggle for power. It may be that in the years ahead the Sandinistas will prove to be totalitarian Leninists, determined to impose a centralized one-party state, but at the moment there is space to work for pluralism. The C.D.N.'s ineffectuality merely encourages U.S. policy; the Sandinistas' current siege mentality understandably pushes them to take more restrictive measures, which then "justify" increased U.S. aggression. It is no wonder that President Reagan wants to "strengthen the democratic center."

Tony Jenkins is the Managua-based correspondent for The Guardian *of London.*

"It is absurd to expect the Sandinistas to accede to 'outside' opposition parties' demands for genuine power-sharing."

viewpoint164

Political Pluralism Is Temporarily Impossible in Nicaragua

Abraham Brumberg

Anyone who returns to Nicaragua after a two-year absence—I recently did—must be struck by a marked deterioration in every facet of life in that country. Two years ago [in 1984], despite the increasing cost of fighting a war on both borders, there was ample evidence of improvement in the life of the average citizen. While the rest of Latin America was experiencing a negative rate of economic growth, Nicaragua's continued to increase steadily. Much of the country's GNP was being eaten up by the war effort; yet enough was left for various agricultural and industrial projects, for education, for health programs, and for a generally higher standard of living.

The government, to be sure, had committed economic blunders and inanities, such as its initial attempt to convert into collective farms all the land seized from the Somoza oligarchy and its cronies. It had relied excessively on food subsidies; it had failed to establish a coherent wage and price policy or a sensible system of graduated incentives to production. The Sandinistas' ideological proclivities had antagonized a good part of the country's middle class, and potentially productive sectors of it had consequently emigrated. Nevertheless, not even the most severe critics of the Sandinista regime could— or did—deny that the average Nicaraguan was living better, and could expect to live considerably longer, than ever before.

Politically, too, things seemed to be looking up two years ago. Censorship, introduced as part of the State of Emergency in March 1982 after several nasty *contra* attacks well inside the country, was still heavy—and heavy-handed. Political parties smarted under restrictions that made it impossible for them to pursue their activities on even remotely equal

terms with the ruling FSLN (Frente Sandinista de Liberación Nacional). Conflict with the Catholic Church, patently a foe of the regime, still raged. Nevertheless, change was in the air. A party that prided itself, not without reason, on maintaining the support of the bulk of the population, and that simultaneously understood its survival to depend on the active sympathy (read: economic and military aid) of Latin America and Western Europe, the FSLN was visibly eager to relax some of its controls and reach an accommodation with its critics.

At that time elections were still nine months off. Preparations, however, were already under way. Discussions with various political parties, even those that discreetly (or not so discreetly) cheered for the *contras*, were proceeding. There was a dialogue with the Church. Most important, the Sandinistas had abandoned the disastrous attempt to "integrate" into the "Revolutionary Project" the indigenous population of the Atlantic Coast (Miskitos and two other Indian tribes, as well as Caribbean blacks, all traditionally hostile to the "Spaniards" of the West). After several massacres and the emergence of a Miskito resistance movement, the Sandinistas recognized their egregious errors and, with apologies, tried to substitute a political and economic compromise.

Current Conditions

Two years later, the landscape looks bleak. More than 50 percent of the GNP now goes to defense, as a result of which numerous social programs have been either curtailed or discontinued. Basic consumer goods are rationed and are in woefully short supply; inflation is at an all-time high; exports, predictably, are at an all-time low. (The official rate of exchange in 1984 was 150 cordobas to the dollar. Now it is 750.) Impoverishment is visible everywhere. In my obscenely posh hotel (posh by any standard, obscenely so when measured against

Abraham Brumberg, "Nicaragua: A Mixture of Shades," *Dissent,* Spring 1986. Reprinted with the author's permission.

the average monthly wage of about 25,000 cordobas), the water was turned off twice a week, as it is all over Managua. The population of the capital has climbed to unmanageable proportions, largely as a result of migrations from the war zones in the north. About a third of the population, over 900,000 people, live in Managua, yet there is no sign of construction, let alone reconstruction. Black market activities thrive openly. And there can be no doubt that popular discontent is growing.

The political horizon has also darkened. The six opposition parties that ran in the election of November 1984 and that have since participated in the deliberations of the National Assembly, openly grumble that they are ignored and bypassed. They complain that legislation is either railroaded through the Assembly by the FSLN, or merely announced— with hardly a word of consultation—by presidential decree. Outside the National Assembly, among opposition parties, hostility toward the regime is more rampant than ever before. The Vatican's appointment of Archbishop Obando y Bravo as Cardinal is seen by the government as a political provocation, and not without reason; this new Cardinal's militant anti-government sallies, expressed within and beyond the borders of Nicaragua, have brought efforts at improving church-state relations (always sporadic) to a virtual standstill.

Nothing has contributed more to the high level of tension than the new provisions of the State of Emergency, enacted [in October 1985]. These provisions may be more fearsome on paper than in practice: freedom of movement, for instance, is suspended, yet there is no sign as far as I could learn that the suspension is being enforced. I spent a full day, together with three other Americans, driving through the northern reaches of the country where contras are still operating. Not once were we stopped and asked to produce documents; not once did local campesinos refuse to talk to us. Nevertheless, the government has now armed itself with legal justification to detain for an indefinite period anyone suspected of committing "crimes against the security of national and public order" and there were indeed many such cases in the first weeks after the decree was passed. The government has banned strikes. It has further restricted the activity of political parties, which must now ask for special permission to hold outdoor rallies. Such measures elicit, both at home and abroad, new apprehensions about Sandinista intentions.

The Cause of the Reversal

What has caused this dismaying reversal? Is it, as some would assert, inevitable, insofar as economic decline and political bloody-mindedness are the essential earmarks of a communist regime, and all communist regimes are hellbent on monopolizing power and crushing any obstacles? (I exclude what

used to be called lunatic fringe conservatism, which out of ignorance or hypocrisy pronounces the contras heirs to Washington and Jefferson.) Or is it, as others would affirm with equal certainty, that the war, openly espoused, financed, and controlled by the United States, has forced the Sandinistas to take repressive measures? Those who condemn American policies do not necessarily excuse the FSLN (here I exclude the groupies, American and West European, who litter the Nicaraguan scene and to whom any criticism of the regime is sacrilege: a delegation of venerable survivors of the Lincoln Brigade; inferior American poets, given to howling their verses to indifferent Sandinista soldiers and gaping tourists; idealistic young "internationalists" helping out with the cotton and coffee harvests; zealots like the Jesuit poet and Minister of Culture, Ernesto Cardenal.) Even members of the FSLN do not always excuse themselves. Generally, the Sandinista officials I talked to were far more ready to concede their mistakes and failures than were their foreign admirers. But they tend to explain even highly disturbing actions as responses dictated by American aggression. . . .

"Demands that the FSLN relinquish its exclusive role . . . are shrugged off."

What the Sandinistas may agree to are some cosmetic changes. The emphasis of their TV "commercials" about the draft has already shifted from defending the Revolution to defending la patria. But the FSLN is dead set against any meaningful concessions in this realm: even the name of the army—Ejército Popular Sandinista—is not negotiable, for symbols can be no less important than realities, indeed, are realities. Demands that the FSLN relinquish its exclusive role in the political education of the army and open it up to representatives of other political parties are shrugged off: "How can you possibly expect us," said Roger Sanchez, a young Sandinista militante who is a well-known cartoonist for the FSLN's newspaper, La Barricada, "to allow parties that are tied, openly or not, to the enemies of our country to conduct their political work [in the army] and possibly even recruit our men for their purposes?" This typical comment reveals the current polarization in Nicaragua, blurring the line between legitimate dissent and outright "counterrevolution." There is no evidence, for instance, that parties in the National Assembly that clamor for a separation of state and army have any "ties" with the contras. They are in fact unanimous in condemning the contra military aggression as both morally reprehensible and politically counterproductive. But suspicion and hostility are close to the surface—on both sides. . . .

A single "model" or explanation—however plausible, seductive or even, to cite my diplomat informant, "true"—is inadequate for understanding Nicaragua today. There are many forces at work in the country, and to focus on any single one of them is to lose sight of the complexity of the situation. The Sandinista system is far from hardened. It is still subject to contradictory impulses and influences, both from within and without. It is still capable of moving—broadly speaking—either toward greater authoritarianism and centralization, or toward a more pluralistic and consensual system.

The Sandinista System

Right now, in Nicaragua and among some writers in the United States, the Latin American "model" seems fashionable. The Sandinistas, you will hear it said, are really reproducing, in their own way, the very system they replaced. Somoza came to power through bullets; so did they. Somoza insisted on total control; they insist on "hegemony." Somoza never looked for competitors, only for cooperators; so too the Sandinistas. Somoza had a system of mock pluralism; the Sandinista version is equally phony. Under Somoza, elections were rigged to give the opposition (Conservatives) about 40 percent of the vote; in the November 1984 elections, the opposition was "allowed" to get some 40 percent (less, in fact). Some of the more bitter opponents of the regime maintain that the Sandinista reign is as repressive as—if not more repressive—than Somoza's (a claim regularly advanced by the Reagan administration, too).

"Political pluralism . . . is not exactly or entirely a sham. But neither can it be understood in the Western parliamentary sense."

As with all hyperbole, there is a germ of truth to this—but not much more. With one exception, leaders of all the political parties—including Domingo Sanchez, head of the "Marxist-Leninist" Socialist Party and a vociferous critic of the FSLN—concede, begrudgingly and despite their suspicions of the Sandinistas, that the elections were "fair and accurate." The one exception is the Nicaraguan Communist Party (PC de N), whose leader angrily told me that the count was "falsified," and that in one voting district where his party has "140 members" the tally showed only "40 votes for our party." (Dr. Mariano Fiallos, chairman of the Supreme Electoral Council and by all lights an honest and honorable man, commented, "Have you looked at the Communist party organ, *Avance*? Read

it. These people live in a world of fantasy. The idea that they would have as many as 140 members in one voting district is simply comical." Having leafed through some issues of *Avance* and the eighty-page program of the party, I can only agree. The PC de N is utterly out of touch with reality.)

The elections were not rigged. There was no need to rig them, if only because there is no doubt whatever that the FSLN still had the backing of the majority of the country. The opposition was and is fragmented into small, squabble-ridden parties. The Latin tradition of *personalismo*—political alliances formed around a single leader—is considerably stronger among the various opposition parties than within the FSLN, which has been able to conceal its internal wranglings (of which, knowledgeable observers say, there is no dearth) behind an impressive facade of unanimity.

A Different Brand of Pluralism

"Political pluralism," then, is not exactly or entirely a sham. But neither can it be understood in the Western parliamentary sense—and those who try to compare Nicaraguan reality with their own desired model, whether of social or liberal democracy, are bound to be disappointed. A distinguished Western diplomat was scathing on the disenchanted who, when they find that the *comandantes* are not "closet social democrats," turn to Reagan's inflated imagery of "totalitarians" and "communist tyrants." "They are," he said, "as dishonest as, in fact more dishonest than Reagan." Opposition parties do not resemble their sycophantic "counterparts" in Eastern European "people's democracies," which cheerfully accept the leading role of the Communist party and almost invariably vote the party line. In Nicaragua, political parties loudly disagree. They oppose, and frequently vote against, legislation introduced by the FSLN (whose members, whatever their private misgivings, always vote en bloc). But their power is limited, both *de facto* and *de jure*, and their freedom of maneuver circumscribed. The Sandinistas make no bones about it. Let me again quote from my interview with Roger Sanchez:

> **AB** (re Sanchez's claim that the opposition parties are "tied to our enemies"): Yes, I know that some of the opposition parties here are in one way or another sympathetic to the *contras*. But surely this does not apply to the parties in the National Assembly, such as the Popular Liberal party, the Democratic Conservatives, or the Popular Social Christian party.
>
> **RS**: Well, I am not entirely sure that they are altogether free of those ties. What is important is that the FSLN led the Revolution, and is the only party that presented a truly national program to the people of Nicaragua. We should be fools to hand over power to political parties that began to develop a political program only after the Revolution. . . . This is a country that only now is embarking on a program of

social transformation, and the bourgeoisie is certainly unable to undertake this task. . . .

AB: Well, then: the attitude of the FSLN is, "We have the power, we conceived the Historic Revolutionary Project, therefore other parties are suspect. Maybe some are allied with the counterrevolution, maybe some are not—but we are suspicious of all of them, and so we arrogate to ourselves the authority to make all the ultimate decisions." But then, what happens to your principle of "political pluralism"?

RS: What we say is that the Revolutionary Project is not under discussion. This does not mean there is no freedom of expression—and I assure you I don't mean this rhetorically. There is a space for pluralism within the Revolution. If we seem to assume such an arrogant attitude about it, it is simply because we have to defend our Revolution. There are parties here that can make a contribution to the Revolution, but then there are those out to destroy us. We do not turn a deaf ear to what other parties are saying—we certainly must have their opinions in order to reach just and correct conclusions. We have been in the struggle for more than twenty years; many of our leaders have laid down their lives in the struggle, and now there are parties that didn't take part in it and want to dispute with us over power. That's really unthinkable.

"counterrevolutionary crimes." (All other prisons, housing either suspects—both criminal and political—or individuals already convicted, are open to organization such as AW and the Red Cross.)

TB: I will certainly look into your request. But I cannot make such an important decision myself—only the National Directorate can do it.

AB: Excuse me, *comandante*, but may I ask you why the National Directorate is to make this decision, and not an appropriate government agency?

TB: Because we must reach decisions collegially. If only one person makes important decisions, this can lead to personal dictatorship and totalitarianism—and we don't want that in this country. That is why we have a collegial mechanism.

AB: I understand why it is infinitely better to have a collective leadership rather than a personal dictator. But my question is, why are decisions like that vested in the party rather than the state?

TB: Because this is the reality of this country. Leaders of the Revolution are also leaders of the state. The president, the ministers, the head of the army, and other state officials are all leading members of the party.

If nothing else, Borge deserves applause for his candor—which also points to some of the serious problems in present-day Nicaragua.

Abraham Brumberg is a contributing editor of The New Republic. *His latest book is* Poland: Genesis of a Revolution.

"The FSLN is History's chosen instrument of social change in Nicaragua, and . . . the party has no intention of relinquishing this role."

Words lend themselves to different interpretations, and in the still fluid conditions of today's Nicaragua their practical application may undergo significant changes. Yet I think that *compañero* Sanchez's candid formulations reflect the basic assumptions of the Sandinista leadership: namely, that the FSLN is History's chosen instrument of social change in Nicaragua, and that the party has no intention of relinquishing this role. To understand this is to understand why, right now at least, it is absurd to expect the Sandinistas to accede to "outside" opposition parties' demands for genuine power-sharing. Even some of the demands voiced by the "loyal opposition" (parties that remain within the National Assembly), such as separation of party and state, and the establishment of the checks-and-balances system of a parliamentary model, are scarcely likely to be met. Let me quote quite an authoritative source, Tomas Borge, minister of the interior, member of the nine-man National Directorate and the only living founder of the FSLN. Our exchange took place during a two-and-one-half hour meeting of Borge and several members of Americas Watch (AW). One member of the AW delegation asked Borge for permission to visit a detention prison for those suspected of viewpoint 165

Americans Should Support the Sandinistas

John L. Hammond

On July 19, 1979, the Sandinista National Liberation Front (FSLN) toppled the Nicaraguan government after a victorious but costly insurrection and disbanded the National Guard which had sustained the Somoza regime for half a century. The FSLN proclaimed a new government and a new type of revolution: it would raise the living standard of the poor while respecting the right of private property in a mixed economy; it would mobilize the masses in the service of collective goals while honoring the rights of individuals in a pluralist political system. By 1986, Nicaragua had spread effective health care to isolated villages, almost eliminated illiteracy, given land and dignity to impoverished peasants, conducted free and open elections, and enabled voiceless people to take control of their lives.

But at the same time, rampant inflation and serious economic shortages have caused rising discontent; young men are fleeing the country to avoid the draft; the Catholic hierarchy is increasingly defiant of the government; and a bloody and brutal war with the US-supported contras has cost the country thousands of lives and millions of dollars.

What has happened . . . to bring this about? US aggression poses almost insurmountable obstacles to the revolutionary program, but the Sandinista leadership has shown some major shortcomings of its own. The western press has criticized the Nicaraguan regime for being totalitarian and despotic; but the criticisms fail to understand the regime's complexity or to explain why these problems have arisen. The Sandinistas have embarked on a unique attempt to create a new kind of society which will hold on to some elements of liberal democracy and at the same time assure social justice and give dignity and political power to the poor. These goals entail real contradictions; but the experiment offers a hopeful model which deserves the political support of progressive North Americans.

Transforming Nicaragua

A principal goal of the revolution is to transform Nicaragua from an underdeveloped society with extreme disparities between the rich few and the masses of poor people to one which meets the minimum needs of all. But the new government declared when it took power that it would respect private property because it hoped to maintain national unity and enlist all classes in the task of reconstruction after the insurrection. The commitment to a mixed economy has become a basic principle. The government has guaranteed that anyone who puts capital or land to productive use can keep it. Property can be expropriated only if its owner abandons the country or leaves resources lying idle.

Economic development under the revolutionary government will be state-led, but it will still count on an integration of state and private capital. Does this represent socialism? Clearly not, at least at present. The government does not declare itself socialist, and the character of the economy remains undefined. Nicaragua is experimenting to create a new model which will preserve the right of private property while denying political dominance to the wealthy.

Transforming the economy meant, first, reconstructing a society wrecked by half a century of Somoza rule. The Somoza dynasty had treated Nicaragua as a private colony, controlling industrial and agricultural development for its private gain. As the end approached, it waged a futile war of enormous destruction: 50,000 people died in the insurrection (in a country of three million), many of them killed in government aerial bombardments;

John L. Hammond, "The Revolution Deserves Enthusiastic Support," *New Politics*, Volume I, No. 1, Summer 1986. © 1986 New Politics Associates, Brooklyn, NY.

200,000 families were left homeless, one quarter of the country's industry was destroyed, and 70% of cropland had gone unplanted in 1978. The last Somoza saddled the country with enormous foreign debts and looted the treasury before he fled. At the end of the war, the fleeing oligarchy had drained resources abroad, investment had practically dried up, production was paralyzed, and the banking system was insolvent. In 1978 and 1979 alone, the country suffered $4.3 million in material damages related to the insurrection.

Among the new government's first steps was to nationalize the holdings of Somoza and his associates, all banking and foreign trade, and some essential industries. Under its guidance the economy recovered strikingly, as cumulative economic growth between 1979 and 1983 reached 22.5%. This performance far exceeded that of the other countries of the region: on the average, the Central American economies *declined* by 5.7% in the same period. . . .

Threatening the Sandinistas' Progress

But an economic crisis, worsening since 1984, threatens to overwhelm the gains in equity which the revolution made in its first five years. Terms of trade for Nicaragua's main exports have grown worse: even as the volume of exports grew (four times as much cotton, and almost twice as much sugar, were exported in 1983 as in 1980), their dollar value declined. Inflation is spiralling (50% in 1984, 251% in 1985); the trade deficit is growing ($560 million on current account in 1985) despite drastic devaluations; wage controls and shortages of imported goods are causing severe discontent.

Contradictions between the goals of guaranteeing a minimum standard of living and upholding the market system have contributed to the crisis: the combination of wage policies, price controls, and tolerance of the black market has spawned a huge nonproductive class in the larger cities which has found that it can make more money at petty commerce than at productive labor. The resulting labor shortage, especially for the harvest of export crops, causes production shortfalls which accentuate the trade deficit, and speculation leads to shortages of goods, higher black-market prices, and greater discontent. The alternative of strict control over the black market, on the other hand, would bring in its wake all the costs of centralization and eliminate the safety valve which the present system provides.

The mixed-economy model also creates a political problem: it calls on the strongest supporters of the revolution, peasants and workers, for major sacrifices while favoring the small and medium bourgeoisie in commerce and agriculture when many of them are overtly opposed to the revolution and eager to use their economic position to sabotage it.

But the major cause of the economic crisis is not the Sandinistas' policy errors; it is United States

aggression. Since 1981, the Reagan administration has cut off aid, pressured allies and international lending agencies to deny credit and aid, and declared an embargo on trade with Nicaragua. Even more costly is the war being waged by the contras and financed by the US: material damages amounted to $196 million between 1980 and 1983, and rose to $184 million in 1984 alone. Forty percent of the budget now goes for defense, forcing postponements of major projects and cutbacks in ongoing social programs.

Education and Health Care

Even with the war, the revolution has achieved amazing successes in health care and education. The most remote areas, previously neglected, now have basic services. The first step in education was the national literacy campaign of 1980, which mobilized tens of thousands of young people and adults as teachers. Many of the crusaders left their towns for the countryside, living in the homes of their adult students and working with them in the fields. The campaign reduced illiteracy from 50% to 13%. . . .

"The measure of a revolution is not only whether it puts food on the table and brings social services to the poor, but whether it gives people power to determine the circumstances of their lives."

Before the revolution medical care had been even more deficient than education. Health services are now widely provided, and the aims of medicine have been gradually transformed to emphasize not curative medicine but primary and preventive care (though, relative to the available resources, there is still an overemphasis on costlier medical procedures). . . .

The measure of a revolution is not only whether it puts food on the table and brings social services to the poor, but whether it gives people power to determine the circumstances of their lives. Experiences like the literacy and health campaigns are thus inherently political; not only because mass involvement is a major factor in their success, but because they provide the empowering experience of working to improve one's condition. The peasant learns that ignorance, the early death of his children, and submission to the landlord or seed merchant are not immutable facts of nature but problems that he can solve; she knows that, as someone who can read and write, she is entitled to the same respect as a rich person. Attending a night school or recruiting for vaccinations is itself a political act, one which only the revolution has made possible.

Like the economic system, the political system is experimental. Nicaragua is attempting to combine a centralized party, pluralist representation, and direct participation through mass organizations. Tensions among these different structures are inevitable, just as they are among the elements of the mixed economy. But Nicaraguans hope to find a synthesis which will enact the will of the people as a whole and protect the rights of individuals but will not allow economic privilege to achieve a dominant political voice.

The mass organizations, the neighborhood-based Sandinista Defense Committees (CDS), the Women's Association (AMNLAE), and the Farmworkers' Association (ATC), arose during the insurrection and since then have become formal channels for popular influence over the government. The mass organizations are closely tied to the FSLN, and they could easily turn into transmission belts for Sandinista ideology or government policy. But they have not; they have often taken an independent role at both the local and the national level. On municipal councils in many towns, they take part in debating the very practical questions of allocating resources in the face of scarcity. Represented in the Council of State (the legislative body until the election of the National Assembly in 1984), they frequently opposed some aspects of government-sponsored legislation and offered alternatives. The ATC in 1979 and 1980 organized its members to occupy abandoned farms not scheduled for expropriation; those occupations forced the government to reverse itself and expropriate some of them.

The Struggle for Autonomy

The FSLN expected the ATC to include small and medium landowners in the same organization with farmworkers. But because their interests are different the farmers founded their own organization, the small and medium farmers' organization (UNAG), in 1981. Thus UNAG's very existence demonstrates that the mass organizations can act autonomously. UNAG represents a constituency which is on the whole much less enthusiastic about the revolution than the members of the other organizations, and it has shown a great deal of independence. It often takes positions on agricultural policy different from those of the government, and it has attempted (with frequent success) to influence government policy in favor of the interests of small and medium growers.

The mass organizations struggle to preserve their autonomy from the FSLN and the government. But it often is a struggle. Many mass organization leaders are also FSLN cadre and are under pressure to orient activities to the party's goals. The FSLN frequently moves them from one position to another without

regard for the needs of the base organizations. Some of the organizations' autonomy appears to be a casualty of war, for they increasingly concentrate on mobilizing members for defense-related tasks like joining the militia and encouraging young men to register for the draft rather than working on their members' immediate problems. At least in the CDSs, the danger of this emphasis has recently been publicly recognized and some efforts are being made to correct it.

"The subject of the Nicaraguan revolution is not any particular class but 'the people' as a whole."

In its attempt to create a mixed political system, Nicaragua is trying to balance direct political participation through mass organizations with pluralist institutions which, for the first time in its history, are giving it a genuinely representative democracy. The mixed economy embodies the quest for national unity, based on the belief that the subject of the Nicaraguan revolution is not any particular class but "the people" as a whole. The political correlative of that premise is that all groups are entitled to representation. . . .

The Costs of War

There is one strong force weighing in favor of centralization, however: the war. The Sandinistas' errors and the conflicts among the principles underlying the political and economic system create problems, but by far the society's most serious problems stem from US aggression.

US efforts to destroy the Sandinista revolution started almost from its inception. Beyond the economic effects already detailed, the war is costly in human lives: according to government figures, contras killed 1,143 soldiers and 281 civilians in 1985 (among the civilians, teachers, health workers and coffee harvest volunteers are favorite targets; *New York Times*, December 31, 1985). Confronting the ongoing military emergency will continue to be costly, and require a centralized command structure; it may force a clampdown to stem the discontent caused by shortages and economic crisis.

Since the triumph, no government measure has been more unpopular than the draft, but it is clearly an unavoidable necessity. A state of emergency has curtailed political activity, although the restrictions have hardly exceeded emergency measures normal in wartime, and they were lifted during and after the election campaign. They were reimposed in 1985, but the terms were lightened by the elected National Assembly exercising its independent powers. The opposition has been highly provocative, and some of its leaders who had claimed to subscribe to the rules of the democratic game have left the country to side openly with the contras.

Many people have been forcibly relocated, not just on the Atlantic Coast but, in increasing numbers, from other combat zones, especially along the Honduran border. Thousands of families were resettled in 1985. Many of them came from areas where the contras had had some support, and resisted dislocation from their home communities. Americas Watch gives the resettlements qualified approval, finding that they were due to genuine military necessity and did not discriminate politically in resettling, but that guarantees of human rights were not always observed in the process: residents were not always given advance notice or allowed to participate in the decision to resettle, and some houses were destroyed as the people were being removed. The integration of these new refugees is a major problem the revolution now faces.

Inevitable Consequences of Revolution

Wartime conditions cannot be dismissed as an aberration affecting the revolution; all revolutions in the twentieth century have faced counterrevolution supported from abroad. The revolutionary government's choices—its military organization, its alliances (foreign and internal class alliances), and its enactment or postponement of programs—must be seen as an outcome of an inevitable condition of revolution.

"I believe we should offer [Nicaragua] our enthusiastic support in the construction of that new society."

But the defense of the country against counterrevolution has also ratified and reinforced popular power. The right to self-defense is a major popular demand, and arms have been distributed to peasants in villages and on cooperatives to defend themselves against attack. The peasants and farmworkers are the backbone of the militia: men voluntarily leave their homes and fields to serve at the front, and those who remain at home, including the women, stand guard nightly. The wide distribution of arms testifies to the close and confident relation between people and leadership.

Most of the information we get from Nicaragua is reported by journalists who, whatever their own sympathies, see little more than the view from Managua. It is then filtered by editors who fear negative reaction from the White House and provide a "balanced" viewpoint which tips ever more in favor of direct US intervention (as the *New York*

Times showed when it printed an Op-Ed article on December 13, 1985, by three contra leaders, making claims which the *Times's* own reporting had shown to be false). . . .

The media have proclaimed terrorism the "story of the year" [for] 1985. The rundowns of the year's terrorist incidents hardly mention the contras (if they do, the report is "balanced" with a reminder that President Reagan accused Nicaragua of being one of the world's five leading authors of terrorism). Why this omission? Perhaps because the readers and viewers (or at least the journalists) can imagine themselves becoming random victims in the Rome airport, but not meeting an ambush on a byroad of the Pan-American Highway. The cultural distance which separates them from Nicaraguan reality leads them to interpret the revolution by the standards of their own very different society. We must take into account the effect of these distortions on our own understanding of what is happening in Nicaragua.

All progressive North Americans agree that we must oppose US aggression against Nicaragua, but the Nicaraguan revolution deserves more. It has brought not just material welfare but active participation to people who are increasingly in control of their own lives. In its experimental economic and political system it is pioneering a new form of society which may provide a model for other peoples. We must be prepared to criticize its shortcomings, but all in all I believe we should offer it our enthusiastic support in the construction of that new society. The bourgeoisie's complaints about freedom of the press and the hierarchy's complaints about the disruption of Church functions must be weighed alongside of the gains made by the vast masses of people who have food on the table, a rifle on the wall, and a voice in their own affairs.

Editor's note: This article was part of a symposium on Nicaragua in which all three participants were opposed to American intervention, although each had different views on the nature of the Sandinista regime. See New Politics, *Summer 1986.*

John L. Hammond teaches sociology at Hunter College and the Graduate Center of the City University of New York. He spent August 1985 as a consultant to the regional government of Las Segovias, Nicaragua.

"The aim of the Sandinista revolution is to crush its society from top to bottom."

Americans Should Not Support the Sandinistas

David Horowitz

Twenty-five years ago I was one of the founders of the New Left. I was one of the organizers of the first political demonstrations on the Berkeley campus—and indeed on any campus—to protest our government's anti-Communist policies in Cuba and Vietnam. Tonight I come before you as the kind of man I used to tell myself I would never be: a supporter of President Reagan, a committed opponent of Communist rule in Nicaragua.

I offer no apologies for my present position. It was what I thought was the humanity of the Marxist *idea* that made me what I was then; it is the inhumanity of what I have seen to be the Marxist *reality* that has made me what I am now. If my former comrades who support the Sandinistas were to pause for a moment and then plunge their busy political minds into the human legacies of their activist pasts, they would instantly drown in an ocean of blood.

The issue before us is not whether it is morally right for the United States to arm the *contras*, or whether there are unpleasant men among them. Nor is it whether the United States should defer to the wisdom of the Contadora powers—more than thirty years ago the United States tried to overthrow Somoza, and it was the Contadora powers of the time who bailed him out.

The issue before us and before all people who cherish freedom is how to oppose a Soviet imperialism so vicious and so vast as to dwarf any previously known. An "ocean of blood" is no metaphor. As we speak here tonight, this empire—whose axis runs through Havana and now Managua—is killing hundreds of thousands of Ethiopians to consolidate a dictatorship whose policies against its black citizens make the South African government look civilized and humane.

A second issue, especially important to me, is the credibility and commitment of the American Left.

In his speech on Nicaragua, President Reagan invoked the Truman Doctrine, the first attempt to oppose Soviet expansion through revolutionary surrogates. I marched against the Truman Doctrine in 1948, and defended, with the Left, the revolutions in Russia and China, in Eastern Europe and Cuba, in Cambodia and Vietnam—just as the Left defends the Sandinistas today.

And I remember the arguments and "facts" with which we made our case and what the other side said, too—the Presidents who came and went, and the anti-Communists on the Right, the William Buckleys and the Ronald Reagans. And in every case, without exception, time has proved the Left wrong. Wrong in its views of the revolutionaries' intentions, and wrong about the facts of their revolutionary rule. And just as consistently the anti-Communists were proved right.

Today the Left dismisses Reagan's warnings about Soviet expansion as anti-Communist paranoia, a threat to the peace, and a mask for American imperialism. We said the same things about Truman when he warned us then. Russia's control of Eastern Europe, we said, was only a defensive buffer, a temporary response to American power—first, because Russia had no nuclear weapons; and then, because it lacked the missiles to deliver them.

Soviet Domination

Today, the Soviet Union is a nuclear superpower, missiles and all, but it has not given up an inch of the empire which it gained during World War II—not Eastern Europe, not the Baltic states which Hitler delivered to Stalin and whose nationhood Stalin erased and which are now all but forgotten, not even the Kurile Islands which were once part of Japan.

Not only have the Soviets failed to relinquish their

conquests in all these years—years of dramatic, total decolonization in the West—but their growing strength and the wounds of Vietnam have encouraged them to reach for more. South Vietnam, Cambodia, Laos, Ethiopia, Yemen, Mozambique, and Angola are among the dominoes which have recently fallen into the Soviet orbit.

To expand its territorial core—which apologists still refer to as a "defensive perimeter"—Moscow has already slaughtered a million peasants in Afghanistan, an atrocity warmly endorsed by the Sandinista government.

"We praised the Soviet Union then, just as the Left praises the Sandinistas."

Minister of Defense Humberto Ortega describes the army of the conquerors—whose scorched-earth policy has driven half the Afghan population from its homes—as the "pillar of peace" in the world today. To any self-respecting socialist, praise for such barbarism would be an inconceivable outrage—as it was to the former Sandinista, now *contra*, Edén Pastora. But praise for the barbarians is sincere tribute coming from the Sandinista rulers, because they see themselves as an integral part of the Soviet empire itself.

A Short Memory

"The struggle of man against power is the struggle of memory against forgetting." So writes the Czech novelist Milan Kundera, whose name and work no longer exist in his homeland.

In all the Americas, Fidel Castro was the only head of state to cheer the Soviet tanks as they rolled over the brave people of Prague. And cheering right along with Fidel were Carlos Fonseca, Tomas Borge, Humberto Ortega, and the other creators of the present Nicaraguan regime.

One way to assess what has happened in Nicaragua is to realize that wherever Soviet tanks crush freedom from now on, there will be two governments in the Americas supporting them all the way.

About its own crimes and for its own criminals, the Left has no memory at all.

To the Left I grew up in, along with the Sandinista founders, Stalin's Russia was a socialist paradise, the model of the liberated future. Literacy to the uneducated, power to the weak, justice to the forgotten—we praised the Soviet Union then, just as the Left praises the Sandinistas now.

And just as they ignore warnings like the one that has come from Violetta Chamorro, the publisher of *La Prensa*, the paper which led the fight against Somoza, and a member of the original Sandinista

junta—"With all my heart, I tell you it is worse here now than it was in the times of the Somoza dictatorship"—so we dismissed the anti-Soviet "lies" about Stalinist repression.

In the society we hailed as a new human dawn, 100 million people were put in slave-labor camps, in conditions rivaling Auschwitz and Buchenwald. Between 30 and 40 million people were killed—in peacetime, in the daily routine of socialist rule. While leftists applauded their progressive policies and guarded their frontiers, Soviet Marxists killed more peasants, more workers, and even more Communists than all the capitalist governments together since the beginning of time.

And for the entire duration of this nightmare, the William Buckleys and Ronald Reagans and the other anti-Communists went on telling the world exactly what was happening. And all that time the pro-Soviet Left and its fellow-travelers went on denouncing them as reactionaries and liars, using the same contemptuous terms with which the Left attacks the President and his supporters today.

Acknowledging Their Crimes

The Left would *still* be denying the Soviet atrocities if the perpetrators themselves had not finally acknowledged their crimes. In 1956, in a secret speech to the party elite, Khrushchev made the crimes a Communist fact; but it was only the CIA that actually made the fact public, allowing radicals to come to terms with what they had done.

Khrushchev and his cohorts could not have cared less about the misplaced faith and misspent lives of their naive supporters on the Left. The Soviet rulers were concerned about themselves: Stalin's mania had spread the slaughter into his henchmen's ranks; they wanted to make totalitarianism safe for its rulers. In place of a dictator whose paranoia could not be controlled, they instituted a dictatorship by directorate—which (not coincidentally) is the form of rule in Nicaragua today. Repression would work one way only: from the privileged top of society to the powerless bottom.

The year of Khrushchev's speech—which is also the year Soviet tanks flattened the freedom fighters of Budapest—is the year that tells us who the Sandinistas really are.

Because the truth had to be admitted at last, the Left all over the world was forced to redefine itself in relation to the Soviet facts. China's Communist leader Mao liked Stalin's way better. Twenty-five million people died in the "great leaps" and "cultural revolutions" he then launched. In Europe and America, however, a new anti-Stalinist Left was born. This New Left, of which I was one of the founders, was repelled by the evils it was now forced to see, and embarrassed by the tarnish the Soviet totalitarians had brought to the socialist cause. It turned its back on the Soviet model of Stalin and his heirs.

But the Sandinista vanguard was neither embarrassed nor repelled. In 1957, Carlos Fonseca, the founding father of the Sandinista Front, visited the Soviet Union with its newly efficient totalitarian state. To Fonseca, as to Borge and his other comrades, the Soviet monstrosity was their revolutionary dream come true. In his pamphlet, *A Nicaraguan in Moscow*, Fonseca proclaimed Soviet Communism his model for Latin America's revolutionary future.

This vision of a Soviet America is now being realized in Nicaragua. The *comandante* directorate, the army, and the secret police are already mirrors of the Soviet state—not only structurally but in their personnel, trained and often manned by agents of the Soviet axis.

Disciples of Fidel Castro

But the most important figure in this transformation is not a Nicaraguan at all. For twenty years, from the time the Sandinistas first arrived in Havana, they were disciples of Fidel Castro. With his blessings they went on to Moscow, where Stalin's henchmen completed their revolutionary course. Fidel is the image in which the Sandinista leadership has created itself and the author of its strategy. Its politburo, the *comandante* directorate, was personally created by Fidel in Havana on the eve of the final struggle, sealed with a pledge of millions in military aid. It was Fidel who supplied the arms with which the Sandinistas waged their battles, just as he supplied the Cuban general—Zenen Casals—who directed their victorious campaign (just as the Soviets supplied the general who directed Fidel's own victory at the Bay of Pigs). *Without Castro's intervention, Arturo Cruz and the other anti-Somoza and pro-democratic contras would be the government of Nicaragua today.*

And it was Fidel who showed the Sandinistas how to steal the revolution after the victory, and how to secure their theft by manipulating their most important allies: the American Left and its liberal sympathizers. . . .

When I listen to the enthusiasts for the Sandinista redeemers, the fate of a hero of the Cuban revolution comes to my mind. For in the year that Jean-Paul Sartre came to Havana and fell in love with the humanitarian Fidel, Huber Matos embarked on a long windowless night of the soul. . . .

The Hangman and the Poet

When Huber Matos saw Fidel's strategy unfolding in Cuba, he got on the telephone with other Fidelistas to discuss what they should do. This was a mistake. In the first year of Cuba's liberation, the phones of revolutionary legends like Huber Matos were already tapped by Fidel's secret police. Huber Matos was arrested.

In the bad old days of Batista oppression, Fidel had been arrested himself. His crime was not words on a telephone, but leading an attack on a military barracks to overthrow the Batista regime. Twelve people were killed. For this Fidel spent a total of eighteen months in the tyrant's jail before being released.

Huber Matos was not so lucky. Fidel was no Batista, and the revolution that had overthrown Batista was no two-bit dictatorship. For his phone call, Huber Matos was tried in such secrecy that not even members of the government were privy to the proceeding. When it was over, he was sentenced to solitary confinement, in a cell without sunlight, for *twenty-two years*. And even as Fidel buried his former friend and comrade alive, he went on singing his songs of revolutionary humanism and justice.

Milan Kundera reveals the meaning of this revolutionary parable of Huber Matos and Fidel. Recalling a French Communist who wrote poems for brotherhood while his friend was being murdered by the poet's comrades in Prague, Kundera says: "The hangman killed while the poet sang."

"This vision of a Soviet America is now being realized in Nicaragua."

Kundera explains: "People like to say revolution is beautiful; it is only the terror arising from it which is evil. But this is not true. The evil is already present in the beautiful; hell is already contained in the dream of paradise. . . . To condemn Gulags is easy, but to reject the poetry which leads to the Gulag by way of paradise is as difficult as ever." Words to bear in mind today as we consider Nicaragua and its revolution of poets.

Revolutionary Cynicism

To believe in the revolutionary dream is the tragedy of its supporters; to exploit the dream is the talent of its dictators. Revolutionary cynicism, the source of this talent, is Fidel's most important teaching to his Sandinista disciples. This is the faculty that allows the *comandantes* to emulate Fidel himself: to be poets and hangmen at the same time. To promise democracy and organize repression, to attack imperialism and join an empire, to talk peace and plan war, to champion justice and deliver Nicaragua to a fraternity of inhumane, repressive, militarized, and economically crippled states.

"We used to have one main prison, now we have many," begins the lament of Carlos Franqui, a former Fidelista, for the paradise that Nicaragua has now gained. "We used to have a few barracks; now we have many. We used to have many plantations; now we have only one, and it belongs to Fidel. Who enjoys the fruits of the revolution, the houses of the rich, the luxuries of the rich? The *comandante* and his court."

To this grim accounting must be added the economic ruin that Fidel's Marxism has wrought. Among the proven failures of the Marxist promise, this is the most fateful of all. The failure of Marxist economies to satisfy basic needs, let alone compete with the productive capitalisms of the West, has produced the military-industrial police states which call themselves socialist today. Nicaragua, with its Sandinista-created economic crisis and its massive military build-up, is but the latest example of this pattern.

"The . . . illusion—that the revolution will mean better lives for Nicaragua's poor—underlies every defense of the Sandinistas today."

Twenty-five years ago we on the Left applauded when Fidel denounced Cuba's one-crop economy and claimed that U.S. imperialism was the cause of the nation's economic plight. It seemed so self-evident. Cuba was a fertile island with a favorable climate, but U.S. sugar plantations had monopolized its arable land, and the sugar produced was a product for export, not a food for Cubans. The poor of Cuba had been sacrificed on the altar of imperialist profit. Whenever we were confronted by the political costs Castro's revolution might entail, we were confident that this gain alone—Cuba's freedom to grow food for Cubans—would make any sacrifice worthwhile. The same illusion—that the revolution will mean better lives for Nicaragua's poor—underlies every defense of the Sandinistas today. . . .

The Aim of the Sandinistas

Nicaragua is now in the grip of utterly cynical and utterly ruthless men, exceeding even their sponsors in aggressive hostility to the United States. The Soviets may be the covert patrons of the world's terrorist plague, but not even they have had the temerity to embrace publicly the assassin Qaddafi as a "brother" the way the Sandinistas have. The aim of the Sandinista revolution is to crush its society from top to bottom, to institute totalitarian rule, and to use the country as a base to spread Communist terror and Communist regimes throughout the hemisphere.

The Sandinista anthem which proclaims the Yankee to be the "enemy of mankind" expresses precisely the revolutionaries' sentiment and goal. That goal is hardly to create a more just society—the

sordid record would dissuade any reformer from choosing the Communist path—but to destroy the societies still outside the totalitarian perimeter, and their chief protector, the United States.

Support for the *contras* is a first line of defense. For Nicaraguans, a *contra* victory would mean the restoration of the democratic leadership from whom the Sandinistas stole the revolution in the first place, the government that Nicaragua would have had if Cuba had not intervened. For the countries of the Americas, it would mean a halt in the Communist march that threatens their freedoms and their peace.

In League with the Dark

In conclusion, I would like to say this to my former comrades and successors on the Left: you are self-righteous and blind in your belief that you are part of a movement to advance human progress and liberate mankind. You are in fact in league with the darkest and most reactionary forces of the modern world, whose legacies—as the record attests—are atrocities and oppressions on a scale unknown in the human past. It is no accident that radicals in power have slaughtered so many of their own people. Hatred of self, and by extension one's country, is the root of the radical cause.

As American radicals, the most egregious sin you commit is to betray the privileges and freedoms ordinary people from all over the world have created in this country—privileges and freedoms that ordinary people all over the world would feel blessed to have themselves. But the worst of it is this: you betray all this tangible good that you can see around you for a socialist pie-in-the-sky that has meant horrible deaths and miserable lives for the hundreds of millions who have so far fallen under its sway.

David Horowitz, the author of several books, was the editor of Ramparts *magazine and a founder of the Vietnam Solidarity Campaign.*

The US Should Help the Contras Win

Michael Johns

I've . . . come before you . . . to discuss what is undoubtedly one of the most important—and dangerous—situations for this country in at least the past decade; perhaps the past three decades. I speak of the advance of international Leninism in our hemisphere—specifically the newest member of this barbaric network, the Sandinista dictatorship in communist Nicaragua.

However, I also come before you to offer my remedy to this situation—which I hope will be embraced by the third generation whose leadership I respect and whose activities will surely have an impact on whether or not democracy ever sees light again in Nicaragua and whether or not the Sandinistas will succeed in their effort to export Marxist revolution throughout Latin America. Simply stated, I think the time has come for the United States of America, part-time leader of the free world, to realize it has a full-time obligation to bring forth an immediate Tet-offensive—both militarily in Nicaragua and intellectually and politically around the world—in an effort to ensure a military victory for the Freedom Fighters—namely, the Nicaraguan democratic force. In this context, I am also proud to come before you to personally relay the messages of these brave fighters—messages which they asked me to relay which, I believe, have been distorted and at times ignored entirely by liberal American institutions and policy makers.

From my visit to the front lines in January of 1984, to several repeat visits to Central America since, to my contact with these brave men and women in the Latin American refugee capital of Miami—where one is still reminded daily of the gutlessness of President Kennedy in not providing the air cover to the Cuban patriots at the Bay of Pigs—I have drawn what I

think is a realistic conclusion—that it is futile for the West to think that the communist thugs in Managua today will ever negotiate an end to the tyranny and modern hell they have created there. Our only hope, I am convinced, is for the free world to come to the conclusion now that it has a moral, ethical, and strategic imperative in promoting a successful democratic revolution that will forcefully and comprehensively oust the illegitimate Marxist junta and foreign occupation forces that currently rule Nicaragua by the sword . . . not by popular mandate.

Military Success Is Possible

To succeed in this mission will not be easy, but I want to emphasize that it can, in fact, be done. The pessimistic doomsayers of American conservatism—who I hope are a minority—that would like to see the revolution succeed, but have since questioned the reality of such an outcome, might as well have never endorsed the Freedom Fighters in the first place. These negative attitudes run rampant here in Washington where policy activists and journalists have not spent their time listening to the brave and ambitious words of the Nicaraguan resistance—who are currently scoring many military victories inside Nicaragua—nor viewing the look in these freedom fighters' eyes that shows brave men and women hungry for nothing less than victory. Rather, many of these Washington conservatives see a very different reality of a democratic process in America that has drug its feet for years on providing the necessary aid, an American society that scarcely realizes there is an expansionist-oriented communist dictatorship closer to Miami than Miami is to Washington, and a media, Congress, State Department, and elements of the Administration who have defied the laws of history and suggested that this whole situation might eventually be solved diplomatically. This last suggestion is perhaps the most frightening. The debate over the $100 million

Michael Johns, "Nicaragua: A Military Victory Over the Sandinistas," a speech delivered to the Heritage Foundation in Washington, DC on September 17, 1986.

in assistance to the FDN [Nicaraguan Democratic Force] did not include many passionate speeches about our moral and ethical imperative in ousting this Soviet base camp to our south. Nor did it include many accurate character sketches about just who these Freedom Fighters are and why we must support them. Rather, the general conservative argument over funding the resistance was first, that if we didn't fund the resistance now, it might become necessary to commit U.S. troops later, and, second, that if we continue to pressure the Sandinistas by funding the resistance, the Sandinistas will then be forced to negotiate a settlement. Perhaps both these arguments were simply part of the realpolitic—empty words that were needed to win over the votes necessary to secure the $100 million. However, I think that conservatives and all those interested in seeing the Nicaraguan problem corrected should feel very uneasy with the concept of negotiation with the Sandinistas—whether it be the direct negotiation of our State Department with the junta—as had been going on in Mexico—or the negotiation of Contadora. In both cases, the Freedom Fighters of Nicaragua would probably be played as pawns in a game that does not render itself to a diplomatic solution. The resistance has consistently relayed to me and others who write frequently on this issue, that as negotiation heats up, the Sandinistas dramatically increase their air attacks on FDN camps. In other words, the communists of Nicaragua will gladly negotiate empty treaties with the West because they realize the only way they will be forced out of power is through military might. At this point, they also know that the resistance is gaining dramatic support in rural Nicaragua and—if financial support continues to come from the U.S.— the chances of a military victory for the resistance are quite good.

"If financial support continues to come from the U.S. . . . the chances of a military victory for the resistance are quite good."

But this victory hedges on U.S. attitudes and especially continued U.S. support for the resistance. The Sandinistas, of course, know this and have thus organized a very effective lobby of grass-roots liberals and Marxists in the United States whose job it is to see that the U.S. abandons the Freedom Fighters to the extermination of Soviet HI-24's and recognizes that the Sandinista presence to our south is something of an inevitability that we might as well start tolerating. They would have us abandon our historical obligation to those brave men and women who are clearly the modern equivalent of our founding fathers.

But to understand this historical obligation, we must first realize why thousands of Nicaraguans have taken up arms in an effort to liberate their homeland. Is it because they seek a negotiated settlement? I think not. These fighters picked up arms because it is the only option they had left. The claims the resistance made about the Sandinista persona several years ago—which were mostly scoffed at at the time by the American left—are now held as common knowledge and even confirmed by individuals like former Borge aide Alvaro Baldizon. Indeed, the Marxist Maryknolls, tenured professors, and underground journalists of the far-left along with a rather impressive list of names from Congress—who once devoted their entire being to promoting the Sandinista cause in their fight against so-called U.S. imperialism—are now quietly eating their words. Others, like Robert Leiken, are at least brave enough to admit they made a drastic mistake.

Reality of the Situation

The reality of the situation is that there really was no Sandinista revolution in Nicaragua. If there was, it lasted only shortly. For the bottom line of what the Sandinistas brought the Nicaraguan people was not domestic revolution but the external ideologies of Marx, Engels, and Lenin in a neatly packaged form. Those in the West who bought the appealing words of the poets in the Sandinista junta are now tasting the poison that was so brilliantly concealed— the obliteration of the Miskito culture, the bogus People's Church, the mob assaults on priests and independent politicians, the schools now handed over to Marxist revolutionary indoctrination, the secret police and so-called neighborhood watch committees, the harassment of those who are trying futilely to retain the Nicaragua they once were proud to call home, the thousands of middle and above class Nicaraguans who have given up hope and fled for the good life in Miami, and—probably most important—the 300,000 in this country of just over two million who couldn't afford to and fled the horror for the underfunded refugee camps of Honduras and Costa Rica.

It isn't a pretty picture. But what about the junta itself? Surely, one would think, they have also participated in all of the so-called sacrifices needed to defend their bogus revolution. Hardly. Rather, the junta has taken for themselves the homes, cars, and luxuries left behind by Somoza and expropriated from other wealthy Nicaraguans. As in other communist countries, an exclusive hard currency store has opened in Managua where foreigners as well as members of the emerging Nicaraguan "nomenklature" may shop for goods otherwise not available. Meanwhile, the Nicaraguan cordoba officially pegged at 70 to the dollar is now going for

2,000 to the dollar in the black market. Stories abound of farmers having to steal food because the socialized economy will not issue them ration coupons even though quotas are being fulfilled. And shortages of just about every food group are common.

Furthermore, the promises the Sandinistas made to the OAS [Organization of American States] about international non-alignment have now turned out to be a cruel facade as the Sandinistas have expressed their support for terrorists around the world from the PLO to the Red Brigade to the Basque ETA and have actively supported Marxist revolution elsewhere from the FMLN in El Salvador to the M-19 in Colombia. Terrorists from around the world have taken haven in Nicaragua. Today, in 1986, it is almost common knowledge in the foreign policy community that the Sandinistas are a destabilizing and malevolent force in Latin America that threatens the existence of democracies and non-communist nations from the southern tip of South America to the Rio Grande . . . and surely they would hope into the United States itself.

In response to these activities, many members of the American left have argued that to really understand the Sandinista actions, one must understand the history of American intervention in Nicaragua. This is nonsense for today Nicaragua is not run by Nicaraguans. It is run by hard-core Marxist Leninists with grand plans for revolution throughout the Americas. So the real historical issue we must consider is the history of Leninism; specifically, what is the history of stopping Leninists and totalitarian nations by way of negotiation . . . and what is the history of stopping them by force. I think you will agree that the latter has generally—if not consistently—proven more effective.

The Need for US Aid

Applying this to the Nicaraguan situation, I must say that the men and women of the Nicaraguan democratic force are pleading that America give them the support necessary to solve this conflict themselves. If they were here now, they would urge you not to buy into the fake promises of a communist dictatorship which has consistently and repeatedly betrayed their word, but to support genuine democrats struggling for political sovereignty and participation.

One of the most significant fallacies surrounding the debate to fund the Nicaraguan resistance is that other Central American leaders and peoples oppose such aid. In Costa Rica, for instance, despite the appeasing words of Oscar Arias, over seventy percent of Costa Ricans support U.S. aid to the Freedom Fighters. Why then does Contadora enjoy support among some Latin American presidents even though others like Salvadoran foreign minister Raldolfo Castillo and Honduran president Jose

Azcona have declared the process a sham? For one thing, for these leaders to remain politically strong they feel they must show independence from the U.S. Many of these nations have communist insurgent groups of their own to deal with— ironically, most of which are fully supported by the Sandinistas—and they feel that vocal support for the resistance in Nicaragua would be like throwing gasoline on fire. But more likely, they simply doubt U.S. resolve to support them should they openly challenge the Sandinistas. For the most part, this doubt stems from our own negotiations with the Sandinistas and our on-again off-again commitment to the democratic forces there. Most obvious in this regard were the comments made by Philip Habib who promised in a letter . . . that the U.S. would end rebel aid once the Sandinistas and their Central American neighbors signed a Contadora treaty. Clearly, this is just what the Sandinistas would most want . . . a treaty that would take solid action in undermining the resistance in exchange for a few empty promises the Sandinistas would never keep.

"The Sandinistas. . . . shot their way into power and they must be shot out of power."

Furthermore, most of the proposals put forth up to now by Contadora refuse to recognize that while the U.S. has committed very limited support to the resistance, over 350 million dollars a year in Soviet military hardware alone has poured into Managua. A freeze in external funding would leave the Sandinistas with a very significant military advantage in the region that they have and would continue to use to their advantage. Already, Nicaragua is the largest military power in Latin American history.

The final criticism I have of Contadora is a criticism I think we hear too infrequently. Contadora likes to bill itself as a non-imperialist, non-interventionist group committed to self-determination in Latin America. However, by trying to impose its will on other nations and peoples it is precisely what it campaigns against. Isn't it a bit presumptuous for the Contadora group to more or less negotiate the future of the Nicaraguan resistance without even inviting their input or giving them a vote in their organization? Clearly, it is also hypocritical for the Contadora nations of Mexico, Venezuela, Panama, and Colombia to spew forth accusations and sometimes outright hatred at the U.S. without allowing or inviting its participation. Indeed, Contadora is in itself a form of intervention which disallows self-determination of the respective parties. In essence, Contadora or any other form of negotiation is bound to be a sham. The Sandinistas are never going to negotiate their way out of the Managua palaces. They shot their way into power and they must be shot out of power.

A Military Victory

So given that the current situation is not at all conducive to negotiation, we must now turn our attention to the best option we have and that is a military victory. Of course, there have already been official U.S. pronouncements in this regard. The now famous line from the Kissinger Commission Report on Central America conceded that "history offers no basis" for the notion that America could sweetly nudge Nicaragua's Marxist government into becoming a pluralist democracy. Force might work, the commission conceded, and so it endorsed aid to the resistance. Preferably this military victory will come from the Nicaraguan Freedom Fighters as opposed to the use of American forces which could be damaging politically for the future of Nicaragua and certainly could possibly be catastrophic for the U.S. But we shouldn't rule out military force, either. We have a successful record of utilizing military force in Latin America and the Caribbean from 1965 in the Dominican Republic to Grenada in 1983. But, clearly, the forces in Nicaragua would be our greatest test of strength and conviction yet in that region. Should military hardware continue to pour into Nicaragua, threatening the fragile democracies in the area and perhaps placing our own national security at stake, we should not hesitate to consider a military blockade to intercept these weapons which are now arriving in outrageous numbers.

But given that we seek a military victory by the resistance, we should ask the next question: Just who are the Freedom Fighters who we are placing our trust in and what are their chances of success?

For the most part, these Freedom Fighters are good people—a significant portion of them are campesinos, others are tradesmen, merchants, and ex-Somoza guardsmen. All are devout Catholics. Recently, criticism has been placed on the resistance that their members are composed of too many campesinos and that, indeed, an effort should be made to incorporate more business people and ex-guardsmen who have more significant leadership backgrounds. I think this is a legitimate criticism. Clearly, with the approval of U.S. aid to the resistance, the Freedom Fighters should be able to go far in enlisting thousands of more fighters, especially those Nicaraguans who before doubted American resolve and are now a bit more convinced.

With the $100 million, the resistance will now be able to learn how to deploy and maneuver units in coordinated attacks. They will begin to receive the weaponry needed to combat the Soviet hardware to which they were previously defenseless. But most of all, with the most powerful free nation in the world

behind them, Freedom Fighter morale will be picked up dramatically. Once again, hope will be restored to their cause, which is now our cause as well. The U.S. support should translate into greater defections from the Sandinista army. It should begin to spark the popular insurrections that will be required for a military victory. In short, the prospects for victory in Nicaragua are greater now than they ever have been and if America continues to lend support, can anyone doubt that the forces of freedom will soon march victoriously through the streets of Managua?

With God and Patriotism

In defining the nature of the resistance to people, I have frequently referred to their motto which I consider indicative of their character and determination. The motto—which rhymes in Spanish—is "con dios y patriotismo, derrateremos al comunismo," meaning "with God and patriotism, we will defeat communism." Seeing 1,000 members of the FDN shout this simultaneously in the fields is a highly emotional and, for me, inspiring event. Now, compare this to the Sandinista national anthem whose lyrics spout out "luchemos contra al yangui, enemigo de la humanidad." This translates to "let's fight against the yankee, enemy of humanity."

Yet many in the West still refuse the reality of communist Nicaragua. Actually, when asking controversial questions about the nature of the Sandinista regime, one frequently need look no further than their own comments for the answer.

"We must now turn our attention to the best option we have and that is a military victory."

Do the Sandinistas want communism? Minister of the Defense Humberto Ortega has said that "Marxism-Leninism is the scientific doctrine that guides our revolution, the instrument of analysis of our vanguard to understand the historical process and to create the revolution . . . our doctrine is that of Marxism-Leninism."

Do the Sandinistas promote and assist communist revolution in El Salvador? David Nolan's book published at the University of Miami clearly quotes the FSLN Declaration of 1969 as saying that "we will struggle for a true union of the Central American peoples within one country, beginning with the support for national liberation movements."

Do the Sandinistas harbor terrorists? Listen to Antonio Farach, former FSLN diplomat, in sworn testimony to Senator Denton's Subcommittee on terrorism: "The Nicaraguan government not only recognizes terrorist organizations, but it instructs its diplomatic officials, such as in my own case, to provide every support and cover when those men from international terrorist organizations are traveling in countries where Nicaraguan diplomatic officials reside."

What about the excellent democratic process in Nicaragua the American left is so proud of? Again listen to Humberto Ortega: "Keep firmly in your minds that these elections are to consolidate revolutionary power, not to place it at stake."

In combatting this barbarity, we must take great steps in countering the awesome level of disinformation that exists regarding the current conflict in Nicaragua. For instance, [since 1984], the radical forces of the news and entertainment media and the academic, political, and religious worlds have led Americans to believe that our level of support for the resistance has been consistent and remarkably high. Consequently, masses of Americans began thinking in terms of "cutting off" U.S. aid to the resistance when the facts clearly show that no military aid has gone to the Freedom Fighters in over two years. Fortunately, Congress did not, for once, buy into this lie. If they had, the credibility and trustworthiness of America as the faithful ally would have suffered a significant blow and popular uprisings against communist dictatorships around the world would have suffered a loss. Today, a glimmer of hope remains.

Immediate Steps

To capitalize on this hope, we need to take several immediate steps: First, we must continue to fund the resistance, giving them all the military hardware they ask for and making sure that we provide enough assistance so that every Nicaraguan who wants to take up arms against the Sandinistas will be given the supplies needed to do so.

"We must continue to fund the resistance, giving them all the military hardware they ask for."

Secondly, we need to do more in the way of applying economic pressures on Managua by ensuring that all free nations cut off economic ties with the country. This will clearly speed up the revolutionary process in Nicaragua.

Next, we must launch an international campaign for truth to combat the outright lies and subtle manipulations of fact by the Sandinistas and their disinformation specialists around the world.

We should call on the OAS and all free nations to follow the Ecuadorian example and cut diplomatic relations with the Sandinistas—as many of these nations did with Anastasio Somoza—and recognize the FDN as part of a government in exile. No free nation should associate itself with the evil that is communist Nicaragua.

Finally, America and the free world must muster the backbone to stand unswervingly with the forces of freedom and to ensure that totalitarianism is never allowed to prosper and especially not allowed to expand. We must realize our moral obligation in seeing that the Nicaraguan Freedom Fighters—much like the freedom fighters in America 200 years ago—are successful in ousting the external forces that in reality rule Nicaragua today.

We must make it clear to the world that communist dictatorships will never stand with our blessing, especially in our own hemisphere.

Michael Johns is assistant editor of Policy Review, *a conservative monthly periodical published by the Heritage Foundation.*

"Trying deliberately to overthrow a legitimate government flies in the face of everything that American citizens believe."

viewpoint **168**

The US Should Not Help the Contras Win

The General Board of Church and Society

[engage/social action *editor's note:*] *On the eve of President Reagan's [1986] mid-March televised appeal for aid to Nicaraguan rebels, the Board of Church and Society [of the United Methodist Church] mounted its own media campaign opposing aid to the anti-government contras. . . .*

The Board called on US Congress to deny support to contra forces "who are inflicting terror, torture and death upon innocent civilians," to refrain from efforts to destabilize the Nicaraguan government and to give active support to the Contadora peace initiative[s] of Mexico, Venezuela, Panama and Colombia. . . .

Here are the comments opposing aid made during the press conference:

Bishop William Boyd Grove, President of the General Board of Church and Society: The General Board of Church and Society of the United Methodist Church is responsible for representing the nine-and-one-half-million United Methodists within this country together with others throughout the world in areas and issues related to social justice. The General Board meeting in St. Louis (March 14) reaffirmed its position on Nicaragua, which was adopted in March 1985. It specifically called upon "the President and Congress of the United States of America to deny support for the Contra forces for inflicting terror, torture and death upon innocent civilians, to refrain from all efforts to destabilize the government of Nicaragua and to give active support for the Contadora peace initiatives of Mexico, Venezuela, Panama and Colombia."

To implement this position, we have asked each member of the Board to contact church leadership in her or his geographical area by telephone today to urge establishment of a telephone chain communication of our concerns to the local churches so as to reach our membership throughout the country. . . . We also have asked Board members to contact their congresspersons . . . , urging them to support peace and diplomatic initiative and to oppose funding for the Contra forces. . . .

Comment from [the] press: The President says that if we don't back the Contras, we are going to have Communism right on our door steps; that's his bottom line.

Bishop Grove: We substantially disagree with that old-line Red-baiting position. We also feel that even if that were true, which we believe it is not, for the government of the United States of America to be involved in the intentional efforts to overthrow the elected government of another sovereign nation is in violation of all the best traditions of our history. Such interference is, from our perspective, not only a violation of international law but a violation of any understanding of morality in the relationship of one government to another.

Comment from press: Ortega's government is not perfect.

Bishop Grove: Of course it is not.

Immoral Action

Shirley Dare, Board member from Evanston, Illinois: I want to respond about the moral right of our country to try deliberately to overthrow another legitimate government. I was in Nicaragua over July 4, [1985,] and our delegation talked with the people—not the Sandinista government per se. They gave us a birthday cake because the people of Nicaragua understood the significance of July 4 for North Americans. This was a layered birthday cake decorated in red, white and blue with an American flag on it—a beautiful expression. Thus, it seems to me that Bishop Grove is saying that trying deliberately to overthrow a legitimate government flies in the face of everything that American citizens believe. Such action is not a part of our heritage, and

The General Board of Church and Society, "In Opposition to Contra Aid," *e/sa*, May 1986. Reprinted with permission.

I think the Nicaraguan people understand this.

Question from the press: Is the President ignorant of what's going on down there or what's the problem?

Shirley Dare: I would not like to say that the President of the United States is ignorant. However, I think each person needs to make his or her own assumptions in light of a President and Administration that continue to act, as far as I am concerned, irresponsible. It would seem to me that the President of the United States has a different understanding of the global perspective than perhaps some church people do, so maybe it is a basic difference in global perspective.

We church people are in contact with other church people in countries around the globe. Perhaps that is an opportunity we have that government leaders do not have. We talk to our brothers and sisters who understand the basic gospel as we understand it, so perhaps we get different information. I would hope, however, that the President and the Administration would listen to some of us who have different opinions. So, I would not say the President is unintelligent; I would say the President is misinformed, and I would hope that he would widen his source of information.

True Representative of the People

Donna Boe, Board member from Pocatello, Idaho: I was in Nicaragua during the elections, and I would like to repeat the fact the government in power now in Nicaragua has a legitimate right to be considered the true representative of the people of Nicaragua. Much has been said about the elections being a fraud, or not being legal, and that they should be redone. I very much disagree. Having been in elective office myself for a while, I recognize campaigning when I see it—whether it's in English or Spanish. There were seven parties on the ballot, and there was wide evidence of vigorous campaigning by all the parties. The government junta that was in charge until the election went to a great deal of trouble to consult with other nations on how to set up the elections, how to inform the people, how to encourage participation for this first free election in Nicaraguan history. We were tremendously impressed with the extent to which they went to encourage everyone to vote. It was not required by law to vote in Nicaragua. However, over 80 percent of the people who were registered did vote. The Sandinista party got a little over 60 percent of the vote. The other six parties got the remainder. All of them were represented, based on a proportional representation in their constituent assembly, which is still in the process of writing the constitution.

Our group made a special effort to talk to people on the street on election day. We especially sought out people who were not going to vote for the Sandinista party or who had not voted for the Sandinista party. No one hesitated to talk to us. They were all very free in their opinions. We talked to people the day after the election, again especially trying to find ones who had not supported the Sandinista party. They were disappointed, of course, that their party did not win but they said, "We are going to work harder the next time and we hope that our party will be more strongly represented."

Our own informal observations on election day, I think, have been confirmed by the official election observers from countries all over the world, especially other Latin American countries and European countries, as well as by political science scholars from the United States and others. There were ample reports available documenting the authenticity of the elections in Nicaragua. . . .

Question from press: Do you think [the President will] get the Contra aid?

Bishop Grove: I don't think so. I hope not. There are many, many people in the Congress and throughout the country—and in the press corps—who share the views that we do. I happen to think, and I can't document this, that our opinion is the majority opinion of America today.

Contra Terrorists

Richard Parker, Board member from New York City: My colleagues have asked me to say just a word about the large numbers of American citizens who have visited Nicaragua over the past several years. Many of them went through an organization called "Witness for Peace," a church-based organization, which has brought approximately 2,000 American citizens to Nicaragua for visits of about two weeks.

"To overthrow the elected government of another sovereign nation is in violation of all the best traditions of our history."

I was part of one of those groups in January. We visited a small remote village in Nicaragua. Other groups have visited other sections of Nicaragua—usually in areas where there has been substantial Contra activity. In the area where we stayed, the small town has been increased radically from a previous population of about 500 to something over 2,000.

Those people who have come into the village have fled from remote mountain settlements where Contra activity has been severe. So we talked with dozens and dozens of people, poor people, used to farming in those remote villages, all of whom had seen members of their families killed, women raped, homes burned, crops destroyed, and who had fled into a more secure area in that little village. That story is repeated over and over again throughout Nicaragua.

We have countless Americans who have first-hand information, leaving us to conclude that the Contra activity in Nicaragua is not a struggle for freedom. It is a terrorist activity spread throughout the country and aimed particularly at teachers, health workers, community leaders, leaders of farming co-ops, and church leaders—known throughout Nicaragua as delegates of the word, lay persons trained to be active in the leadership of their local congregations.

We find ourselves devastated by the constant stream of stories from these people, and we find it absolutely impossible to give any credibility to American claims that the Contra persons are freedom fighters.

Praying for Peace

Martin Deppe, Board member from Hinsdale, Illinois: I would like to underscore the fact that we are not just opposed to funding the Contra forces. We are supporting and encouraging and praying for the peace process. In the year that we finally as a nation have made official the birthday of Martin Luther King, Jr., we want to underscore the role of the church—and hopefully the government—in pursuing diplomatic and peaceful alternatives to the situation. Obviously we need a resolution. We have an incredible crisis. We have a huge debate in Congress and on the streets. We have people dying in Nicaragua. We need a solution, and the position of this Board and this denomination is that we support the Contadora process and support self-determination in Central America and the right of those people in those countries to resolve the situation. We have confidence that they will do so.

Question from press: It is fair to say that when you all visited, you saw a very different kind of society in Nicaragua?

Dare: A participatory society. I think that is what impressed me. It's such a small country; I think it reflects the New England town meeting kind of organizational structure in which local people certainly do have direct influence in the governmental politics. So I would describe it as participatory.

Democratic Traditions

Parker: It certainly is struggling to maximize the democratic traditions that we are familiar with here, but that's not easy in a nation that has not had a long history with democratic structures and in participation on the part of the people. I think the government made honest and effective efforts to establish a democratic process. The major political leaders of the government, major Sandinistas, have a policy of spending time out in the countryside. The President and cabinet members go out into the villages and sit down in the town square, or some community building in the village, and talk with the people, listen to them. They make an honest effort to involve the citizens of the country in the government.

"The Contra activity in Nicaragua is not a struggle for freedom. It is a terrorist activity."

When we were in Nicaragua, major streets in Managua had many, many billboards advertising several political parties. The Sandinistas had their own political billboards up, the FSLN, but so also did four or five other parties. Political dissent is common in Nicaragua, the arguments go on openly all the time. We never saw any sign of repression or interference in the life of local churches.

That is not to say that the Sandinistas have not made mistakes. They have done some silly and stupid things, I think, from time to time. Part of that is a result of their anxiety over the present situation in which they see themselves at war with the United States—the major power in the hemisphere.

The General Board of Church and Society represents the views of the United Methodist Church on social justice issues.

"Established procedures for making national security decisions were ignored."

viewpoint 169

The Tower Commission Report: An Overview

John Tower, Edmund Muskie, and Brent Scowcroft

Editor's note: The following viewpoint is an excerpt from the report of the President's Special Review Board, otherwise known as the Tower Commission.

The arms transfers to Iran and the activities of the NSC [National Security Council] staff in support of the Contras are case studies in the perils of policy pursued outside the constraints of orderly process.

The Iran initiative ran directly counter to the Administration's own policies on terrorism, the Iran/Iraq war, and military support to Iran. This inconsistency was never resolved, nor were the consequences of this inconsistency fully considered and provided for. The result taken as a whole was a U.S. policy that worked against itself.

The Board believes that failure to deal adequately with these contradictions resulted in large part from the flaws in the manner in which decisions were made. Established procedures for making national security decisions were ignored. Reviews of the initiative by all the NSC principals [the Vice President, Secretary of State, Secretary of Defense, National Security Advisor, White House Chief of Staff, and Director of the CIA] were too infrequent. The initiatives were not adequately vetted below the cabinet level. Intelligence resources were underutilized. Applicable legal constraints were not adequately addressed. The whole matter was handled too informally, without adequate written records of what had been considered, discussed, and decided. . . .

Contradictory Policies

The record of the role of the NSC staff in support of the Contras is much less complete. Nonetheless, what is known suggests that many of the same

John Tower, Edmund Muskie, and Brent Scowcroft, *The Tower Commission Report.* New York: Random House, 1987.

problems plagued that effort as well. . . .

The arms sales to Iran and the NSC support for the Contras demonstrate the risks involved when highly controversial initiatives are pursued covertly.

The initiative to Iran was a covert operation directly at odds with important and well-publicized policies of the Executive Branch. But the initiative itself embodied a fundamental contradiction. Two objectives were apparent from the outset: a strategic opening to Iran, and release of the U.S. citizens held hostage in Lebanon. The sale of arms to Iran appeared to provide a means to achieve both these objectives. It also played into the hands of those who had other interests—some of them personal financial gain—in engaging the United States in an arms deal with Iran.

In fact, the sale of arms was not equally appropriate for achieving both these objectives. Arms were what Iran wanted. If all the United States sought was to free the hostages, then an arms-for-hostages deal could achieve the immediate objectives of both sides. But if the U.S. objective was a broader strategic relationship, then the sale of arms should have been contingent upon first putting into place the elements of that relationship. An arms-for-hostages deal in this context could become counter-productive to achieving this broader strategic objective. In addition, release of the hostages would require exerting influence with Hezballah [a terrorist group in Lebanon], which could involve the most radical elements of the Iranian regime. The kind of strategic opening sought by the United States, however, involved what were regarded as more moderate elements.

The U.S. officials involved in the initiative appeared to have held three distinct views. For some, the principal motivation seemed consistently a strategic opening to Iran. For others, the strategic opening became a rationale for using arms sales to obtain the release of the hostages. For still others, the initiative appeared clearly as an arms-for-hostages deal from first to last.

Whatever the intent, almost from the beginning the initiative became in fact a series of arms-for-hostages deals. . . .

Rewarding Terrorism

It is true that, strictly speaking, arms were not exchanged for the hostages. The arms were sold for cash; and to Iran, rather than the terrorists holding the hostages. Iran clearly wanted to buy the arms, however, and time and time again U.S. willingness to sell was directly conditioned upon the release of hostages. Although Iran might claim that it did not itself hold the hostages, the whole arrangement was premised on Iran's ability to secure their release.

While the United States was seeking the release of the hostages in this way, it was vigorously pursuing policies that were dramatically opposed to such efforts. The Reagan Administration in particular had come into office declaring a firm stand against terrorism, which it continued to maintain. In December of 1985, the Administration completed a major study under the chairmanship of the Vice President. It resulted in a vigorous reaffirmation of U.S. opposition to terrorism in all its forms and a vow of total war on terrorism whatever its source. The Administration continued to pressure U.S. allies not to sell arms to Iran and not to make concessions to terrorists.

"The arms-for-hostages trades rewarded a regime that clearly supported terrorism and hostage-taking."

No serious effort was made to reconcile the inconsistency between these policies and the Iran initiative. No effort was made systematically to address the consequences of this inconsistency—the effect on U.S. policy when, as it inevitably would, the Iran initiative became known.

The Board believes that a strategic opening to Iran may have been in the national interest but that the United States never should have been a party to the arms transfers. As arms-for-hostages trades, they could not help but create an incentive for further hostage-taking. As a violation of the U.S. arms embargo, they could only remove inhibitions on other nations from selling arms to Iran. This threatened to upset the military balance between Iran and Iraq, with consequent jeopardy to the Gulf States and the interests of the West in that region. The arms-for-hostages trades rewarded a regime that clearly supported terrorism and hostage-taking. They increased the risk that the United States would be perceived, especially in the Arab world, as a

creature of Israel. They suggested to other U.S. allies and friends in the region that the United States had shifted its policy in favor of Iran. They raised questions as to whether U.S. policy statements could be relied upon. . . .

Ignoring Political Risk

The activities of the NSC staff in support of the Contras sought to achieve an important objective of the Administration's foreign policy. The President had publicly and emphatically declared his support for the Nicaragua resistance. That brought his policy in direct conflict with that of the Congress, at least during the period that direct or indirect support of military operations in Nicaragua was barred.

Although the evidence before the Board is limited, no serious effort appears to have been made to come to grips with the risks to the President of direct NSC support for the Contras in the face of these Congressional restrictions. Even if it could be argued that these restrictions did not technically apply to the NSC staff, these activities presented great political risk to the President. The appearance of the President's personal staff doing what Congress had forbade other agencies to do could, once disclosed, only touch off a firestorm in the Congress and threaten the Administration's whole policy on the Contras.

Decision-Making Process Flawed

Because the arms sales to Iran and the NSC support for the Contras occurred in settings of such controversy, one would expect that the decisions to undertake these activities would have been made only after intense and thorough consideration, in fact a far different picture emerges. . . .

At each significant step in the Iran initiative, deliberations among the NSC principals in the presence of the President should have been virtually automatic. This was not and should not have been a formal requirement, something prescribed by statute. Rather, it should have been something the NSC principals desired as a means of ensuring an optimal environment for Presidential judgment. The meetings should have been preceded by consideration by the NSC principals of staff papers prepared according to the procedures applicable to covert actions. These should have reviewed the history of the initiative, analyzed the issues then presented, developed a range of realistic options, presented the odds of success and the costs of failure, and addressed questions of implementation and execution. Had this been done, the objectives of the Iran initiative might have been clarified and alternatives to the sale of arms might have been identified.

Expertise Not Used

Because of the obsession with secrecy, interagency consideration of the initiative was limited to the cabinet level. With the exception of the NSC staff and, after January 17, 1986, a handful of CIA officials, the rest of the executive departments and agencies were largely excluded.

As a consequence, the initiative was never vetted at the staff level. This deprived those responsible for the initiative of considerable expertise—on the situation in Iran; on the difficulties of dealing with terrorists; on the mechanics of conducting a diplomatic opening. It also kept the plan from receiving a tough, critical review.

Moreover, the initiative did not receive a policy review below cabinet level. Careful consideration at the Deputy/Under Secretary level might have exposed the confusion in U.S. objectives and clarified the risks of using arms as an instrument of policy in this instance. . . .

"There appeared little effort to face squarely the legal restrictions and notification requirements applicable to the operation."

A thorough vetting would have included consideration of the legal implications of the initiative. There appeared little effort to face squarely the legal restrictions and notification requirements applicable to the operation. At several points, other agencies raised questions about violation of law or regulations. These concerns were dismissed without, it appears, investigating them with the benefit of legal counsel.

Finally, insufficient attention was given to the implications of implementations. The implementation of the initiative raised a number of issues: should the NSC staff rather than the CIA have had operational control; what were the implications of Israeli involvement; how reliable were the Iranian and various other private intermediaries; what were the implications of the use of Mr. [Richard] Secord's private network of operatives; what were the implications for the military balance in the region; was operational security adequate. Nowhere do these issues appear to have been sufficiently addressed.

The concern for preserving the secrecy of the initiative provided an excuse for abandoning sound process. . . .

The only staff work the President apparently reviewed in connection with the Iran initiative was prepared by NSC staff members, under the direction of the National Security Advisor. These were, of course, the principal proponents of the initiative. A portion of this staff work was reviewed by the Board. It was frequently striking in its failure to present the record of past efforts—particularly past failures. Alternative ways of achieving U.S.

objectives—other than yet another arms-for-hostages deal—were not discussed. Frequently it neither adequately presented the risks involved in pursuing the initiative nor the full force of the dissenting views of other NSC principals. On balance, it did not serve the President well. . . .

An Unprofessional Operation

The manner in which the Iran initiative was implemented and LtCol North undertook to support the Contras are very similar. This is in large part because the same cast of characters was involved. In both cases the operations were unprofessional, although the Board has much less evidence with respect to LtCol North's Contra activities. . . .

Because so few people from the departments and agencies were told of the initiative, LtCol North cut himself off from resources and expertise from within the government. He relied instead on a number of private intermediaries, businessmen and other financial brokers, private operators, and Iranians hostile to the United States. Some of these were individuals with questionable credentials and potentially large personal financial interests in the transactions. This made the transactions unnecessarily complicated and invited kick-backs and payoffs. This arrangement also dramatically increased the risks that the initiative would leak. Yet no provision was made for such an eventuality. Further, the use of Mr. Secord's private network in the Iran initiative linked those operators with the resupply of the Contras, threatening exposure of both operations if either became public.

The result was a very unprofessional operation. . . .

Congress Not Told

Congress was not apprised either of the Iran initiative or of the NSC staff's activities in support of the Contras.

In the case of Iran, because release of the hostages was expected within a short time after the delivery of equipment, and because public disclosure could have destroyed the operation and perhaps endangered the hostages, it could be argued that it was justifiable to defer notification of Congress prior to the first shipment of arms to Iran. The plan apparently was to inform Congress immediately after the hostages were safely in U.S. hands. But after the first delivery failed to release all the hostages, and as one hostage release plan was replaced by another, Congress certainly should have been informed. This could have been done during a period when no specific hostage release plan was in execution. Consultation with Congress could have been useful to the President, for it might have given him some sense of how the public would react to the initiative. It also might have influenced his decision to continue to pursue it. . . .

Iran Arms Sales and the Law

The Board was unable to reach a conclusive judgment about whether the 1985 shipments of arms to Iran were approved in advance by the President. On balance the Board believes that it is plausible to conclude that he did approve them in advance. . . .

Under the National Security Act, it is not clear that mere oral approval by the President would qualify as a Presidential finding that the initiative was vital to the national security interests of the United States. The approval was never reduced to writing. It appears to have been conveyed to only one person. The President himself has no memory of it. And there is contradictory evidence from the President's advisors about how the President responded when he learned of the arms shipments which the approval was to support. In addition, the requirement for Congressional notification was ignored. In these circumstances, even if the President approved of the transactions, it is difficult to conclude that his actions constituted adequate legal authority. . . .

The Presidential Finding of January 17, 1986, formally approved the Iran initiative as a covert intelligence operation under the National Security Act. This ended the uncertainty about the legal status of the initiative and provided legal authority for the United States to transfer arms directly to Iran.

The National Security Act also requires notification of Congress of covert intelligence activities. If not done in advance, notification must be "in a timely fashion." The Presidential Finding of January 17 directed that Congressional notification be withheld, and this decision appears to have never been reconsidered. While there was surely justification to suspend Congressional notification in advance of a particular transaction relating to a hostage release, the law would seem to require disclosure where, as in the Iran case, a pattern of relative inactivity occurs over an extended period. To do otherwise prevents the Congress from fulfilling its proper oversight responsibilities.

Legal Questions Ignored

Throughout the Iran initiative, significant questions of law do not appear to have been adequately addressed. In the face of a sweeping statutory prohibition and explicit requirements relating to Presidential consent to arms transfers by third countries, there appears to have been at the outset in 1985 little attention, let alone systematic analysis, devoted to how Presidential actions would comply with U.S. law. The Board has found no evidence that an evaluation was ever done during the life of the operation to determine whether it continued to comply with the terms of the January 17 Presidential Finding. Similarly, when a new prohibition was

added to the Arms Export Control Act in August of 1986 to prohibit exports to countries on the terrorism list (a list which contained Iran), no evaluation was made to determine whether this law affected authority to transfer arms to Iran in connection with intelligence operations under the, National Security Act. This lack of legal vigilance markedly increased the chances that the initiative would proceed contrary to law.

> *"Consultation with Congress could have been useful to the President, for it might have given him some sense of how the public would react to the initiative."*

The NSC staff activities in support of the Contras were marked by the same uncertainty as to legal authority and insensitivity to legal issues as were present in the Iran initiative. The ambiguity of the law governing activities in support of the contras presented a greater challenge than even the considerable complexity of laws governing arms transfers. Intense Congressional scrutiny with respect to the NSC staff activities relating to the Contras added to the potential costs of actions that pushed the limits of the law.

In this context, the NSC staff should have been particularly cautious, avoiding operational activity in this area and seeking legal counsel. The Board saw no signs of such restraint.

President at Fault

The NSC system will not work unless the President makes it work. After all, this system was created to serve the President of the United States in ways of his choosing. By his actions, by his leadership, the President therefore determines the quality of its performance.

By his own account, as evidenced in his diary notes, and as conveyed to the Board by his principal advisors, President Reagan was deeply committed to securing the release of the hostages. It was this intense compassion for the hostages that appeared to motivate his steadfast support of the Iran initiative, even in the face of opposition from his Secretaries of State and Defense.

In his obvious commitment, the President appears to have proceeded with a concept of the initiative that was not accurately reflected in the reality of the operation. The President did not seem to be aware of the way in which the operation was implemented and the full consequences of U.S. participation. . . .

The President's management style is to put the principal responsibility for policy review and implementation on the shoulders of his advisors. Nevertheless, with such a complex, high-risk operation and so much at stake, the President should have ensured that the NSC system did not fail him. He did not force his policy to undergo the most critical review of which the NSC participants and the process were capable. At no time did he insist upon accountability and performance review. Had the President chosen to drive the NSC system, the outcome could well have been different. As it was, the most powerful features of the NSC system—providing comprehensive analysis, alternatives and follow-up—were not utilized. . . .

Advisors at Fault

President Reagan's personal management style places an especially heavy responsibility on his key advisors. Knowing his style, they should have been particularly mindful of the need for special attention to the manner in which this arms sale initiative developed and proceeded. On this score, neither the National Security Advisor nor the other NSC principals deserve high marks.

It is their obligation as members and advisors to the Council to ensure that the President is adequately served. The principal subordinates to the President must not be deterred from urging the President not to proceed on a highly questionable course of action even in the face of his strong conviction to the contrary. . . .

"The NSC system will not work unless the President makes it work."

All had the opportunity. While the National Security Advisor had the responsibility to see that an orderly process was observed, his failure to do so does not excuse the other NSC principals. It does not appear that any of the NSC principals called for more frequent consideration of the Iran initiative by the NSC principals in the presence of the President. None of the principals called for a serious vetting of the initiative by even a restricted group of disinterested individuals. The intelligence questions do not appear to have been raised, and legal considerations, while raised, were not pressed. No one seemed to have complained about the informality of the process. No one called for a thorough reexamination once the initiative did not meet expectations or the manner of execution changed. While one or another of the NSC principals suspected that something was amiss, none vigorously pursued the issue. . . .

If but one of the major policy mistakes we examined had been avoided, the nation's history would bear one less scar, one less embarrassment, one less opportunity for opponents to reverse the principles this nation seeks to preserve and advance in the world.

The Tower Commission was appointed by President Reagan to investigate the Iran-contra Affair. John Tower is a former Republican senator from Texas; Edmund Muskie is a former Democratic senator from Maine who served as secretary of state under President Carter; Brent Scowcroft is a retired air force general who served as national security advisor under President Ford.

"The [Tower] report contains ample evidence that the sloppiness of the president and his men repeatedly shaded off into disregard for—or plain violation of—the law of the land."

viewpoint **170**

The Tower Report Denounces President Reagan

The New Republic

> Throughout the Iran initiative, significant questions of law do not appear to have been adequately addressed.
>
> —from the Tower Commission report

In the immediate aftermath of the Tower Commission report, attention has centered on President Reagan's "management style," to use the prevailing euphemism. Well, the Constitution doesn't say the president has to be a candidate for Mensa. It does, however, admonish him to "take care that the laws be faithfully executed." The Tower panel's mandate didn't include determining the criminal culpability of anyone involved in the byzantine Iranamok dealings, and it was careful not to offer any hard-and-fast judgments on such matters. Nevertheless, the report contains ample evidence that the sloppiness of the president and his men repeatedly shaded off into disregard for—or plain violation of—the law of the land. Despite the commission's own mealymouthed language, this is the most damning finding.

Policy Ignores Law

In August 1986 the Arms Export Control Act was amended to prohibit arms sales to countries that the State Department identified as supporters of terrorism. Iran was on the list. The White House sold arms to Iran in October 1986.

Under the Arms Export Control Act, a president wishing to transfer arms to *any* country, terrorist or not, must meet a series of requirements to ensure, first, that countries receiving U.S. weapons don't resell them and, second, that Congress is notified in advance of any transactions involving weapons worth more than $14 million. In the case of Iranamok, Reagan ignored the first requirement.

True, the Arms Export law says he could have waived it on grounds of national security, but such a waiver requires prior congressional notification. Needless to say, Reagan ignored that, too.

Much has been made of whether or not Reagan approved an arms transfer to Iran via Israel in August 1985. After saying he did, then saying he didn't, Reagan now says he can't remember. But even if the president *did* give some kind of "oral" approval, that vague gesture probably didn't satisfy the National Security Act, which requires a formal intelligence finding to authorize such covert activity, as well as congressional notification—if not in advance, then at least in "a timely manner."

On January 17, 1986, Reagan finally did sign a presidential intelligence finding authorizing the arms-for-hostages covert action, and giving the United States legal authority to sell arms directly to Iran. Actually, Reagan never studied the finding himself, and didn't even sign it with his own hand. Rather, he listened as national security adviser John Poindexter described the document to him; then he approved it. Poindexter scribbled the president's initials—"per JMP"—at the bottom.

Congress Not Notified

The finding called for a delay in notifying Congress, apparently until the hostages were safely in U.S. hands. The administration maintains that postponing notification was justified by a desire to avoid a congressional leak that might jeopardize the deal, and was therefore allowed by the law's "timely manner" provisions. But as the Tower Commission points out, this rationalization lost whatever force it might have had after the Iranians failed to release the hostages as promised. In the event, the White House *never* informed Congress until the story became public by other means.

Obviously fear of leaks cannot be a permanent justification for not informing Congress of

The New Republic, "White House Outlaws," March 23, 1987. Reprinted by permission of THE NEW REPUBLIC, © 1987, The New Republic, Inc.

intelligence operations, or the law's requirement that Congress be informed would be meaningless. Implicit in the law is a decision that the benefit of democratic review is worth the risk of leaks. The remarkable stupidity of this very operation illustrates the law's wisdom in allowing a congressional kibitzer or two to oversee intelligence operations. Someone might have said, "Are you crazy?"

"It's against the law to lie to Congress, whether or not you're under oath."

From late 1984 to mid-1986, Congress prohibited U.S. government support for the *contras*. Although the prohibition was phrased in terms of financial expenditures—as are many legal prohibitions—the purpose was clear. The Tower report offers fewer details about Oliver North's "private" network to funnel military aid to the Nicaraguan *contras* than it does about the Iran project. Nevertheless, the report overwhelmingly confirms that North—with the knowledge of his superiors on the NSC, and more than likely with the knowledge and cooperation of other officials—violated the law by shipping military aid to the *contras*. In fact, he put together a vast network, called "Project Democracy," of shell corporations, ships, and bank accounts dedicated to getting arms and ammunition to the *contras*. Siphoned-off money from the arms sales to Iran probably wound up in one of Project Democracy's Swiss bank accounts.

The supposedly private *contra* aid network and the Iran project were linked in other ways, too. Indeed, at one crucial juncture, the Iran deal could not have gone forward if the outlaw *contra* network hadn't been in existence. On November 22, 1985, North suddenly found himself without the aircraft he needed to deliver HAWK missiles to Iran. His pal retired Gen. Richard Secord filled the gap, offering the services of an aircraft he had planned to use for a supply drop to the *contras*. "Will meet w/Calero tonite to advise that the ammo will be several days late in coming," North wrote.

Obstructing Justice

It's against the law to lie to Congress, whether or not you're under oath. On several occasions in 1985, former national security adviser Robert McFarlane responded to inquiries from House members with carefully hedged but basically false denials of North's role in the *contra* network, which he was fully aware of. North himself did the same thing in testimony to the House Intelligence Committee in August 1986—a deception that earned him a "Well Done" from McFarlane's successor, John Poindexter.

Then there's obstruction of justice. North was interviewed last November by Attorney General Ed

Meese during the White House's belated attempts to put together a coherent story about the Iran dealings. After talking to Meese, North reportedly shredded documents and doctored memos, in what looks transparently like an effort to keep evidence of his wrongdoing, and that of others, away from investigators.

Finally, the Tower report leaves unresolved serious questions about the conduct of high officials other than those on the NSC staff. One is former CIA chief William Casey, whose name crops up in connection with North's secret *contra* operation. For example, in a May 1986 memo Poindexter warned North to be more discreet, in a way that suggests North had been in the habit of talking freely to Casey about his activities in Central America: "From now on, I don't want you to talk to anybody else, including Casey, except me about any of your operational roles." The report barely touches on the possible role that may have been played by Vice President Bush and his staff in the *contra* network. Key members of that staff apparently had contact with the supervisors of covert *contra* resupply flights out of El Salvador's Ilopango air base. Another official with a lot of explaining to do is Assistant Secretary of State Elliott Abrams. He had frequent discussions with North about *contra*-related matters, but has nevertheless denied, both in the Tower report and in past congressional testimony, that he knew about North's illegal network.

A Matter of Character

We're not baying for blood. Perhaps no one in the administration will ever be prosecuted for Iranamok. None of the relevant arms export or anti-*contra* aid laws contain specific criminal penalties. Even the issue of obstruction of justice is not as clear-cut as it might seem, since North could argue he didn't know he was, or soon would be, under criminal investigation. But the issue of the president's duty to "take care that the laws be faithfully executed" is different from the issue of specific indictability. If no one is ever convicted in connection with Iranamok, that will be heralded in some quarters as "proof" that there was "no wrongdoing." But it will be no such thing. The record already assembled—even before key players such as North, Secord, and Poindexter have told their stories—demonstrates a pattern of official disregard for the law and the truth. And that's a matter of basic character, not "management style."

The New Republic *is a weekly public affairs journal.*

*"For all its hyped 'toughness,' the
Tower Commission responds . . . with a
clear recommendation to save, not
abort, the Reagan presidency."*

viewpoint 171

The Tower Report Excuses President Reagan

Revolutionary Worker

At the heart of empire, a ruling class shudders: their champion is visibly tottering. Their government, their alliances, their "global initiatives" threaten to drift. Sordid secrets gush into the domain of Everyman. Even ignorant loyalists feel gripped by disillusionment, a sense of betrayal, a fear that the future may not be as simple, as bright, or as triumphant as promised. Political crisis has burst upon Resurgent America.

The Tower Report

If this wasn't already clear, [the] Tower Commission report brought the point crashing home. Most of their information wasn't new; but here it was, made official and stacked in one place. Hundreds of pages detail the casual flow of hi-tech weapons back and forth across a planet. Elaborate flowcharts document dummy corporations and stables of cutthroats dangling from the White House chain of command. America exposes itself, bartering human flesh from Nicaragua to the Persian Gulf. Once again, the secret records of America's chieftains reveal an utter disdain for even their own legality and institutions.

The commission had been advertised as "tough" and "critical," and in a way they were. Their report rains fire on certain "initiatives" of the Reagan administration. They denounce "casual decisionmaking." They complained that the expertise and professionalism of the State Department and CIA bureaucracies were bypassed in favor of ad-hoc networks of foreigners, private adventurers, and "unsupervised self-starters." They gripe that "alternative options" were not "fully vetted" in lively in-house debate.

But to explain what is going on here we first have to mention what has *not* come under criticism:

The bombing of Libya? Apparently the Tower commission thinks this was quite fine. The rape of Grenada? Clearly acceptable. Overt and covert support for South Africa's butcher regime? Hardly a basis for a scandal. The *doubling* of CIA covert operations during the '80s? Above reproach; in fact, they think the CIA should have been *more* involved in planning and debate over the Iran initiative. Seven years of terrorist war against Nicaragua? Hardly illegal, certainly not immoral. What about the whole idea of maneuvering for a "geostrategic opening," the need to capture dominance, in Iran? *That* "no one doubts," says the Tower Commission. A worldview rooted in hostile confrontation with the Soviet bloc? Eight years stampeding toward nuclear war? *None* of this is an issue of dispute!

All of *these* policies, you see, unfold *within* the bounds of acknowledged American interests. As imperialist figures on an imperialist commission investigating an imperialist president . . . the Tower Commission did not question these matters.

A Friendly Investigation

This was the report of a friendly, in-house commission, hand-picked by the president himself. John Tower, the chairman of the commission, has been of the Senate's "military lobby," a key architect of the last decade's war buildup, and was director of the 1984 Reagan reelection campaign in Texas. Edmund Muskie, "balancing" the commission for opposition Democrats, was a former Secretary of State under Carter who knows a lot about Iran debacles. And the final member of the Tower troika is Brent Scowcroft, a former Air Force general and technocrat/expert on nuclear war-fighting strategies.

Together they formed a "band of wise men," supposedly above personal or "partisan" bias. In reality they were commissioned to exercise a

Excerpted from *Revolutionary Worker,* "Three Wise Men and The Emperor," March 2, 1987. Some subheads have been changed by Greenhaven Press editors. Reprinted with permission.

particular kind of partisanship: to approach this explosive crisis from the interests of the *overall* ruling class. The cover of the Tower report bore the Latin inscription *"Quis custodiet ipsos custodes."* "Who watches over the guardians?" Their purpose was hardly to challenge America's global crusade. It was to salvage. They had no beef with "successful" American aggressions, their focus was on the embarrassment of failures.

And even then they were not interested in dragging *all* recent failures before the world. They declined to dissect the failure of American Contra policy, and even refused to touch the secrets of funding-by-diversion. They virtually ignored the debacle of Reykjavik. Their method was cautious. They centered on debacle, the sale of arms to Iran, and belabored the "decision-making process" that led to it.

The fact that their final product is still so lurid and leaves their Great Communicator looking so fallible is merely a sign of how damaging Reagan's errors have been to his own cause.

Reagan Criticized for Weakness

"The president's policy," the commission concluded, "was a mistaken policy." The report remarks, "The Reagan administration in particular had come into office declaring a firm stand against terrorism, which it continued to maintain. In December of 1985, the Administration completed a major study under the chairmanship of the Vice President. It resulted in a vigorous reaffirmation of U.S. opposition to terrorism in all its forms and a vow of total war on terrorism whatever its source. The Administration continued to pressure U.S. allies not to sell arms to Iran and not to make concession to terrorists. No serious effort was made to reconcile the inconsistency between these Policies and the Iran initiative. No effort was made systematically to address the consequences of this inconsistency—the effect on U.S. policy when, as it inevitably would, the Iran initiative became known."

No argument here, obviously, against the "vow of total war on terrorism." *That* has been a policy commanding near universal approval in the American government. It has served to cover preparations for wider, global war. The commission inquires: Why screw up a good thing? The problem noted is that once made public, the administration's "inconsistency" would weaken the ability of the United States to enforce a unified policy by its own bloc.

In the end, the most damning charge was that the life and death decisions for the whole West were made with casual improvisation. And seen from the whole *global* plane of prewar strategy, Reagan's trade of "arms for hostages" is indicted for an untimely and unacceptable appearance of *weakness in the face of enemies.*

Those are the public charges Reagan faces from his own kind. Reagan criticized for being a Carter-like wimp? This is heavy with irony. But it's a grim reminder: apparently not even *Reagan's* approach is *hard* enough to suit those he serves.

Report Easy on Reagan

Scandal erupted because Reagan could not be allowed to continue the string of failures that stretched from Iceland to Iran. The result: an administration flopping on the ground like a wounded bird. At this point a basic dilemma arises: the ruling class can't afford two years of a weakened, rudderless government. And yet, they can hardly accept the political cost of disgracing *yet another* president, especially one like Reagan invested with so much of Resurgent America's moral capital. Crises can spiral out of control from just such an absence of recognizable solutions.

For all its hyped "toughness," the Tower Commission responds to that dilemma with a clear recommendation to save, not abort, the Reagan presidency. That was not just their conclusion, it was one of their purposes. Their analysis of *causes* underlying the "mistakes" is classic apologetics: they claim that the honorable but inattentive monarch was "ill-served" by his advisers.

Over and over again the commissioners praise Reagan: his "openness," his "genuine commitment" to "getting the facts out." Tower said, "Mistakes were made, but . . . the Iran-Contra affair was clearly an aberration." He added, "The president, I think, is an inherently honest man."

Essentially, the commission moved across the political battlefield simply shooting the already dead and wounded a second time. Their aim rarely went farther than the already well-battered five: Lt. Col. Oliver North, Vice Admiral Poindexter, Robert McFarlane, William Casey, and Donald Regan.

"This was the report of a friendly, in-house commission, hand-picked by the president himself."

The feverish White House attempt to "cover-up," which in November 1986 produced a "doctored chronology" for public consumption, is blamed solely on Donald Regan and his subordinates. Reagan, the commission suggests, is guiltless; the world is expected to believe that he was merely the unknowing *beneficiary* of the deceit. Similarly, they absolve Reagan of any criminal activity. They acknowledge that there is no evidence that *anyone* in the White House ever bothered to pay attention to laws. But the commission shrugs it off; Scowcroft insists that many of these laws were "murky, complex and ambiguous'' anyway. If crimes are suspected, look to the underlings as fall guys. . . .

Raw Fiction

In short, the Tower Commission followed the White House's own "rogues and stupidity" defense; they depicted a befuddled president, cut off from debate and "alternative options" by his close advisors, while zealous underlings were left free to romp in unsupervised "rogue" adventures. President Reagan was criticized but only for "detachment," for a "hands off management style," and for excessive-but-genuine "sentiment" regarding hostages. These are hardly new charges, and they are designed not to be lethal. They are certainly not the "high crimes and misdemeanors" for which American chieftains are formally beheaded. NBC's Chris Wallace passed on the intended message: "No real bombshells here, no smoking guns."

This picture is raw fiction, of course: new evidence surfaces daily (as if any more were needed!) that links Reagan personally to the whole array of covert actions, secret dealings, and certainly with the continuing support for his Contra terrorist army. Claiming he was guided by "genuine compassion" is a deliberate attempt to reissue the mythology about the nuclear warrior with a heart of gold. Reagan's real concern for "the hostages" was to recoup the major intelligence loss following the capture of CIA station chief William Buckley in Beirut. One of the major prizes the Iranians had to barter was the 400-page "confession" Buckley had written under torture.

"The Tower Commission followed the White House's own 'rogues and stupidity' defense."

But truth is hardly the issue here. Policies are being sharply criticized, while Reagan is being painted as your "basic nice guy." And the purpose is obvious: Reagan is being given another chance to pull it all together. CBS's Dan Rather made the point with a heavy hand: "The thought occurs that the old admonition, 'Don't rush to judgement' may advantageously be applied here. We all need time to reflect on this, to consider it, ponder it." . . .

Back on Deadly Course

The White House spokesman explains that this Tower report contained "many new facts" that Reagan had not previously understood. Accordingly, he added, Reagan was "rightfully angry about the mismanagement described in this report, and he intends to make changes as soon as possible." And lo, within hours Chief of Staff Regan slinks offstage defeated. Howard Baker strides into his slot, to

"bipartisan" praise; here is the Watergate moderate, the proven reformer. What better symbol of "housecleaning"?

What theater! Now, finally, the evil advisers have been exposed and scattered; the well-intentioned Tsar finally seems aroused to "take command." All the hype that accompanied the Tower Commission report will now be turned around and used as proof that "the worst has now come out, it is all on the table." Reagan will have "taken it on the chest" again, and will claim redemption as the reward for his manly courage. Who can doubt that the world will be offered an orchestrated ending for this passion play? Soon will come announcements that all is well again, and that Resurgent America is back on its deadly course.

Revolutionary Worker is the weekly publication of the Revolutionary Communist Party of the USA.

"Everything that our president did . . . merely followed from an impulse of lawless glory by which all policy was answerable to the demands of fantasy and spectacle."

The Iran-Contra Affair Proves Presidential Incompetence

David Bromwich

For the past twenty-two months, almost since the day of President Reagan's second inauguration, the foreign policy of the United States has been controlled by a handful of military officers and their pals: freelance spies, itinerant jobbers from think tanks, adepts of "sailing close to the wind" in the illegal export of arms. The president is not, exactly, part of this company, though nobody has ever been better at toasting them, with a wink and a nod. But it was his office, the common knowledge of his opinions, and his ignorance that provided the necessary cover for them to join together. By christening their head organizer "a national hero," he has lately endorsed the very acts he claims to have known too little to ratify at the time.

The Swill of Empire

Who are these men? We have only begun to glimpse, in the half light of their hints and hesitations, the curious underground life that the Reagan administration fostered for the Norths, Poindexters, and Secords, whom it had silently raised to power. One thing is certain. It was a life of soldiers playing at government; of fledgling citizens, barely acquainted with the rules of a democracy; of sly executants and solid henchmen, whose loyalty to the Constitution was nothing beside their faith in the great man they served. But again, who were they? Gunrunners; the sponsors, or concocters of aliases, for armies of mercenaries; ex-CIA agents (but what *is* an ex-CIA agent?) and their cronies from the world of munitions and lobbying: in short, facilitators of terrorists-in-need, along with the usual foot soldiers, who turn up as drug peddlers on the return trip. They are the swill of empire. But the deals they cooked up were elaborate—the packages they assembled heavy to load and unload. It is not to be

supposed that they did their secret work without many well-placed accomplices up and down the halls of State and Defense.

Americans have lived these last many months by the whims of a state within the state. Everything we seem to stand for, every commitment our leaders seem to affirm, is puzzling, questionable, recondite. The president himself is a personified *double entendre;* and he does not wait for an answer. In every picture you see, these days, he is waving goodbye.

Back in early 1985, some of Ronald Reagan's friends came up with an idea to win a mid-term election. Get back the American hostages in Lebanon by arranging a payoff to Iran. What! Iran, the stronghold of Moslem fanaticism? Iran, whose every success we have deplored, and instructed all Europe (in terms of no uncertain moral advantage) to help us stop? No. This was another Iran, one we had almost forgotten; the Iran of geopolitical renown, the "bulwark against Soviet penetration" in the Persian Gulf. The idea, for this second Iran, was to send a few shipments of weapons—not enough to win the war, our president believed or might have believed; though, in fact, Iran may now be winning the war, thanks to the same negligible supplies. We pitched in with two thousand missile-launchers, which the president thought were handheld until, at a press conference, a reporter informed him that they were mounted. With these, the Iranians can fire missiles that burn through the lead plating of tanks; the spare parts that we added give them enough to equip their air force once again. But all of it (we were told at first) "could easily fit into a single cargo plane." No taking of sides was involved.

An Impulse of Lawless Glory

The home of the Ayatollah Khomeini's freedom fighters bought our weapons, all the way down the line. But in another sense the Iranians were not

David Bromwich, "Contragate: The Swill of Empire," *Dissent,* Spring 1987. Reprinted with permission.

buying: the chance to wreck one more American presidency was too perfect to resist. Besides, this time they could have their revenge on Israel into the bargain. The president's motive appears to have been a pathetic mix of sentimentality and opportunism. Israel's motive was more canny, from one point of view. It came to betting on a nation of evangelical Moslems, which is committed to the destruction of Israel, against a nation of the Arab League, which has held the same commitment for a longer time. It is difficult to conceive how this gamble could prove to be other than disastrously wrong. But in offering to help the United States, the leadership of Israel was at any rate conducting policy, however wrong the help and however imprudent the policy. By contrast, everything that our president did, at the bidding of the Colonel, the Admiral, and their friends, merely followed from an impulse of lawless glory by which all policy was answerable to the demands of fantasy and spectacle. In such a mood, a "wild idea" that would "sock it to the president's opponents" was already halfway to being realized.

> *"The president's motive appears to have been a pathetic mix of sentimentality and opportunism."*

It had occurred to a few people all along—people, like the current secretary of state, who do not consistently aspire to the status of outlaws—that these military deals and geopolitical rationalizations would cast a suspicious light on our anti-terrorist "line." Meanwhile, it was occurring to some even less trustful Americans that there never had been a line. We were proterrorist when it suited our aims of the moment: as witness our support for the *contras.* So why not Iran? Still, in all the administration's doings and in the shuffling quasi-legal apologetics that followed their discovery, nobody could have guessed the final turn of the story that the president's artists-in-uniform had contrived. While Iran was paying good money for the weapons we sent, it was paying bad money too, over the market value of the items purchased, to show its appreciation for the mob of geniuses at the White House. And that money went—*not* straight to the mob; for these were supply-side men. It went, instead, to our second set of terrorist friends, the *contras.*

The White House was thus paying a hefty bribe to retrieve hostages from terrorists, who could then recapture them, or others, at will. At the same time, it was chiseling a few extra dollars (thirty million, if we can trust Edwin Meese with a fact) from the first set of terrorists, for the sake of conveying them to a second set. All this it did at a moment when such payment appears to have been prohibited by the ever more freely interpretable laws of the Congress of the United States.

Truth and Generosity

Let us turn from these lofty considerations to the patchwork of rumor and innuendo that confronts a reader of the daily papers. And, in particular, to the two interesting personalities at the heart of the case: our new national hero, Colonel North; and the distributor of medals who was the first to acclaim him. Americans easily confound truthfulness and generosity by supposing that together they form a compound virtue called "good nature." Truthfulness and generosity, honesty and altruism, are in fact widely different traits. Everybody has known direct, plain-spoken, even compulsively truth-telling persons without a particle of generous feeling. Likewise it is possible for an altruist—someone who is "generous to a fault"—to have only the vaguest familiarity with a great many ordinary habits of truth-telling. In imagining, and then bringing into being, a cause or a set of persons worthy of his self-sacrifice, the altruist has to be a ready believer from the first in one kind of fiction. His calling is simply to make it come true. And if he is aided by self-deception, there is no telling where he will stop. The hero, Pyle, of Graham Greene's *The Quiet American,* was modeled on this sort of person. Some foreign observers have supposed him to be an American type.

Nobody pretends that Admiral Poindexter is an inveterately honest man. He seems well versed in the arts of skulduggery and manipulation, and his management of the press, at the invasion of Grenada, was itself enough to establish his character. But what if one chose to credit the picture of Colonel North that his admirers have tried to make current: that he is an ingenuous fellow, an enthusiast of freedom, with a big streak of decency. Why should we therefore expect him to tell the truth? He *made up* the cause he served, that of the *contras,* before it had a proper existence outside his mind. He had to lie about it, or dissimulate, or redefine the truth, in order to keep it alive through its days of adversity the ugly past of its leaders, the scrappiness of its political program, the grinding inhumanity of its guerrilla tactics: these facts had to be kept in obscurity; or, if they did come to light, they had to be placed on an infinitely adjustable schedule of reformation. Doubtless to the *contras* themselves, North has been a straight dealer, within the limits of his competence. But they were his whole economy of truth. Other truths—that civil wars are to be avoided, particularly when they are not one's own; that Iran today remains a terrorist power; that there is not, and never yet has been, anything resembling a majority popular sentiment against the Sandinistas—these were outside his province. From day to day, it was Colonel North's business to sell out all these truths, in order to keep afloat the one cause that he did care something about. For him now to say what actually happened, after the initial profession of bafflement, the shredding of documents, and the sudden siege of prudence and the Fifth Amendment, would be to begin an unfamiliar conversation. Since he first came to prominence on William Buckley's *Firing Line*, with a defense of the army after the massacre at My Lai, Colonel North has been called a "maverick," a "cowboy," a "rogue elephant." But truth is a maverick, too. It will not be hired out by anyone who pleases.

North Dishonorable

Colonel North received a medal for heroic service on the occasion of his successful wheedling in Congress to cry up votes for selling AWACS to Saudi Arabia. It was the finding of still more arms, for still another war, which, if fought, the United States would observe from the sidelines, with its customary geopolitical acumen. How many faraway deaths it takes to feed the hearty decency of this president's helper! It would seem that he is a man who lives for, and is kept healthy by, war. Yet we are told he performed none of these acts for private gain. A ruling passion like war can sometimes be its own reward, and in any case a large share of his reversion took the form of personal (not public) vanity. He was secure in his knowledge that the president loved him for what he did. But to the view of every person of sense, dishonor was written over everything he did: dishonor for the word of his country, and for the cause of constitutional democracy itself, which he was busy dismembering at home in the dubious hope of forging a counterfeit of it some day south of the border.

"He [Ronald Reagan] has bequeathed to us a confusing legacy of debts and corruption, with a vacant air of good feeling."

As for the distributor of medals, he remains a less enigmatic, but finally a more mysterious, phenomenon. He is no stranger to dishonor. He presided over the slaughter of our marines in Lebanon, and then withdrew without a whisper. James Watt and Michael Deaver sat at the places he set for them. These memories belong to his life without having joined his reputation. Has there ever before been a public figure to whom people felt so kindly disposed, whose record of public kindness was such an absolute zero as his? When, in the mid-1940s, Americans said that they loved Roosevelt, they had in view an impression of selfless activity that they could read in the lines of his face; there was also perhaps the impression that he was one of the rich, who had not sold the country to the rich, but helped to widen its promise in a time of crisis. Nothing like these impressions can explain the dream of Reagan from which we are only beginning to awake. This awakening is unprecedented in our history—never, before, was there such a sleep—and it will be painful. He has bequeathed to us a confusing legacy of debts and corruption, with a vacant air of good feeling. Whatever emerges from the scandal of Iran and Nicaragua, it will be recorded of Ronald Reagan that he was a spellbinder, who enchanted his countrymen when they could least afford that luxury, but whose charm may have ended in time to repair some of the things he almost destroyed. He was, and is, the ultimate front man.

David Bromwich is a member of the editorial board of Dissent *magazine.*

The Iran-Contra Affair Does Not Prove Presidential Incompetence

Aaron Wildavsky

Editor's note: This viewpoint was written in response to an essay by James David Barber, in which Barber criticized President Reagan's policy making.

How did the President and his NSC [National Security Council] staff get sucked ever deeper into this morass? Easy! It happens all the time, and not only to Presidents. The objectives one has in mind are both long- and short-run, general and concrete. How often have students of policy observed that the long-run and general (Iran after Khomeini) often give way to the short-run and specific (the hostages)? Aphorisms abound: "The measurable drive out the more important but impalpable."

The incremental illusion is also common. Which of us has not discovered himself swearing he would put only so much effort or money or trust into a venture only to go further and further on the grounds, sometimes valid, usually not, that doing a bit more would bring home the grand prize?

I do not say this to absolve the President. He is a professional politician and public official responsible for his actions. My point, rather, is that the errors in regard to Iran are not extraordinary, revealing of exceptional incapacity, but of the garden variety by which the high and mighty, as well as the rest of us, are brought low.

A Political Failure

It is said that we had a teflon President who either mesmerized the public with nonsense syllables or was apparently so charming that nothing could stick to him. Now we know better. A reasonable conclusion would be that when the President speaks sense to the people they go along with him, and when he appears to speak nonsense, whether this is about the Daniloff swap or the Iranian swap of arms

for hostages, the people reject what they are being told. The flipside of the coin is that the President was apparently making sense to the people before, but I hear very little about this. I am pleased to confirm that our people have a reasonable sense of discrimination.

The failure in Iran is political. The President undertook an action that, when it became known, would be rejected by the vast majority of the citizenry as well as political elites. By me too. For this political failure there has been substantial political punishment. The Iran policy has been reversed, the NSC has been reorganized, and the President's popularity has plummeted. Since the President lives by his deep intuition of the American public, it is not inappropriate that he should suffer when this insight leaves him. But I do not think you [columnist James David Barber] make a case that the President's personality or organizational apparatus is fatally flawed. Indeed, one could imagine, reading your columns and those of many other people, that the ideal President, the one who knew everything about most things, and who was a great detail man, was none other than the nationally beloved Jimmy Carter.

You write that Reagan is obviously not a man in charge: ". . . in the face of his own revelations that he did not know what his National Security Council was up to regarding the most sensitive area of his entire foreign policy." This is overheated; moreover, it appears to be wrong. What would you say of our relations with the Soviet Union or with the NATO nations or with Japan if Iran is "the most sensitive area"? You write further that "major military moves were undertaken without even the obviously appropriate deliberations." On the contrary, the evidence we have reveals that the internal deliberations were appropriate and that all the major players had their opportunity to say their piece. The NSC was involved. And the military significance of

Aaron Wildavsky and James David Barber, "What The Hell Is Going On?" *The American Spectator*, April 1987. Reprinted with permission.

the arms shipments was small. While I am not among those who think readily of moderates in the Iranian administration, a dispassionate observer would point out that the Israelis, who are known for hard-headed thinking, and who are certainly in touch with the minute facts regarding these matters, thought this a good idea.

Classical Planning

Therefore, I believe that the charge of triviality and nonsensicalness does not carry weight. Indeed, this episode has all the hallmarks of classical planning. What the President thought he was doing was not allowing events to take their course, not allowing the market of international relations to dictate what would happen, not merely reacting to events. Rather, believing he would save the nation much greater difficulty should the Iranian regime collapse and Communist elements take over, the President wished to anticipate this danger by taking preemptive action. Must he always be right? Do we say this is bad judgment and pass on to the next matter? Or do we go on, as you do, to claim a fatal flaw? . . .

You speak of ". . . wild risk taking by Reagan executives." There is in fact no evidence of this, at least none that you or others have provided. On the contrary, the history of the Reagan Administration thus far is one of extraordinary caution, the sole exceptions being Grenada (which I approved) and Lebanon (which I didn't). Can you say that you thought that when Ronald Reagan became President you would be in the seventh year of his presidency and have only to report these two minor military ventures?

His Hands Were Tied

You gloss over the profound differences between the Reagan Administration and the Democratic Congress on what our foreign policy ought to be. When there is such agreement, as in regard to the Philippines, then you do find them working together. But when there is utter dissensus, as in Central America, one finds quite the opposite. Indeed, what you are actually urging, given the disposition of opinion in Congress, is that the President not do what congressmen dislike, which would give him no foreign policy at all. Do you teach your students that Presidents and Congresses agree on who has the power to do what? Scholarship suggests not only perennial disagreement about the division of power but also that conflict over who is constitutionally empowered to act is part and parcel of disputes over what kind of action should be undertaken. Far from failing to perform its representative functions, Congresses may well have exceeded them by tying the President's hands in so many ways that they create additional incentives not to have themselves informed.

Evidently, the degree of trust necessary to make the intelligence committees work has been damaged, if not lost. Whether this trust had previously eroded, I do not know. But when informing others becomes the equivalent of being unable to undertake a policy, the stage for distrust is already set. . . .

So Many Restrictions

I have said nothing about the diversion of funds because sufficient facts are not yet evident. Evidently we cannot countenance illegality. Especially not in the White House. Why, then, is this operation located there? Obviously, the more such operations are located outside the executive office, especially the inner sanctum of the White House, the easier it is for the President to disavow them. Obviously, self-protection is not the main thing in the President's mind. One possible reason is that there were now so many restrictions, restrictions that would not have applied in earlier times, that the operation could not have been run elsewhere. Like you, I think this was a strong sign it ought not to have been done. But I remind you that in the past the President had triumphed by going against his main advisers. I will wait for further information before making up my mind on the President's part, if any, direct or indirect, in the funds transfer.

"I think that broad delegation does work for this President most of the time, and that is all one can ask of any procedure."

Should Reagan have known about the diversion of funds to the contras? Presumably, Presidents are not expected to know about everything, in fact most things, going on in government. How about the White House? There are dozens, hundreds even, of top people. How could (and, I would add, why should) a President know what they are doing in fulfilling an agreed purpose, subject to a presidential Finding? Surely the time spent in surveillance of associates, aside from its denigration of their loyalty, would be a waste of presidential time. How much less likely, then, would an unauthorized action, such as fund diversion, come to presidential attention? I read that Zbigniew Brzezinski, as NSC head, read over forms describing what the fifty or so people reporting to him were doing every day. Yet, if an action were left out, how would he have known? Of course, one can trivialize the matter by saying that Presidents should know about all illegal actions. But how and, more importantly, at what cost? . . .

It used to be that good executives were those who gave their subordinates the freedom to make mistakes, who encouraged them to make creative improvisations, subject only to general guidelines. Certainly these are the conditions under which you and I would like to work. Subordinates who require detailed supervision are not worth having. Why, then, do we hear that the White House should be full of people constantly reporting to the chief, looking back to see who is gaining on them? Such a system would stultify every White House, not merely that of the incumbent President.

There is nothing wrong with (and much to be said in favor of) delegation so long as it works. If it breaks down, however, is one better off shoring it up or engaging in detailed supervision? As an observer of a wide range of policies, I think that broad delegation does work for this President most of the time, and that is all one can ask of any procedure. But why would the President give so much leeway to a mere lieutenant colonel? Because this is America, where strict adherence to hierarchy is not the norm, we escape the sclerosis that affects gerontocracies.

Too Much Absolutism

There is an awful lot of absolutist talk going around as if people were purely good or evil or actions were either all of one thing or all of another. The President thought of arms for hostages as a partial retreat from a policy that otherwise stood in force. Indeed, the Administration could presumably have undertaken large-scale weapons shipments and that would not have been the same as the amount of arms that were actually sent. If a little is the same as a lot, we lose an important sense of discrimination. Similarly, if any violation is the same as the grossest violation, I cannot think of any President, or of any human being, who could make the grade.

The President thought he was acting in the national interest. Others may not know but you as a scholar do know how often Presidents, even our greatest (Jefferson and Lincoln come immediately to mind), disavowed adherence to strict canons of legality in order to preserve the essence of liberty. The latest *This Constitution* cites Jefferson's justification for condoning serious extra-legal action done to curtail Aaron Burr's activities: "To lose our country by scrupulous adherence to written law would be to lose the law itself with life, liberty, and property . . . thus absurdly sacrificing the ends to the means." Of course, Jefferson may well have been mistaken, as I think President Reagan was this time. But as my mind searches for parallels, I am less inclined to be censorious. . . .

Don't Hamstring the Presidency

The other day on the radio, I heard a local congresswoman, Barbara Boxer, say that Congress must act to assure that no illegality ever occurs again in the White House. One way to do this would

be to strip the White House of all the accretions it has developed in past decades. Need I remind you, as a student of the presidency, that most of these units have been put there at the insistence of Congress, including, as I recall, the NSC? What have liberals (who think of themselves as the party of positive government) to gain by weakening what our colleague Nelson Polsby has called The Presidential Branch? Soon enough, calls for presidential action will be heard. And who will there be to respond? The anti-third term amendment already creates unnecessary pressure to speed up action so as to shoehorn events into the last years. The only way to assure that an institution will do no harm is to render it powerless. Hamstringing our common heritage, the presidency, is not, I think, a worthy legacy.

Role of the Media

American hostages obviously create problems for our people and politicians . . . from Korea to Vietnam to Daniloff in the USSR to Iran. If they are really prisoners of undeclared wars, why do the media keep building up their importance? Surely this visibility, as President Carter discovered, highlights the impotence of the Administration. If the government is then not allowed to do what is required to get them back—ransom them or invade the offending nation or take hostages of our own— why are their families given so much publicity, thus suggesting action ought to be taken? Though no one intends to do so, the result is to condemn Presidents either for weakness or recklessness (poor Jimmy Carter got it both ways). When one reads in the funny papers that the President either is lying or ignorant, the same effect is secured: whatever we find out, he is damned.

"The President thought of arms for hostages as a partial retreat from a policy that otherwise stood in force."

Did the President ship arms to Iran to free hostages, or to intervene in its internal affairs? Since it must be one or the other, we are told, he is deceiving us whichever way he chooses to explain his behavior. In the normal course of events, we speak of motives invariably being mixed; we also know that they are retrospectively rationalized to suit our future behavior. Yet here we persist in setting up a procrustean category—at once too short and too long—so the President is condemned whichever one he chooses.

I am impressed, as you can tell, with how many things we used to believe about administration, the presidency, foreign policy, human behavior (and more) that we go against when Presidents we do not like on wholly other grounds are involved.

You say that the people and the press have been too easy on this President's grievous faults. False charge, I reply. The only difference between now and before, unless one is utterly insensitive to barrage after barrage of criticism, is that this time the charges stuck. As usual, the implications run two ways: the charges were unbelievable before but in this instance they are believable. What should be done?

Do No Harm

The policies have been reversed, the NSC reformed, a high political price exacted. What more? The congressional mantra—we've always done it this way—does not move me. Between the President's review panel, the special prosecutor, and Congress, a joint committee would have been more than enough. Endless hearings have begun to fray everyone's nerves; they are a lousy way to get information; and the public interest in getting the facts could well be served by three rather than four investigations. But there may yet be worse to come.

"The charges [of incompetence] were unbelievable before but in this instance they are believable."

Watergate in its time was properly regarded as an aberration. Another effort to impeach or to force a President to resign, thus reversing the result of the election without recourse to the people, would create a crisis of legitimacy. Conservatives would conclude that they could not rely on the ballot box not merely to elect but to keep the people's choice in the White House. We should not exchange a small temporary problem for a large permanent one.

Evidently, it is easier to say what should not be done—make this case a capital crime—than to say what should be done. Absent something splendid to do beyond what has been done, with each cure far worse than the disease, we have our negative clue: adopt the policy version of the Hippocratic oath: Do no harm. "Iranamok" should not become a historical designation for how we made a bad situation much worse.

Aaron Wildavsky is a professor of political science and public policy at the University of California-Berkeley.

"I know of no great advance in the cause of freedom . . . that has been achieved through covert action or espionage."

viewpoint **174**

The Iran-Contra Affair Proves That Covert Actions Are Wrong

Ronald Goetz

America long ago lost its innocence, and thus one can expect to be censured by the "realists" among us if one argues for a return to morality in the conduct of the country's international affairs. Nonetheless, in view of the Irangate fiasco—which is but the latest in a long list of debacles into which our nation has lurched since World War II—I would offer for consideration the following "moralist" cliché: the only way effectively and finally to combat terrorism or any other form of fanatical agitation is to strive toward a just, democratic world order. This "truism" is grounded in the contention that injustice, inequality, deprivation and the cynicism of the haves toward the have-nots constitute the fertile soil upon which fanaticism feeds. Activities designed to create chaos and revolution are the result of despair over the inadequacy of political orders to address legitimate grievances.

Such may be true enough in an abstract, utopian sense, the hardheaded will acknowledge. However, since "a just, democratic world order" does not in fact exist at present, we must, they argue, predicate our policy on the realities of international disorder. We must fight fire with fire. We must match the surreptitious treachery and deceit of our nation's enemies with our own treachery and deceit, lest we be made patsies and perhaps even victims of destruction. Kill or be killed.

No Covert Triumphs

If our national survival is indeed dependent on cloak-and-dagger skulduggery and secretive double-dealing, then we are in deep trouble, for we simply aren't very good at it. I know of no great advance in the cause of freedom since World War II that has been achieved through covert action or espionage. I do know of genuine triumphs in U.S. interests that

have come about through open diplomacy—for example, the Marshall Plan, NATO, and various arms control agreements. To be sure, we can all cite instances of humiliating national dishonor occasioned by covert and/or extralegal activities—for example, the Bay of Pigs episode and the schemes to assassinate Fidel Castro; the overthrow of Arbenz in Guatemala, Mossadegh in Iran, Lumumba in the Belgian Congo and Allende in Chile; and now the Iran-*contra* disaster—but no triumphs of the spy's art.

Too often in this kind of activity the only ones we fool are ourselves. The Gulf of Tonkin affair, for example, was a deceitfully engineered "event" designed by the Johnson administration's intelligence service to suck us into the Vietnam war. The North Vietnamese knew that our government was lying, but the overwhelming majority of the members of Congress were misled, and President Johnson got carte blanche to wage his catastrophic war.

The Central Intelligence Agency, which came into being during the Truman administration, had an ambiguous mandate from the outset. Its primary task was the gathering of intelligence data. The desire of governments to obtain all the information they can is understandable and valid, though there is always in this function a temptation to conduct espionage of a dubious and problematic sort. But in regard to the CIA, there was also a veiled implication that it would carry out aggressive covert operations overseas. In the aftermath of the Vietnam war and during the Carter administration, the CIA was curbed considerably. President Reagan, however, in conjunction with his pledge to let America "stand tall" again, sought to strengthen the agency. Finding himself unable to untie its hands completely, he in effect opened his own branch office in the White House basement. Clearly, Jimmy Carter, in his recognition of the extreme danger to U.S. interests in allowing extralegal, amoral governmental activities, was right, as the current scandal involving Reagan illustrates.

Government via covert activity is inherently undemocratic, if for no other reason than the fact that policies arrived at and carried out in secret make an intelligent exercise of one's franchise to vote in a liberal democracy as impossible as the communists claim it to be—for in such a situation one can never know what the real issues are. Democracy requires that the state's powers be severely limited. There are things that a democracy must forego which a totalitarian state can indeed, must—do. For the sake of democracy we must sacrifice such "guarantees" of state security as a secret police, political arrests, secret trials and torture, and even the macho self-image we conjure up for ourselves by means of covert activities. But apparently some Americans would view it as a tragedy were we to let go the latter.

> ## "Government via covert activity is inherently undemocratic."

Beneath his show of piety, Ronald Reagan is quite the world pirate; think of Grenada, Nicaragua (which brought a judgment against the U.S. in the World Court), the duplicitous support of both Iran and Iraq, and so on. But it has not been only conservative superpatriots who have endorsed and conducted secret illegalities. One is reminded of the liberal John F. Kennedy, whose seemingly forthright acceptance of responsibility for the abortive Bay of Pigs operation obscured the fact that he was not eschewing covert espionage, as his later complicity in the coup that led to the murder of Ngo Dinh Diem in Vietnam indicates.

Won't Address Real Issues

Reagan's television address to the nation will not, of course, put an end to the Irangate infamy. We will witness a series of investigations designed to root out the specific stupidities and crimes of the whole messy situation, but in all probability the government will fail to address the real issue: getting out of the sabotage business altogether.

Until such practices are challenged, we will continue to shoot ourselves in the foot. Even if covert aggressions did not make a mockery of internal democratic procedures, they must fail because they are dependent for their success on a secrecy that is doubly impossible. Not only must our partners in double-dealing be trusted, in our particular case, to cease double-dealing and "honorably" keep the secret (in the ransom payment to Iran, for example, we had to trust the Khomeini regime to maintain silence!). But in a democracy

such as our own, the governmental infrastructures are—thank God—awash with leaks. No secret *can* remain so for long. Covert operations—even if by some miracle a brilliant one were to be conceived—must finally embarrass us because nothing stays covert.

Since World War II, espionage and sabotage have been invested with a certain perverse romanticism. Spy movies and novels purvey the bogus notion that the interests of nations are advanced not through diplomacy but by the subterranean machinations of amoral conspirators. Agent 007 types or even cruder extralegals like Sylvester Stallone's Rambo character are able to cut through the profoundly vexing political problems confronting world leaders and come up with neat if bloody solutions, or so we are led to believe. If one must read spy novels, the truth is much more closely approximated in those of John Le Carré, who reveals the sordid dead end that international treachery really is.

A Flat Contradiction

On the basis of his Irangate speech, however, President Reagan still seems to be a true believer in the myth of the overriding value of covert activities. Now that the National Security Council has been caught redhanded in illegally resorting to secret actions, Reagan promises "no ifs, ands or buts" in prohibiting its members from further criminality. But illicit covert deeds will continue; only henceforth they will somehow be "in compliance with American values." Surely this is a flat contradiction, for espionage itself is a violation of democratic American values.

The resort to terrorism and abductions that so frustrates us these days is a reflection of the weakness of desperate people who, lacking any other means, seek to affect affairs in a manner vastly out of proportion to their actual strength. And our own counterconspiracies undermine our interest in international order, since such illegalities serve only to legitimize and inflame the illegalities of terrorists and violent revolutionaries.

If the U.S. were in a state of declared war, the situation might be different. Once the mania of war is loosed upon the world, espionage and sabotage become extensions of a nation's avowed public policy, which is to destroy the enemy. But the time now is one of fragile, spasmodic peace. Unless we buy into the Marxist idea that the whole of history consists of incessant class warfare, there is a real difference between a world at war and a world at peace. If our enemies endanger the peace by terrorism and international subversion, we need not follow them into that self-defeating maelstrom.

Ronald Goetz is an editor at large for The Christian Century *magazine.*

The Iran-Contra Affair Does Not Prove Covert Actions Are Wrong

Charles Krauthammer

The Iran scandal has set off a frantic search for causes. Even before the investigations begin, the suspects have been rounded up. First is character: a detached, out-of-touch president; a chief of staff afflicted with a deadly combination of arrogance and incompetence; a lieutenant colonel on a National Security Council staff convinced that his own ideas of the national interest (on the whole, correct ideas) transcend such constitutional niceties as respect for law and the will of Congress.

Then there is structure: a decentralized executive where so much is delegated that an entire foreign policy can be conducted in the White House without the president knowing; a rogue National Security staff become independent and operational when it was only intended to be deliberative and advisory; Cabinet officers so detached from a policy with which they disagree that they fail to raise a hand to constrain it.

A Recurring American Crisis

All true. There is no doubt that the sentimental and anecdotal character of the president (which let him bend national interest to the entreaties of hostage families) and the looseness of his foreign policy apparatus had much to do with the origins and execution of this debacle. But these causes are insufficient. The current crisis is not unique to this president. Its origins transcend both the personalities of this administration and the peculiar way in which it runs foreign policy. This affair is not a Reagan crisis nor a presidential crisis, but a recurring American crisis, rooted ultimately in the tension between America's need to act like a great power and its unwillingness to do so. Into the breach between will and necessity have stepped people willing to violate the law. The result is disaster.

Charles Krauthammer, "Divided Superpower," *The New Republic,* December 22, 1986. Reprinted by permission of THE NEW REPUBLIC, © 1987, The New Republic, Inc.

Watergate was paranoid, mean-spirited, and partisan in a way that the North affair is not. But ultimately it evolved out of the same contradiction: an administration, constrained by a divided polity from pursuing an intervention abroad, seeks surreptitious means to evade those constraints, and destroys itself trying to cover up the means. Watergate began when Nixon, trying to cover his secret actions in Cambodia and to prevent press leaks about the Vietnam War, turned matters over to his plumbers. In the current case, an administration prevented by a deeply divided Congress from funding the Nicaraguan *contras* used the Iranian arms deal to get around the law.

No Inclination

The United States has a vital interest in preventing the consolidation of a Soviet satellite in Central America. There are compelling moral reasons, too, for preventing Nicaragua from suffering the fate of Cuba. But the major point, and the major contradiction, is strategic. The United States has the responsibilities of a superpower, but not the national inclination to carry them out. In retrospect, it is the bipartisan internationalism of the first two postwar decades, and not the isolationism of the subsequent "Vietnam syndrome," that constitutes the historic aberration. America has reverted to its natural foreign policy instincts: a feeling of national moral superiority harnessed to a desire for isolated quiet. The result is a willingness to influence the world by example only.

Last year a French commando team was caught redhanded blowing up a Greenpeace ship in New Zealand. That pathetic little vessel was harassing French forces conducting nuclear tests in the South Pacific. One man died in the sinking. When the French cover story collapsed and the operation was revealed to be the work of the French secret service, there was a brief whiff of *scandale* in Paris. Brief. A few weeks of newspaper revelations. A principled resignation or two. There was even some halfhearted attempt by the French press to ask what President Mitterrand knew and when he knew it. And then . . . nothing. One got the distinct impression that the initial burst of muckraking enthusiasm was an exercise, perhaps an imitation of Watergate, that the French just could not pull off. They could not overcome the native feeling that France had important interests in the South Pacific, beside which all other considerations pale.

"In what business is the CIA, if not interfering in the affairs of foreign countries? Agriculture?"

Compare the French reaction with the following. Two weeks into the Iran affair, Bob Woodward's lead story in the *Washington Post* revealed this: "The covert action authorized by Reagan's January 17 secret intelligence 'finding'"—the document authorizing arms sales to Iran—"allows the Central Intelligence Agency to interfere in the affairs of a foreign government." Goodness. In what business *is* the CIA, if not interfering in the affairs of foreign countries? Agriculture?

France is not exactly a model for constitutional emulation. National interests are not the only consideration. But they do count for something. Any country that deems it necessary *specially* to authorize its secret service to interfere in the affairs of other countries and that deems such authorization to be front-page news is going to find pursuing its interests abroad a distasteful and exceedingly difficult project.

A Sentimental Anachronism

No one doubts that American life would be happier and more prosperous (less defense spending) and less riven by division were we to be free of the responsibilities of leading the alliance of free nations. Who would not prefer that we adopt the foreign policy of 19th-century America or Switzerland today? But neutrals can enjoy the luxury of neutrality precisely because they can take shelter behind the protection of superpower. America did that for a century behind the British navy, as Switzerland now does behind the United States.

But American abhorrence of sordid realpolitik is nothing more than a sentimental anachronism. America can never again be a hemispheric Switzerland. As Walter Lippmann pointed out 35 years ago, the United States cannot even be 20th-century Britain or France. Unlike Europe, which could always rely on the reserves of the United States to come to its rescue, "we have to shape our policies with the knowledge that there are no

strategic reserves upon which we could draw if our plans miscarried."

Congress is paralyzed by a faction—half the House—that acts as if the United States had unlimited reserves, some greater power to protect it from the consequences of its own irresponsible inaction. And that paralysis has produced the irresolvable contradiction between America's objective responsibilities and American will. The result—before North, after North—is crisis after crisis. Either the Executive accedes to congressionally mandated passivity, the result being a geopolitical crisis (the successive defeats of the late Carter years). Or the Executive tries to circumvent its constraints, the result being a constitutional crisis (the lawbreaking of the Nixon and now the Reagan administrations).

Divided Popular Will

What North did was wrong. One cannot sacrifice the rule of democracy in pursuit of even the most obvious and disinterested national objective. But until we resolve whether or not to accept the responsibilities of a superpower, we must expect more debacles of this sort.

The problem is not democracy. Democracy is instrumental. Its role is faithfully to transmit popular will. The problem is American popular will, which is deeply divided on whether to accept the responsibilities of a great power. (France, for example, is a democracy too, but its national consensus supports going to even the most cynical extremes to preserve France's status as a world power.) The result is that the presidency finds itself in the permanent bind: to fulfill its obligations as leader of a superpower or to fulfill its obligations as leader of a democracy. Confronted with the choice, a president must choose the latter. But it is the choice itself—not the identity of the president or his management style—that is the source of our recurring crisis.

Charles Krauthammer is a sydicated columnist and a senior editor of The New Republic.

bibliography

The following bibliography of books, periodicals, and pamphlets is divided into chapter topics for the reader's convenience. The topics are in the same order as in the body of this *Opposing Viewpoints SOURCES*.

The US and Africa, Case Study: South Africa

Heribert Adam and Kogila Moodley	*South Africa Without Apartheid.* Berkeley: University of California Press, 1986.
Arnaud de Borchgrave	"Botha: Other Countries Just Don't Understand Apartheid," an interview, *The Washington Times,* March 4, 1986.
Peter Brimelow	"Why South Africa Shrugs at Sanctions," *Forbes,* March 9, 1987.
Mangosuthu G. Buthelezi	"The Future of South Africa," *Vital Speeches of the Day,* January 15, 1987.
Horace Campbell	"The Dismantling of the Apartheid War Machine," *Third World Quarterly,* April 1987.
J.M. Coetzee	"Tales of Afrikaners," *The New York Times Magazine,* March 9, 1986.
Christopher Coker	*The United States and South Africa, 1968-1985: Constructive Engagement and Its Critics.* Durham, NC: Duke University Press, 1986.
Alan Cowell	"A Farewell to South Africa," *The New York Times Magazine,* January 25, 1987.
William Finnegan	*Crossing the Line: A Year in the Land of Apartheid.* New York: Harper & Row, 1986.
Otto Friedrich	"United No More," *Time,* May 4, 1987.
Joseph Hanlon	*Beggar Your Neighbours: Apartheid Power in Southern Africa.* Bloomington, IN: Indiana University Press, 1986.
Adam Hochschild	"Green Is Detained. Yellow Is Missing. Red Is Confirmed Dead. An Eyewitness Account from South Africa," *Mother Jones,* September 1986.
John Hospers	"A Visit to South Africa," *The Freeman,* February 1987.
Michael Isikoff	"Marching from Pretoria: The Bottom Line," *The Washington Post National Weekly Edition,* December 1, 1986.
Frances Kendall	"South Africa's Only Hope?" *Reason,* January 1987.
David Lewis	"Voting in South Africa," *The Nation,* April 25, 1987.
Richard Manning	"South Africa's Civil War," *Newsweek,* June 23, 1986.
Michael Massing	"The Business of Fighting Apartheid," *The Atlantic Monthly,* February 1987.
Michael Massing	"The Chief," *The New York Review of Books,* February 12, 1987.
Warren L. McFerran	"A Meeting of Minds," *The New American,* March 2, 1987.
Steven Mufson	"The Fall of the Front," *The New Republic,* March 23, 1987.
Steven Mufson	"Who Is the ANC?" *The New Republic,* August 25, 1986.
Richard John Neuhaus	*Dispensations.* Grand Rapids, MI: Eerdmans, 1986.
Conor Cruise O'Brien	"What Can Become of South Africa?" *The Atlantic Monthly,* March 1986.
Vic Razis	*The American Connection: The Influence of U.S. Business on South Africa.* New York: St. Martin's Press, 1986.
Ronald Reagan	"U.S. Economic Relations with South Africa," *Vital Speeches of the Day,* August 15, 1986.
Sheila Rule	"Nothing Prepares You for Apartheid," *The New York Times Magazine,* May 4, 1986.
Helen Suzman	"What America Should Do About South Africa," *The New York Times Magazine,* August 3, 1986.
Mark Swilling	"Living in the Interregnum: Crisis, Reform, and the Socialist Alternative in South Africa," *Third World Quarterly,* April 1987.
Mark A. Uhlig, ed.	*Apartheid in Crisis.* New York: Vintage Books, 1986.
Mark Whitaker	"South Africa's Civil War," *Newsweek,* June 23, 1986.
Oliver F. Williams	*The Apartheid Crisis: How We Can Do Justice in a Land of Violence.* New York: Harper & Row, 1986.

The US and Central America, Case Study: Nicaragua

Lucia Annunziata	"Democrats and the Arias Plan," *The Nation,* April 18, 1987.
E. Bradford Burns	*At War in Nicaragua: The Reagan Doctrine and the Politics of Nostalgia.* New York: Harper & Row, 1987.
Beverly May Carl	"The Nicaraguan Economic System," *America,* February 21, 1987.

Shirley Christian	*Nicaragua: Revolution in the Family.* New York: Random House, 1986.
Alexander Cockburn	"Ground-Level Agony of the U.S. Contra Policy," *The Wall Street Journal,* April 30, 1987.
Peter Davis	"Managua Is Waiting," *Esquire,* March 1987.
Peter Davis	*Where Is Nicaragua?* New York: Simon & Schuster, 1987.
Christopher Dickey	*With the Contras.* New York: Simon & Schuster, 1986.
Linda Drucker	"A Contra's Story," *The Progressive,* August 1986.
Mark Falcoff and Robert Royal	*The Continuing Crisis: U.S. Policy in Central America and the Caribbean.* Washington, DC: Ethics and Public Policy Center, 1987.
Donald C. Hodges	*Intellectual Foundations of the Nicaraguan Revolution.* Austin: University of Texas Press, 1987.
Morton Kondracke	"Into the Jungle," *The New Republic,* April 6, 1987.
Michael Kramer	"The Case for the Contras," *U.S. News & World Report,* June 1, 1987.
Saul Landau	"The Way of the Sandinistas," *The Progressive,* August 1986.
Charles Lane	"Pack It In," *The New Republic,* April 6, 1987.
Robert S. Leiken	"The Battle for Nicaragua," *The New York Review,* March 13, 1986.
Robert S. Leiken	"Reform the Contras," *The New Republic,* March 31, 1986.
John Norton Moore	*The Secret War in Central America: Sandinista Assault on World Order.* Frederick, MD: University Publications of America, 1987.
Joseph E. Mulligan	"Religion and the Nicaraguan Constitution," *The Christian Century,* April 29, 1987.
David Munro	*The Four Horsemen.* Secaucus, NJ: Lyle Stuart Inc., 1987.
The New Republic	"The Case for the Contras," March 24, 1986.
Conor Cruise O'Brien	"God and Man in Nicaragua," *The Atlantic Monthly,* August 1986.
Frank M. Oppenheim	"A Report on Nicaragua," *America,* March 8, 1986.
William Safire	"Better the Contras," *The New York Times,* April 9, 1987.
Nina H. Shea	"Human Rights in Nicaragua," *The New Republic,* September 1, 1986.
Max Singer	"Can the Contras Win?" *National Review,* February 13, 1987.
Carlos M. Vilas	*The Sandinista Revolution.* New York: Monthly Review Press, 1986.
W. Bruce Weinrod	"Thirty Myths About Nicaragua," *Vital Speeches of the Day,* May 15, 1986.
Richard Brookhiser	"The Public Brawl, the Secret War," *National Review,* January 30, 1987.
Commonweal	"A Shadow Government," February 27, 1987.
Frances FitzGerald	"Reagan's Band of True Believers," *New York Times Magazine,* May 10, 1987.
Morton H. Halperin	"The Case Against Covert Action," *The Nation,* March 21, 1987.
Christopher Hitchens	"Minority Report," *The Nation,* March 14, 1987.
Walter Isaacson	"A Council of 'Wise Men' for Reagan," *The New York Times,* December 7, 1986.
Michael Kinsley	"A Case for Glee at Reagan's Comeuppance," *Los Angeles Times,* December 4, 1986.
Michael Kinsley	"Hostage to Hypocrisy," *The New Republic,* December 12, 1986.
Lewis Lapham	"Fade to Black," *Harper's,* May 1987.
Anthony Lewis	"Seeing Iran Plain," *The New York Times,* February 3, 1987.
Carnes Lord	"Executive Power & Our Security," *National Review,* Spring 1987.
Robert S. McElvaine	"Why the Debacle Shouldn't Hearten Liberals," *The New York Times,* December 9, 1986.
Burton Yale Pines	"Policy on Iran: Right and Wrong," *The New York Times,* December 5, 1986.
The Progressive	"Government by Plumbers," January 1987.
Ronald Reagan	"The President's Response to the Tower Commission Report," *Vital Speeches of the Day,* March 15, 1987.
Michael Reisman	"Should We Just Write Off Hostages?" *The New York Times,* December 3, 1986.
James Reston	"America Takes the Fifth," *The New York Times,* March 8, 1987.
Roger Rosenblat	"The Too Personal Presidency," *Time,* November 24, 1986.
William Safire	"Ten Myths About the Reagan Debacle," *The New York Times Magazine,* March 22, 1987.
Peter Dale Scott	"The Secret Team Behind Contragate," *The Nation,* January 31, 1987.
George Shultz	"Iran and U.S. Policy," *Department of State Bulletin,* February 1987.
Robert W. Tucker	"Fouling Up," *The National Interest,* Spring 1987.
Leon Wieseltier	"What Went Wrong?" *The New York Times,* December 7, 1986.

The US and the Middle East, Case Study: The Iran-Contra Affair

Terrell E. Arnold	"The King Is Hostage," *National Review,* April 10, 1987.
James David Barber	"A Government in Disarray Drifting Toward Accidents," *Los Angeles Times,* December 7, 1986.
David Bar-Ilan	"The Iran-Contra Uproar: A Travesty," *The New York Times,* January 11, 1987.
Robert Bresler	"Covert Action and National Policy: Beyond North and Poindexter," *USA Today,* March 1987.

index

Afghanistan, 288
Africa
  black rule in, 218, 224
  human rights in, 223-224
  South Africa's effect on, 223, 247, 251
  US relations with, 221, 249-250
African National Congress (ANC), *see* South
  Africa
Afrikaners, *see* South Africa
Angola
  US policy toward, 249, 251
Anti-Apartheid Act (1986), 228, 247
apartheid
  and sanctions, 255-258, 260
  is beneficial, 221-224
  is oppressive, 215-219
  reforms in, 224
    are minor, 218, 251
  white attitudes toward, 216, 218-219,
    234-235, 241
  see also South Africa
Arms Export Control Act, *see* Iran/US arms
  transfers; terrorism

Bromwich, David, 313
Brumberg, Abraham, 279

Central America
  imperialism in, 264
  Sandinista threat to, 291, 293, 294
  supports contras, 293
  US role in, 293, 294
Central Intelligence Agency (CIA)
  and Iran/US arms transfers, 311, 324
  history of, 321
  Reagan's impact on, 321-322
  role of, 324
China, 288
communism
  American Left's support of, 287-290, 291
  and negotiations, 242, 293
  in China, 288
  in Soviet Union, 287-288
  threatens Latin America, 291
Congress, US
  hampers foreign policy, 318, 319, 324
  President and, 303-304, 307-308
constructive engagement, *see* South Africa
Contadora process, 287, 292, 293
  is anti-US, 293-294
contras
  and Iran/contra scandal, 301-324

are freedom fighters, 291-295
are terrorists, 298-299
can win war, 291-292, 294
have popular support, 294
Reagan's support of, 302
US aid to
  is immoral, 297-298
  is imperialist, 263
  must continue, 290, 291-295, 323
    con, 297-299
  through private groups, 277
see also Nicaragua; Sandinistas
covert actions
  are necessary, 323-324
  are wrong, 321-322
Crocker, Chester A., 227-228, 247
Cuba
  American Left's support of, 289-290
  and Sandinistas, 288, 289
  communist takeover in, 239

Fierce, Milfred C., 251
foreign policy
  and morality, 321
  Congressional role in, 303-304, 307-308,
    318-319
  media coverage of, 215
  US
    as imperialist, 309-311
    as isolationist, 323-324
Foy, Colm, 229
freedom fighters, *see* contras

General Board of Church and Society, 297
Goetz, Ronald, 321

Hammond, John L., 283
Haugen, Gary A., 215
Horowitz, David, 287
hostages
  and foreign policy, 319
  in Lebanon, 301-305, 311, 313

Ingraham, J.H., 269
Iran/Iraq war, 302
Iran/US arms transfers
  and drug deals, 313
  and Watergate, 320, 323
  attempted cover-up of, 308, 310
  Congressional hearings on, 320, 322
  Congressional role in, 303-304, 307-308,
    318-319

Oliver North's role in, 303, 308, 314-315
proves covert actions are wrong, 321-322
  con, 323-324
Reagan's role in
  ignored the law, 307, 323
    con, 318
  is responsible for, 304-305, 310-311, 313
    con, 319-320
  proves incompetence, 313-315
    con, 317-320
  secrecy of, 302-303
  were well-planned, 317-318
  were hostage exchange, 301-302, 314, 319
  were strategic mistake, 301
  see also Tower Commission Report
Israel
  and Iran/US arms transfers, 307, 314

Jenkins, Tony, 275
Johns, Michael, 291

Karis, Thomas G., 243
Kennedy, John F., 322
Kissinger Commission, 294
Krauthammer, Charles, 323

Lebanon
  hostages in, 301-305, 311, 313

McAlvany, Donald S., 237
McFerran, Warren L., 221
Mandela, Nelson, 217, 225-226
  is a communist, 226, 238
Minter, William, 255
Mozambique, 249
Muskie, Edmund, 301

National Security Council
  and Iran/contra scandal, 301-305, 317,
    320, 322
New Republic, The, 307
Nicaragua
  and US leftists, 283-286, 287, 292, 295
  Catholic church in, 270-271, 273, 277, 280
  communist threat to, 239, 323
    myth of, 297
  economy of, 267
    private ownership in, 270, 278, 283
    US has harmed, 284, 299
    war's effect on, 279-280, 298-299
  elections in
    were a sham, 295

were fair, 276-277, 298
government of
    allows pluralism, 275-278, 298, 299
        con, 279-282, 294
    and grassroots organizations, 265-266,
        285
    has popular support, 276, 298, 299
        con, 280, 291
    is communist, 269, 291
    is democratic, 264-266, 299
        myth of, 269-270, 280
    human rights violations in, 269
    is Soviet puppet, 287-290
    military in, 264-265, 285, 293
    opposition in
        is democratic, 291-295
            con, 275-278
        is unwilling to negotiate, 275-276
        lacks popular support, 276-277
    press censorship in, 271-272, 276
    US relations with, 264, 291-292
    war in, 299
        effects of, 279-280, 285
        Sandinistas are winning, 263-264
    see also contras; Sandinistas
Nicaraguan revolution (1979)
    and human rights issue, 273, 292
    and Somoza's rule
        was beneficial, 271, 273
        was harmful, 281, 283-284
    benefits of, 283, 284
North, Oliver, see Iran/US arms transfers

Rainbow Warrior scandal, 323-324
Revolutionary Worker, 309
revolutions
    communism's role in, 289-290
Ruchwarger, Gary, 263

Sandinistas
    Americans should support, 283-286
        con, 270, 280, 287-290
    are communists, 269, 289-290, 294
    have improved Nicaragua, 263-267,
        283-284
        con, 269-273, 290
    must be overthrown, 291-295
    popular support for, 275, 284-285
        con, 273
    threaten Latin America, 291, 293, 294
    will not negotiate, 291-292
    see also contras; Nicaragua
Scowcroft, Brent, 301
South Africa
    African National Congress (ANC)
        and violence, 217, 240-241, 243
        Freedom Charter of, 227, 237
        is communist movement, 218, 237-242
            con, 243-246
        Soviets control, 224-225, 227, 239
            con, 217-218, 245
    blacks in
        are oppressed, 215-219
            con, 221-228
        fighting among, 217, 227, 233-234
            casualties from, 234, 240-241
            is government-sponsored, 230-231
            will take over government, 229-232

con, 233-235
Congressional policy toward, 228, 231,
    243
economy of, 218, 221-223
    and neighboring countries, 222, 235,
        247
    is weak, 231, 252
Eminent Persons Group visit to, 231, 248,
    253
government of
    and 1984 constitution, 217-218, 224
    and censorship, 219, 230, 231, 235
    homelands in, 216, 223
    human rights violations in, 217, 230,
        231-232
        myth of, 223-224
Inkatha, 234
media coverage of, 215, 233
minerals in, 222, 224-225
reforms in
    are minor, 218, 251
    are significant, 224
    white backlash against, 234-235
sanctions against
    are ineffective, 259-262
    are needed, 231, 252-253, 255-258
    Rhodesia case, 235, 256
    South Africa's reaction to, 235, 247-248,
        259-260
    will hurt blacks, 248, 260
        con, 255, 258
Sharpeville protest (1960), 217, 252
South African Communist Party (SACP),
    243, 245
Soweto protest (1976), 217, 229
tribalism in, 217, 222-223
United Democratic Front, 226, 232
US policy toward
    aid program, 248, 250, 261
    can promote peaceful change, 247-250
    has failed, 251-253
    helps communists, 228, 242
whites in
    are becoming more right-wing, 234-235
    factions among, 234, 241, 252
    racial attitudes of, 216, 218-219
Soviet Union
    human rights violations in, 288
    involvement in
        Central America, 291
        South Africa, 225, 227, 239
    Stalin's rule in, 288
    threatens world peace, 287-288

terrorism
    ANC role in, 240
    and Arms Export Control Act, 304, 307
    causes of, 321
    and covert actions, 321-322
    Iran arms sales encouraged, 302
    Reagan policy against, 301, 310
    Sandinista role in, 293, 294
    US supports, 310, 313, 314, 322
Tower Commission Report, 301-305
    blames Reagan, 307-308
    supports Reagan, 309-311
    see also Iran/US arms transfers
Tower, John, 301

United Methodist Church
    and contra aid, 297

Vietnam, 239, 321
Villiers, Fleur de, 259

Wildavsky, Aaron, 317

cumulative index

This index is cumulative for viewpoints 101-175,
1985, 1986, and 1987 annuals.

as immoral, 48
necessity of, 71-73
with trade sanctions, 85, 86
US relations with, 264, 291-292
war in, 299
effects of, 279-280, 285
Sandinistas are winning, 263-264
see also contras; Sandinistas
Nicaraguan revolution (1979)
and human rights issue, 273, 292
and Somoza's rule
was beneficial, 271, 273
was harmful, 281, 283-284
benefits of, 283, 284
Nidal, Abu, 134, 150
Nixon, Richard, 73
doctrine of, 80
North, James, 55
North Korea, 107
North, Oliver, *see* Iran/US arms transfers
Novak, Robert, 164
Nunn, Sam, 172
Nygard, Richard, 40

O'Neill, Thomas P., 71
Ongpin, Jaime, 165, 188
Oppenheimer, Harry, 51
Orwell, George, 6, 8
Owen, Ken, 197

Pakistan, 100-101, 107
Palestine Liberation Organization (PLO), 29,
31, 137
support of Nicaragua, 88
Papandreou, Andreas, 101
Pastora, Eden, 71, 89
murder of, 5
Paton, Alan, 52
Patterson, Eric, 83
Perez de Cuellar, Javier, 2, 34, 151
Philippines
and the communist NPA (New People's
Army), 163, 164, 165, 171-172, 175, 177
Catholic church in
as bulwark against communists, 171-172
is infiltrated by communists, 187
CIA involvement in, 176, 189
difficulty of sustaining democracy in, 105
election was fraudulent, 173, 177-183
was not fraudulent, 168, 185-191
Lugar commission's role in, 173, 182, 186
media involvement in, 168-169, 171, 178,
182, 186
resemblance to Vietnam, 167
role of Corazon Aquino in
and capitalism, 165
as beneficial, 165, 171-174
did not help defeat communism, 169,
191
role of Ferdinand Marcos in
and communism
helped defeat, 168
con, 163, 164, 173, 175
and democracy, 164-165
and freedom, 164, 168
as an ineffective ruler, 163-165, 171-174,
177
con, 168, 186

as a victim, 187-188
US policy in
bipartisan support for, 172-173
did not promote democracy, 175-176
was not successful, 175-176
was successful, 171-174
withdrawing support for Marcos
as beneficial, 167-169
as betrayal, 163-165
Pineiro, Manuel, 124
Poland, 48
Price, Raymond, 155
PSN (Nicaraguan Socialist Party), 87

Qaddafi, Muammar, 126, 139, 140, 142,
149-157, 160-161
see also terrorism

Rainbow Warrior scandal, 323-324
Reagan, Ronald, 2, 69-70, 118, 129, 137,
149, 159, 172, 174
and Nicaragua, 72, 85, 89
anti-terrorist policies of, 9, 75-77, 86,
93, 140
as immoral, 22, 49, 56, 83-86
effectiveness of, 78-81, 136, 149-150,
155-157
ineffectiveness of, 11-12, 151, 153
doctrine of, 79-81, 107, 139
soundness of, 79-81
wrong, 83-86, 116
Revolutionary Worker, 309
revolutions
communism's role in, 289-290
in Central America, 80, 84
Robelo, Alfonso, 124
Robinson, Jackie, 45
Rogers, William, 175
Rosenthal, A.M., 99, 107
Rostow, Eugene, 133
Rubin, Jeffrey Z., 145
Ruchwarger, Gary, 263
Rusk, Dean, 160

Sakharov, Andrei, 53
Sandinistas, 102
Americans should support, 283-286
con, 270, 280, 287-290
are communists, 87, 269, 289-290, 294
myth of, 94, 96
attacks on civilians, 90
Catholic opposition to, 95
exporters of revolution, 90
have improved Nicaragua, 93, 263-267,
283-284
con, 269-273, 290
human rights violations committed by,
88-89, 90
myth of, 93, 94
military force of, 88
misuse of aid, 91
must be overthrown, 291-295
popular support for, 275, 284-285
con, 273
threaten Latin America, 291, 293, 294
will not negotiate, 291-292
see also contras; Nicaragua
Sandino, August Cesar, 94

Savimbi, Jonas, 130
Scowcroft, Brent, 301
Seko, Mobutu Sese, 101, 119
Seoka, Joe, 193
Shevchenko, Arkady, 118
Shipler, David, 111
Shultz, George P., 9, 11, 25, 77, 79, 85, 89,
135, 136, 141, 149, 151, 152, 156, 172,
173, 175, 190
and Nicaragua, 12
Sin, Cardinal Jaime, 182, 187, 188
Sithole, Masipula, 211
slavery
as terrorism, 1, 30
Smith, Ian, 213
Smith, Nico, 194, 198
Solarz, Stephen J., 76, 77, 169, 172
soldiers, 5
Solzhenitsyn, Alexandr, 8
Somoza, Anastasio Debayle, 71, 83, 87, 102
South Africa
African National Congress (ANC), 195-198
and violence, 217, 240-241, 243
Freedom Charter of, 227, 237
is communist movement, 218, 237-242
con, 243-246
Soviets control, 224-225, 227, 239
con, 217-218, 245
apartheid in, 45-68
and the churches, 201
and pass laws, 200
black boycotts of, 194, 198
blaming Britain for, 213
history of, 212-213
compared to Nazi Germany, 47, 67
as fallacy, 49, 53
improvements in, 49-53, 59
inhumanity of, 45-48, 53
oppresses blacks, 203-206
con, 199-202, 211
ways to improve
constructive engagement, 49
failure of, 37, 68
Sullivan Code, 51, 56, 63-64
failure of, 67
white opposition to, 199-202
white support of, 203-210
blacks in
are oppressed, 215-219
con, 221-228
fighting among, 195, 217, 227, 233-234
casualties from, 234, 240-241
is government-sponsored, 230-231
will take over government, 229-232
con, 233-235
Congressional policy toward, 228, 231,
243
democracy unsuitable, 51
disinvestment
reasons against, 51, 53, 59-61, 63-65
cannot improve apartheid, 67-68
harms blacks, 59-61, 208, 209
reasons for, 55-57, 67-68
aids blacks, 55-57, 67-68
can improve apartheid, 63-65
supported by Africans, 56
myth of, 52, 60
drought in, 52

economy of, 218, 221-223
  and neighboring countries, 222, 235, 247
  is weak, 231, 252
Eminent Persons Group visit to, 231, 248, 253
government of, 198, 212
  and 1984 constitution, 217-218, 224
  and censorship, 219, 230, 231, 235
  destroying black history, 45-46
  oppression through language, 46
  shooting blacks, 46-47
homelands in, 51, 216, 223
human rights violations in, 68, 217, 230, 231-232
  myth of, 59, 223-224
increasing black militancy in, 193-195, 198, 208
Inkatha, 234
media coverage of, 215, 233
minerals in, 222, 224-225
oppression of blacks, 45
reforms in
  are minor, 218, 251
  are significant, 224
  by creating federation system, 209
  by economic sanctions, 208
  one-person-one-vote is harmful, 209
  should be gradual, 208-209
  white backlash against, 234-235
  will come only through pressure, 211-213
  will not come through violence, 208-209
sanctions against
  are ineffective, 259-262
  are needed, 231, 252-253, 255-258
  Rhodesia case, 235, 256
  South Africa's reaction to, 235, 247-248, 259-260
  will hurt blacks, 248, 260
    con, 255, 258
settlement of, 45-46
Sharpeville protest (1960), 217, 252
South African Communist Party (SACP), 243, 245
Soweto protest (1976), 217, 229
tribalism in, 217, 222-223
United Democratic front, 226, 232
uprisings in, 55, 64, 195
US policy toward
  aid program, 248, 250, 261
  can promote peaceful change, 247-250
  has failed, 251-253
  helps communists, 228, 242
  should leave, 67
white opinion of black rule in, 197
whites in
  are becoming more right-wing, 234-235
  factions among, 234, 241, 252
  racial attitudes of, 216, 218-219
South Korea, 107
Soviet Union
  aid to Ethiopia, 35, 39
  as model for revolution
    myth of, 80
  as terrorists, 6, 9, 13, 15
    myth of, 2, 3
  expansionist ambitions of, 102, 123-124,

126-127, 131
  human rights violations in, 288
  involvement in
    Central America, 291
    Eastern Europe, 8, 15
    South Africa, 225, 227, 239
  Stalin's rule in, 288
  support to Nicaragua, 96
  support to the PLO, 29
  threatens world peace, 287-228
  US opposition to, 76
Speakes, Larry, 85
Stalin, Josef, 7
Steinberg, David, 164
Stevenson, William, 135
Sullivan Code, 51, 56
  effectiveness of, 63-64
  unsuccessful, 67
Sullivan, Leon H., 63
SWAPO (Namibia), 111
Symms, Steven D., 77

Tambo, Oliver, 196, 198, 208
Taylor, Humphrey, 59
terrorism
  ANC role in, 240
  and Arms Export Control Act, 304, 307
  and capitalism, 1-3
  and covert actions, 321-322
  and the PLO, 29-31
  and totalitarianism, 5-8
  as attack on US, 18
  as crime, 7, 10
  causes of, 321
  chemical, 18-19
  combatting
    by economic sanctions, 137
      failure of, 139-140, 149-150, 156
    by force
      as ineffectual, 159-161
      failure of, 134-135
      is justified, 139-140, 151-153
      successes of, 135
    by ignoring, 141-143
    by increasing airport security, 141
    by issuing arrest warrants and bounties, 136
    by political alliances, 137
    by reprisals, 137
      creates more terrorism, 140, 142, 151
      con, 150, 157
  control possible, 13-15
    as impossible, 17-20
  from Lebanon, 161
  from Libya, 139, 160-161
  getting worse, 13
  government's right to squelch, 8, 133
  in Iran, 21-24, 29, 30
  in Lebanon, 25-27
  innocent victims of, 4, 6, 13, 16-18
  in Turkey, 14, 112
  in the US, 1, 17, 18, 19
  Iran arms sales encouraged, 302
  politics of, 5, 6
  raid against Libya
    was justified, 149-150, 155-157
    was not justified, 151-153
  Reagan policy against, 301, 310

Sandinista role in, 293, 294
successes of, 16
US need to fight, 9-10, 30, 133
  as threat to human rights, 11-12, 23
    impossibility of, 11-12
US-sponsored, 25-27, 310, 313, 314, 322
terrorist states
  emergence of, 30
  need for US to pull out, 25-27
  need for US to punish, 29-32
  need for US to seek reconciliation with, 21-24
Thatcher, Margaret, 151
Thomas, Franklin, 67
Tinoco, Victor Hugo, 89
Tower Commission Report, 301-305
  blames Reagan, 307-308
  supports Reagan, 309-311
  see also Iran/US arms transfers
Tower, John, 301
Truman, Harry S., 73
  doctrine of, 79
Tutu, Desmond, 45, 52, 56, 207, 208, 241
  support of disinvestment, 68

Ulc, Otto, 49
United Methodist Church, 297
United Nations
  as useless, 31
  condemnation of US, 8
  inadequacy of, 39
  Soviet proposal before
    as good, 2-3
    as propaganda, 8
Ury, William, 146
US
  and dictatorships, see dictatorships
  and Ethiopian famine, 37-38, 39
    aid to alleviate, 42
      should be stopped, 40
      slow to respond, 35
  and intervention in foreign countries, see intervention
  and Nicaragua, 69-98
    and Contadora process, 98
    attempts to overthrow government, 97
      myth of, 87, 93-98
    need to combat communism, 79-81, 86
    should recognize Sandinistan government, 98
    supporting democracy, 90-91
    support of the contras, 75-77
      immorality of, 69-70, 83-86
      morality of, 71-73, 85, 87
    trade sanctions, 86
  and the Philippines, 176, 189
    was not successful in, 175-176
    was successful in, 171-174
  and South Africa
    corporations
      as a force for change, 63-65
        myth of, 67-68
    disinvestment
      reasons against, 51-52, 59-61
      reasons for, 55-57
  and terrorism, 9-10, 21
    attacks against, 18
    ineffective policies of, 9, 13-15